Authoritarian Journalism

JOURNALISM AND POLITICAL COMMUNICATION UNBOUND

Series editors: Daniel Kreiss, University of North Carolina at Chapel Hill, and Nikki Usher, University of San Diego

Journalism and Political Communication Unbound seeks to be a high-profile book series that reaches far beyond the academy to an interested public of policymakers, journalists, public intellectuals, and citizens eager to make sense of contemporary politics and media. "Unbound" in the series title has multiple meanings: It refers to the unbinding of borders between the fields of communication, political communication, and journalism, as well as related disciplines such as political science, sociology, and science and technology studies; it highlights the ways traditional frameworks for scholarship have disintegrated in the wake of changing digital technologies and new social, political, economic, and cultural dynamics; and it reflects the unbinding of media in a hybrid world of flows across mediums.

Other books in the series:

Journalism Research That Matters
Valérie Bélair-Gagnon and Nikki Usher

Reckoning: Journalism's Limits and Possibilities
Candis Callison and Mary Lynn Young

News After Trump: Journalism's Crisis of Relevance in a Changed Media Culture
Matt Carlson, Sue Robinson, and Seth C. Lewis

Borderland: Decolonizing the Words of War
Chrisanthi Giotis

The Politics of Force: Media and the Construction of Police Brutality
Regina Lawrence

Imagined Audiences: How Journalists Perceive and Pursue the Public
Jacob L. Nelson

Pop Culture, Politics, and the News: Entertainment Journalism in the Polarized Media Landscape
Joel Penney

Democracy Lives in Darkness: How and Why People Keep Their Politics a Secret
Emily Van Duyn

Building Theory in Political Communication: The Politics-Media-Politics Approach
Gadi Wolfsfeld, Tamir Sheafer, and Scott Althaus

Authoritarian Journalism

Controlling the News in Post-Conflict Rwanda

RUTH MOON

OXFORD
UNIVERSITY PRESS

Oxford University Press is a department of the University of Oxford. It furthers
the University's objective of excellence in research, scholarship, and education
by publishing worldwide. Oxford is a registered trade mark of Oxford University
Press in the UK and certain other countries.

Published in the United States of America by Oxford University Press
198 Madison Avenue, New York, NY 10016, United States of America.

© Oxford University Press 2024

All rights reserved. No part of this publication may be reproduced, stored in
a retrieval system, or transmitted, in any form or by any means, without the
prior permission in writing of Oxford University Press, or as expressly permitted
by law, by license, or under terms agreed with the appropriate reproduction
rights organization. Inquiries concerning reproduction outside the scope of the
above should be sent to the Rights Department, Oxford University Press, at the
address above.

You must not circulate this work in any other form
and you must impose this same condition on any acquirer.

Library of Congress Cataloging-in-Publication Data
Names: Moon, Ruth, author.
Title: Authoritarian journalism : controlling the news in post-conflict Rwanda / by Ruth Moon.
Description: New York : Oxford University Press, 2024. |
Series: Journalism and pol commun unbound series |
Includes bibliographical references and index.
Identifiers: LCCN 2023017302 (print) | LCCN 2023017303 (ebook) |
ISBN 9780197623428 (paperback) | ISBN 9780197623411 (hardcover) |
ISBN 9780197623442 (epub) | ISBN 9780197623459
Subjects: LCSH: Press—Rwanda. | Journalism—Objectivity—Rwanda. |
Journalistic ethics—Rwanda.
Classification: LCC PN5499 .R84 M66 2023 (print) | LCC PN5499 .R84 (ebook) |
DDC 079 .67571—dc23/eng/20230717
LC record available at https://lccn.loc.gov/2023017302
LC ebook record available at https://lccn.loc.gov/2023017303

DOI: 10.1093/oso/9780197623411.001.0001

Paperback printed by Marquis Book Printing, Canada
Hardback printed by Bridgeport National Bindery, Inc., United States of America

Contents

Acknowledgments   vii

1. On the Margins: Understanding Peripheral Journalism   1
2. Strong State, Weak Field: The Forces Shaping Journalism in Rwanda   28
3. Founding Myths: Stories as Building Blocks of Journalism Practice   55
4. Underbaked or Unrealized: "Underdevelopment" as a Journalistic Keyword   82
5. Money Matters: The News Values of Business Pressure   109
6. Bridging Worlds: Working Global While Living Local   133

    Conclusion: What Is Weak Journalism Good For? The Power and Potential of Peripheral Practice   156

Appendix: Note on Methods   173
Bibliography   181
Index   201

Acknowledgments

This project was, of course, a team effort. Its earliest cheerleaders were my doctoral committee—Phil Howard and Matt Powers (cochairs) and Ron Krabill—who saw a book in my dissertation and encouraged me to pursue it. As the book project grew, so did my support team: I owe a great deal of thanks to Angela Chnapko at Oxford University Press for her patient and thorough editing and advice throughout the revision process. Series editors Daniel Kreiss and Nikki Usher were equally supportive and thoughtful with their feedback; all three of these editors shaped this manuscript into a more readable and engaging book.

Fieldwork was a fantastic and strange experience enriched by unexpected and often enduring relationships. Chief among these, of course, were the anonymous journalists and others I interviewed for the project, to whom I owe much gratitude. Many of them volunteered time out of their days, changed travel plans so I could accompany them to field sites, drove me home after late production nights, and otherwise invited me into their lives. Their time, perspectives, and friendships made this project and my time in Rwanda better than I could have expected. Nikhila Gill welcomed me to the community of expats in Rwanda, showing hospitality through food, friendship, and more. Of course, fieldwork does not happen without money, and this project was funded by a variety of sources, including University of Washington graduate student support and a National Security Education Program Boren Fellowship.

Colleagues supported this project in ways large and small. Alison Estep, my boss at Seattle Pacific University during two crucial years of writing, was consistently curious and encouraging about this work, even though it was a side project and not part of my day-to-day work. Colleagues and supervisors at Louisiana State University's Manship School supported my project with course releases, funding, and cheerleading—notably Martin Johnson, who hired me, and Josh Grimm, who stepped in as interim dean and led our department admirably for several years. Fanny Ramirez, a colleague at the Manship School, offered thoughtful, detailed edits that helped me frame the manuscript. Alicia Cohn, now an editor at Bloomberg Industry, read and ripped apart almost every chapter with characteristic journalistic attention to craft. Developmental editor Heath Sledge helped focus my arguments when I hit a wall, and Manship School graduate student Hayley Booth fact-checked, labeled, and sorted information through the final steps of manuscript preparation.

My family—parents, siblings, husband, kid, and dog—have been my biggest cheerleaders through this project. My mom was my first teacher and applauded my educational goals even when they stopped making financial sense. My parents both made the trek to Great Lakes Africa to visit during fieldwork. My siblings supported my project as well, visiting me in the field and coaching me to explain my work to broader audiences. This book would not exist without my husband Will, who supported me from afar through fieldwork, encouraged me through the long process of writing and revision, and wrote most of my chapter titles. And finally, the kids keep me grounded—my dog, Roux, and my son, Theo, who joined our family hours after I finished manuscript revisions. Without my family's sense of perspective and priorities, I would probably still be tweaking sentences and puzzling over arguments, rather than turning this book loose into the world so I can take the dog for a walk and play with Theo in the backyard.

* * *

Portions of chapter 3 originally appeared in R. Moon (2021), When Journalists See Themselves as Villains: The Power of Negative Discourse, *Journalism & Mass Communication Quarterly* (98)(3), 790–807.

Portions of chapter 6 originally appeared in R. Moon (2019), Beyond Puppet Journalism: The Bridging Work of Transnational Journalists in a Local Field, *Journalism Studies* 20(12), 1714–1731.

1
On the Margins
Understanding Peripheral Journalism

On a warm evening toward the end of June 2017, a group of Rwandans and expats gathered at Café Neo, a trendy rooftop coffee shop near the city center, often full of Americans and Canadians working on tech startups and other business ventures. Tables had been pushed to the edges of the room to accommodate rows of folding chairs and rain flaps rolled up to expose the clear evening sky. Empty Primus, Mutzig, and Skol bottles multiplied on the countertops as three panelists discussed the role journalism could play in Rwanda's upcoming election. The panelists—a local journalist who worked for the Rwandan Media Commission and the *East African* (a regional weekly newspaper), the European Union ambassador to Rwanda, and a Kenyan professor who studied the media system—used the example of Kenya's 2013 election to describe how journalists could foster violent or peaceful election processes. The audience included Rwandan journalists working for local and international media outlets, expats working for NGOs and other organizations, local journalism professors, and me—a white, American woman doing doctoral research. I was six months into fieldwork, trying to understand why Rwandan journalists neglected investigative reporting, flocked to government press conferences, and generally produced party-aligned reports while claiming that journalists should critique power and that laws and professional organizations encouraged and protected their right to independence and creativity. I joined the meeting late, alerted to it by Caleb,[1] a journalist friend, but quickly caught the gist.

People tend to see Rwandan journalism in extremes, shaped in part by their perspective on the political environment. Some downplay the role of governance and politics in enforcing journalism practice, as the Café Neo panelists did (McIntyre and Sobel 2018, 2019). This approach tends to focus on the ways that individual journalists' perceptions, abilities, and training

---

[1] Not his real name. For a list of the pseudonyms used in this book, see Table 1.1.

influence news production. Others see the political environment as so potently dangerous to critics that journalists have no choice but to pursue party-line journalism; this approach emphasizes the ways that journalists are controlled by others (Reyntjens 2013; Sundaram 2016). Both approaches miss crucial aspects of control and freedom woven into the fabric of Rwandan journalism—not by politics or professional training, but through stories that are so powerful that they become myths shaping the rules of journalistic reality.

The panel's presumption that Rwanda is governed by an emerging, if troubled, democracy comparable to Kenya's is nonsense but is an important fiction with implications for journalism practice. Rwanda is one of a number of countries committed to image management as a strategy to bolster international legitimacy as a state that is "stable, responsible, and even democratic" (Dukalskis 2021, 143). Kenya is a transitioning democracy characterized by intense and violent transfers of power and political conflicts. Rwanda is an authoritarian country with peaceful persistence of one-party rule, despite democratic symbols like regular elections. This is clear on several dimensions. Kenya's elections are hotly contested; in 2013, the winning candidate received just over 50 percent of the vote, and the runner-up garnered 43 percent of the vote (African Democracy Encyclopedia Project 2013). In contrast, Rwandan elections are practically unanimous. In 2010, the incumbent Paul Kagame took 93 percent of the vote, while the nearest runner-up, Jean Damascene Ntawukuriyayo, earned only 5 percent of the vote. In Kenya, ethnic divisions are public and frequent topics of discussion, and important determinants of political party (Wolf 2013). Ethnicity is important in Rwanda but nearly invisible in public discourse, because discussing it is illegal (Lacey 2004). Kenya's parliament in early 2017 comprised a nearly even split between the two most popular political parties, with 167 members from the Jubilee Party and 141 members from the primary opposing Orange Democratic Party (Oluoch 2017). After the 2018 parliamentary election in Rwanda, President Paul Kagame's party—the Rwandan Patriotic Front—garnered 40 of 53 seats up for election, while the opposition Democratic Green Party gained two seats for the first time (Uwiringiyimana 2018). In short, Kenyan politics is chaotic, full of open debate that often turns violent, while Rwandan politics is ordered and controlled by the strong influence of the majority party, with little political opposition.

These observations all show that Rwandan journalists do not work in a democracy. Instead, with a growing number of journalists around the world, they work in a contemporary autocracy that incorporates democratic symbols into functionally authoritarian regimes. Different labels capture nuances in governance styles, but journalists working in these "competitive," "soft," or "developmental" authoritarian contexts share the distinction of working in "boring and tolerable" non-democratic regimes (Levitsky and Way 2002; Matfess 2015; Pepinsky 2017; Tripp 2004). In this book I examine Rwandan journalism to show how control works in these contexts—how journalists and other social actors set, learn, and maintain the boundaries of acceptable practice in a place where the overt rules encourage democratic engagement while the subtext pressures journalists into a different direction.

The panel discussion also reinforced an assumption that Rwandan journalists can be easily manipulated by political parties and others in power, and that they might unwittingly collude to cause chaos. The bulwark against this manipulability is individual training in skills and professional expectations. This emphasis on journalists as highly manipulable social actors is also reflected in, for instance, media assistance programs that aim to cultivate individual professionalism and critical thinking through workshops and codes of ethics. As one media program assessment puts it, "Journalists who are well educated, who know journalism-ethics and who are conscious of their social responsibility are not easy to manipulate" (Alexis and Mpambara 2003, 27). This approach is buttressed by research proposing that strong media dependency lent radio a seemingly powerful role in exacerbating the 1994 Genocide against the Tutsi, in which an estimated 800,000 to 1 million people, primarily of Tutsi ethnicity, were killed in a 100-day span from April 7 to July 15 (Kellow and Steeves 1998; Prunier 1997).

Putting these assumptions together, the panel's message was that Rwandan journalists are free to stir up violence and chaos, and they might do so, even unwittingly, unless they become more professionalized and learn to think for themselves. This message clearly invoked a cultural memory of the genocide, suggesting that journalists might be manipulated or even choose to produce provocative content again and that they would be free to do so if they wished. Audience members pushed back, pointing out that Rwandan journalists are hardly free to critique just anything when most of the advertising, and hence the paychecks, comes from government and big businesses. Why would journalists risk their paychecks by criticizing the government officials who pay the bills? Murmurs of assent swept the room. The panelists, though, stuck with their message, treating Rwandan journalism as a democratic institution with the freedom to spread information and—whether by inclination or manipulation—stir up violence.

At this point, I had been in Rwanda—a small, landlocked country in the Great Lakes region of Africa with a population of about 12 million—since January 2017. I had spent most of that time in newsrooms watching and interviewing reporters, editors, photographers, and others involved in news production. This evening helped me frame Rwandan journalism by clarifying the contradictions that shape so much of journalists' work. It also encapsulated the problematic assumptions that shape observers' views of journalism practice in the country. By ignoring the history and lived reality guiding Rwandan journalists to behave differently, the panel discussion reinforced a message that social and political pressures were not, in fact, important forces shaping journalistic behavior. This approach neglects important aspects of reality; it also pushes journalists and observers away from recognizing the real constraints on their practice and leaves them blaming individual journalists for failing to produce news the way they think they should.

The evening's discussion implied that the upcoming election could foster violence, and that Rwandan journalists had the power to either exacerbate or calm the violence through their decisions about how to cover the coming months' events. Both assumptions were wrong. Caleb predicted, accurately, that the election would be no contest, with no accompanying violence. And, as I will argue in this book, by this point in Rwandan history, local journalists had little, if any, power to affect the election or social response to it. Instead, Rwandan journalists operate with such a low level of autonomy—reinforced, ironically, by myths about their powerful role in the genocide and their ability to write critical news if it is reported well—that the enforcement of a few standard journalism routines is enough to ensure that provocative, critical, or potentially inflammatory news never makes it to publication.

The assumptions perpetuated by this roundtable discussion are common, both about journalism in Rwanda specifically and about journalism in other modern authoritarian societies. The idea comes down to this: journalists have enough autonomy to fulfill a liberal democratic role as government watchdogs and guardians of the people's interests, if only they will exercise that power—which they can do if they become more professional and learn more reportage skills. Furthermore, if journalists don't have that autonomy already, they will fight to gain it. This assumption is rooted in research; scholars studying journalism around the globe find that journalists prioritize autonomy as a central feature of their professional identities (Carlson 2017; Waisbord 2013). Journalism schools and professional workshops—often funded and staffed by foreign aid agencies—teach "critical thinking" on the assumption that journalists do not currently have enough of it. If they did, the logic goes, they would surely have autonomy and, by extension, more liberal democratic orientations to news production. Rwandan journalists themselves share the assumption that it's their own fault they are not more powerful, dismissing their work as "PR for the government" and critiquing their colleagues for lacking professionalism on one hand while failing to stand up for themselves on the other (sentiments shared by many journalists I interviewed). It is true that Rwandan journalism is, like journalism across the continent, often characterized by bandwagonism and mimicry, with an emphasis "less on thinking than on doing, less on leading than on being led," but the reasons for this are complex and rooted in history, social understanding, and Western intervention as well as local constraints (Nyamnjoh 2015, 37).

To understand journalism in this contemporary, authoritarian state, I approach it as a field of power where journalists are playing a game, with moves and rules like soccer or chess. In this field, actors with varying levels of prestige and resources interact with each other and with members of other social fields (like politicians and corporate leaders). Using this lens, I analyze ethnographic data from seven months of fieldwork and 80 interviews with journalists in and around Rwanda. News content tends to follow the pattern one might expect from journalism in an authoritarian system: it is fairly government aligned and generally uncritical. However, the process by which this news is created has several surprising lessons for scholars, policymakers, and practitioners. Among the most surprising is that journalists themselves embrace a position of limited autonomy, motivated by field-defining myths rooted in shared history and serving as a cautionary limit on contemporary practice. Rwanda presents an important model of contemporary journalism, one where journalists relinquish their autonomy because of limited and unreliable support from legal and social systems *but also* because shared stories take on the power of professional myths reinforcing the boundaries and rules of appropriate journalism practice. These journalists recognize the distance between the reality of practice and the hypothetical world of education and training but strategically choose a self-reinforcing path of continued dependency. They are often just passing through the field of local journalism, where they play by the rules until they have earned enough prestige and resources to get a different job in Rwanda or a journalism job defined by transnational, rather than local, rules.

Over the past decade journalism scholars have increasingly used field theory to explain aspects of journalistic behavior and news production, primarily focusing on journalism practice in Western democracies (Maares and Hanusch 2022). Within this approach, studies often focus on the concept of "field," using it to examine the common tension between market pressure and autonomy or the ability to pursue professional values (Leeds 2022; Maares and Hanusch 2022). The field concept is especially useful for scholars seeking to unpack the variety of approaches journalists take to their work. It highlights, for instance, the problems with characterizing "African media" or even journalism within a particular African country as a monolithic entity, when in fact different media outlets can perpetuate vastly different media narratives (Wahutu 2017, 2018c). As James Wahutu shows in his forthcoming book on African media coverage of the Rwanda and Darfur conflicts, it can illuminate the complex power dynamics at play within coverage and source decisions by media organizations and fields (Wahutu, in press). It positions journalism as a contributor to culture and community, aligned with the African concept of Ubuntu and collective knowledge production (Fourie 2010). The game approach to journalism practice also can pinpoint areas where incorporation of dominant Western journalistic paradigms generates harmful tension within local African fields (Wahutu 2019). In short, field theory provides tools to complicate the Global North-oriented assumption that there is one way of doing journalism (Mutsvairo et al. 2021). In this book, I continue this conversation, examining a journalistic field as construed by key practitioners in an authoritarian African context. I show how, in Rwanda, the tension between market pressure and professional values is softened and redirected by a variety of implicit and explicit factors, including narratives about journalist roles, financial pressure, and organizational norms. As a result, the rules of local journalism shape a porous field whose rules and rewards incentivize departure.

This argument contributes to scholarship, practice, and policy. Common research findings about journalism practice and motivations fail to explain the complexity of news production in Rwanda and, by extension, many places around the contemporary world. My analysis demonstrates how existing theories fall short of adequately capturing the complexity of news production in non-democratic countries and how these theories can benefit from fresh encounters with new sources of data. Scholars should continue to examine the nuanced reality of news production in the context of, but not limited by, current (often Northern) theoretical approaches to create a clearer and more thorough understanding of reality. This book can serve local journalists by describing the shared reality of Rwandan journalism and critically assessing the capacity and limitations of local journalism practice. While local journalists say they value an autonomous watchdog role, they do not practice it (McIntyre and Skjerdal 2022). This book explains why, and in so doing provides shared language that journalists, policymakers, and others can use to discuss and shape the future of the Rwandan journalism field. With a clear, shared understanding of the current reality, journalists in Rwanda and other authoritarian contexts may find new paths to expanding autonomy while also developing a journalism practice grounded in local reality rather than Global North ideals. Journalists and those supporting the profession might benefit from relinquishing an ideal of watchdog journalism and embracing instead values of development journalism adapted for local needs and pressures.

Finally, this book reinforces the importance of grounding journalism education and professional development programs in knowledge of local practices and context. Locally illiterate international aid interventions aimed at strengthening media capacity are at best ineffective and at worst counterproductive as they allow authoritarian governments to signal transparency without improving journalists' security, access, or paths to publication.

Post-conflict Journalism in a Strong State

Journalism in Rwanda is a high-profile and low-reward profession where journalists are the subjects of frequent surveillance, observation, and critique. It is particularly high profile because of Rwanda's post-conflict context, its centralized government, and that government's mission to cultivate a positive international image from a global periphery position. Each of these factors contribute unique pressures to the journalistic work environment, which is shaped by popular narratives about media role in the genocide, state policies, and government publicity efforts. However, Rwandan journalism also shares similarities with journalism practice around the world—particularly in post-conflict or authoritarian environments. Some of these pressures even show up in the United States, where President Donald Trump repeatedly targeted journalists with negative rhetoric, even calling them "the enemy of the people" (Carlson et al. 2021). This book unpacks the challenge of practicing journalism in a context where journalists are high-profile targets of critique burdened—fairly or not—with a negative social role.

Journalism in Rwanda is indelibly shaped by the effects of the 1994 genocide. Aid and development studies show that Rwanda has transitioned past the "post-conflict" phase of recovery, but in practical terms the genocide is inextricably woven into the fabric of governance and social life in ways that deeply affect journalism practice. State surveillance, while it predates the genocide and even colonial rule, has become increasingly visible and central to social organization since 1994 (Purdeková 2015, 2016). The post-genocide government's international image management reinforces the importance of democratic symbolism and security while enhancing authoritarian control (Dukalskis 2021; Samset 2011). Government messages reinforce official, often selective genocide narratives, sometimes at the expense of nuance, in public spaces, including news reports (Kelley 2017; King 2010; Waldorf 2009). The Rwandan genocide is a particularly extreme case of conflict, but journalists in Colombia, Bosnia-Herzegovina, Ireland, and other countries emerging from conflict grapple with similar attempts to control post-conflict memory and construct official narratives while being closely surveilled for their ability to shape public messages (Atanesyan 2020; Bratic 2008; Fiedler and Mroß 2017; Jukes et al. 2021; Lundy and McGovern 2001; Takševa 2018). The social and political factors shaping Rwandan journalism highlight how the post-conflict context presents powerful barriers to some practices and incentives toward others.

Rwanda also offers insight into the nature of journalism practice in the growing number of non-democratic countries around the world. In 2020, Rwanda was one of 54 authoritarian countries around the world, and the number of authoritarian regimes is increasing—up from 52 countries in 2018 (Economist Intelligence Unit 2020; Shapiro 2017). These countries house more than one-third of the world's population; meanwhile, just 8 percent of the world's population lives in a full democracy (The Economist 2021). And democratic backsliding—in which governments disrupt or remove existing democratic political institutions—is on the rise (Bermeo 2016; Mechkova et al. 2017; Vachudova 2020; Waldner and Lust 2018). Non-democratic media systems increasingly demand scholarly attention, and Rwanda provides a window into mechanisms of control in such a context. Rwanda's contemporary authoritarianism is emblematic especially of countries with low levels of power in the global economy, where appearing democratic brings important political and economic benefits. Across sub-Saharan Africa, governments have instituted symbolic events and institutions such as elections, independent media governance, and judicial systems, which seem democratic but are in fact closely controlled by central authorities to prevent opposition (Levitsky and Way 2002). In another neo-authoritarian move, the Rwandan government controls the country's major business interests, with government-owned organizations dominating domestic manufacturing and agricultural business (Gökgür 2012; Mann and Berry 2016). These neo-authoritarian features are increasingly widespread and have powerful effects on journalism practice.

Some of the hybrid aspects of Rwandan governance likely stem from the country's reliance on global aid and development funds, which often come from Western democracies that require some semblance of democratic governance to grant aid (Tripp 2004). In this, Rwanda joins most countries in the world on the periphery of global power, with its relatively low GDP and low levels of global political and military power, making it financially dependent on the goodwill of a small group of core countries, which include the United States and other strong democracies (Chase-Dunn et al. 2000). These democracy-related governance expectations spill over into journalistic regulation and thus affect practice, especially since many Western funders see functional and independent media organizations as a bellwether for and fundamental aspect of healthy democratization (Bläsi 2004; Hanitzsch 2004; Laplante and Phenicie 2009; Mattes and Bratton 2007; Paluck and Green 2009; Shaw et al. 2011). The image-conscious Rwandan government relies heavily on PR firms to promote an image of peace, prosperity, and unity to the international community to maintain the flow of international aid, which constitutes a major portion of the country's budget—50 percent in 2008 (Dukalskis 2021). As a result of aid incentives, global policy pressure, and increasingly porous national boundaries allowing information to spread between countries, governments today are more likely to control news coverage by buying news outlets and withholding advertising than by, for instance, censoring negative content or arresting journalists for critiques (Hughes 2006; Repnikova 2017; Roudakova 2017; Waisbord 2000).

This context has fundamental implications for news production in Rwanda. Journalists are immersed in globalized journalism culture—primarily oriented to Western contexts and needs—through education and training, and overt messaging from government and journalism leaders promotes independence, freedom, and protection of journalists. However, shared myths within the field, poor legal enforcement, limited training, and strong financial pressures reinforce a weak field that is defined by limited autonomy and a set of orthodox news values at odds with those promoted by training and global journalism culture.

This finding is important for several reasons. It expands journalism and mass communication scholarship by showing in a fresh context how building a study from Western theory and expectations without grounding it in local context can miss or even deflect from the nuances of journalism on the ground. A core assumption of journalism scholarship—that journalists value and seek autonomy—falls apart on inspection in the Rwandan field. Instead, most Rwandan journalists embrace limited autonomy, and the common routines of journalism practice serve to reinforce the value of following rules rather than questioning authority. To understand why, we must explore a complex system of control that includes powerful myths alongside ethical norms, laws, and other shaping pressures. Journalism's power is set in part by legal and political structures, but it is also negotiable and subject to change through shared stories about the occupation. These myths about journalism and journalists—retold by the public and by journalists—shape the collective imagination of journalism's potential to benefit or harm society, affecting public support of the profession and how journalists think of their own potential and limits. I show how this happens in Rwanda, but my argument helps explain the underpinnings of self-censorship across many non-democratic societies.

This research contributes to policymaking as well. Journalists often play a powerful role in political processes like elections and judicial processes; they can foster peace or conflict, and they are important actors in democratic transitions (Bläsi 2004; Hanitzsch 2004; Laplante and Phenicie 2009; Mattes and Bratton 2007; Paluck and Green 2009; Shaw et al. 2011). Newspapers create community identity, which is an important component of state consolidation (Anderson 2006; Höhne 2008). In sub-Saharan Africa in particular, journalism plays a critical role in post-conflict transitions, and, moreover, journalists want to help; journalists in Kenya, for instance, say they want to promote social change and provide information to the public (Ireri 2017; Nkurunziza 2008). In light of this, the international community since the end of the Cold War has dedicated hundreds of millions of dollars and other support to assisting the news media in post-conflict and democratizing societies (Howard 2003; Murphy and Scotton 1987). However, those interventions are often poorly planned. Instead of using country-specific knowledge to develop tailored programs, international donors base their interventions on broad, inaccurate generalizations from their own experiences (Karlowicz 2003). In reality, of course, models of governance are diverse, coexisting with a variety of media systems, even across Western European democracies (Hallin and Mancini 2004, 2012; Strömbäck and Dimitrova 2006; Waisbord 2013). And poorly designed interventions are not just inefficient; to the extent that liberal democratic models have been incorporated in Rwandan journalism, they are in fact counterproductive, serving to intensify an authoritarian system rather than aiding democratization. This book shows the complexity of motivations and other pressures driving journalism in Rwanda—information that policymakers can use in designing interventions to Rwanda and other small, post-conflict authoritarian countries. It also highlights the importance of location-specific research in devising effective assistance programs.

Finally, my research provides insights for practicing journalists. By unpacking the contradictions I observed in Rwandan journalism practice, I highlight points of breakdown and potential reconstruction that can be difficult to observe while immersed in daily work routines. Rwandan journalists and those practicing journalism in similar contexts may find this useful in their efforts to further professionalize the field, especially by developing locally aware approaches in journalism education, training, and ongoing incentives. This book can also inform journalists in established democracies about the complex mental labor involved in non-democratic journalism practice.

Contemporary journalists working on the periphery of global power occupy precarious positions in many ways (de Bustamante and Relly 2021). They must constantly negotiate competing frames of reference to meaningfully motivate everyday decisions. Especially in places where journalism was first instituted as a state-building enterprise in a colonial context, overlapping global and local fields contribute to the complexity of journalism practice by introducing layers of competing norms and pressures for journalists to accommodate. Rwandan journalists work within boundaries set by local society and politics alongside global forces. Global forces encouraging autonomy and independence compete with local narratives supporting loyalty and acquiescence. This book highlights the tension inherent in doing journalism in Rwanda and other countries where governments combine symbolic democratic practices with functional authoritarianism. In these places, journalism constitutes a border zone between global and local views of power, governance, and action. I contribute to a global view of journalism by identifying and unpacking the work of constructing personal and professional identity in a field that is both globalized and local.

Globalizing the Journalism Field

Rwandan journalists face constraints and incentives similar to those journalists face around the globe, in that their work is shaped by systemic and social forces, institutions, organizations, routines, and individual preferences and identity (Shoemaker and Reese 2013). However, Rwandan journalism highlights the ways that globalization mixes the levels together, creating new, complex situations (Appadurai 1996). The result is organizations like Rwanda's most prominent English-language newspaper, the *New Times*, where global and local pressures layer in a confusing cacophony. Organizational norms are officially shaped by globally grounded ethics and an unbiased "editorial line" mandating neutrality. However, the organization relies heavily on advertising from government agencies, and several editorial board members have close ties with the country's main political party, the RPF, leading to a pro-government publication bias. As a result, journalists learn by trial and error that, while spoken rules embrace global journalistic practices such as objectivity and independence, editors in fact reward and publish news that supports government policies.

Cross-national flows of information, people, and tools can increase uncertainty in the journalistic profession, as happens at the *New Times*. They also give journalists larger potential audiences and increased international attention, thus raising the profession's profile as well. In places like Rwanda, journalists are an important part of the nation's international reputation and local power. Their news tells locals what is happening but also contextualizes government behavior as normal or odd; at the same time, they are under close observation from international organizations that treat journalism as an indicator of democratic health. As journalists channel and shape information for their audiences, they are shaped by global processes and also become agents of globalization (Castells 2009). Western influence permeates journalism practice in the Global South, extending even to sourcing practices among African journalists, who tend to prioritize Western over local voices in continental coverage (Serwornoo 2021; Wahutu 2018a, 2018b). Journalists today regularly receive and send information across national borders through wire services such as Reuters, the Associated Press, Agence France-Presse, Inter Press Service, and Xinhua. They also repackage information for their own audiences, shaping those wire stories by adding context to make stories more relevant to local geographic, political, or social realities. News media thus channel global power by strategically repackaging information for crucial local audiences while signaling local context to international observers.

Thinking of journalism as a game played on a field or board helps unpack the effect of globalization and its intersection with local pressures to shape news production. Field theory is rooted in the belief that one must examine social actors' relationships with each other and with actors in other fields to really understand how they behave and why (Krause 2017). In general, as I noted earlier, Bourdieu and others who have built and used field theory think of the field as a flat space resembling a chessboard or a soccer field. In this flat space, players take different roles depending on their skills and motivations; financial security and internal prestige are key, opposing motivations that drive players' moves. Most journalists are to some extent motivated by desires to be both financially stable and to be respected professionally. However, some, like news aggregators in the United States, hold roles where money is a bigger motivation, while others, like journalists at nonprofit organizations, hold roles where fulfilling a journalistic ideal is central (Coddington 2019; Konieczna 2018). Fields can be relatively strong or weak, depending on how much autonomy the members have to set their own goals and pursue them and on how closely the members agree on those goals and best practices (Steinmetz 2008; Vauchez 2008, 2011). Individuals can also choose to leave fields altogether, and boundary-crossing behavior can reveal important points of tension and weakness in the field—as, for instance, when actors move between journalism and political roles in Zimbabwe (Chibuwe 2021).

Globalization adds a third dimension to the playing field, and a nondemocratic context changes the way journalistic motivations intersect. As Rwanda shows, the result is a slippery field with holes in the borders, where journalists tend to leave for either local political positions on one hand or international journalism positions on the other. Journalists on the global periphery—in countries with limited power relative to major global forces— know about and must make sense of messages from international forces as well as the traditional layers of social forces within an area (Ferguson 2006). Journalists also can work for organizations based in different countries and thus in different journalism fields without physically moving. A Rwandan journalist in Kigali could work for the *New Times* or *KT Press*, but they could also work for Reuters (a global wire service based in the UK), Deutsche Welle (based in Germany), or Xinhua (based in China). Each of these international positions requires the journalist to follow production rules from multiple countries—reporting in Rwanda and writing news for an audience elsewhere—thus adding a transnational layer to the concept of a field. This added layer also changes the ways journalists can gain power: rather than looking for a better-paying job or more prestige within local journalism, they can move to a position where they gain prestige or money playing by German, Chinese, or transnational journalistic rules.

The ability to play by different rules without physically changing locations suggests that journalism fields can overlap in one location and are not always defined by national borders. Journalists leaving the *New Times* to work for Reuters, for instance, leave the Rwandan field to work in a global journalism field; Reuters is headquartered in London but produces news for subscribers around the (primarily Western) world, and has bureaus and stringers worldwide as well. Global fields often carry different values and incentives than their national counterparts, while still requiring members to have credibility in local spaces (Buchholz 2016; Go 2008). This field layering also changes the ways that journalists can gain and use power: journalists with minimal credibility at the *New Times* because of their inclination to write investigative pieces, for instance, might find that taking a job for the Associated Press or Deutsche Welle provides a better opportunity to influence Rwandan politics because of the power globalization gives to international image management (Sassen 2007).

Finally, globalization affects the rules and roles that journalists adopt within a field. Especially in contemporary authoritarian contexts, journalists often must make sense of contradictory values leading to different social roles, some imposed by global journalism communities and others imposed by local needs and restrictions. Across Africa, journalists must integrate liberal democratic values with inherently contradictory but equally democratic "African notions of personhood and agency" (Nyamnjoh 2005, 20). Journalists are thus tasked to promote democracy, save face with foreign dignitaries, and support pro-African interests, all at the same time— often an impossible contradiction of roles. In Cameroon, these pressures lead journalists to become partisan, politicized, and militant, and to promote authoritarianism over democracy (Nyamnjoh 2005). In Rwanda, this means that there is a wide gap between role conception and role performance: journalists say they should fill a watchdog role but actually support the political regime, and the more autonomy they say they have, the larger the gap (McIntyre and Skjerdal 2022).

Setting Field Boundaries

Whether a particular journalism field is global, transnational, or local, it is defined by boundaries establishing what is and what is not appropriate, what counts as journalism and what does not. Boundary work defining "real" journalism happens in relationships between journalists, audiences, sources, lawmakers, and others (Carlson 2017; Gieryn 1983).

A major contribution to the boundaries of journalism usually comes from the political sphere, where laws and informal expectations shape how journalists should act in general and how they should act with reference to the political system (Freedman 2008). Politicians and laws have shaped the boundaries of journalism by, among other things, taxing ink and paper and raising shipping costs; providing subsidies for periodical postage in the US mail system; and controlling who has access to information via freedom-of-information acts and other laws (Cook 1998; Hallin and Mancini 2004; Kielbowicz 1983; Nielsen 2014; Overholser and Jamieson 2005; Schudson 1978; Starr 2004; Winsbury 2013). National and local governments contribute important boundaries to journalism practice. Journalism practice looks different in Rwanda than in Uganda, in large part because the national border defines different laws and political systems that in turn encourage different sorts of social interaction (Hanitzsch and Mellado 2011).

Economic systems, also contained within national boundaries, are another force shaping the borders of appropriate journalism. More commercially oriented journalism fields—like the one in the United States—tend to produce news that is relatively sensational, episodic, and ideologically similar, while less commercially driven media tend to be more ideologically diverse and detailed in their coverage (Benson 2013). Within one field, organizations can span this range, with mass-oriented news outlets prioritizing entertainment values and elite-oriented news outlets prioritizing more thorough background and policy information.

These relationships look different in authoritarian contexts than in democracies such as the United States. In Rwanda and places like it, financial constraints and incentives can be closely linked with politics through funding, ownership, and small circulations. In some places, the government openly owns some or all media outlets. In Uganda, for instance, the highest-circulation English-language newspaper, the *New Vision*, is majority owned by the national government (Vision Group). In other countries (like Rwanda), the state has a financial stake in media outlets, but it might be hidden beneath layers of private ownership. While this sort of ownership gives the appearance of distance between the political system and news organizations, research in China, Russia, Turkey, and other authoritarian countries has shown that "independent" ownership does not lead to independent journalism. In fact, it can make media organizations more effective self-censors and state messengers because they now appear to be independent but in reality still face pressure from advertisers to produce news in a certain, often state-aligned, way (Stockmann and Gallagher 2011; Coskuntuncel 2018; Roudakova 2017).

Often, scholars don't look past national boundaries in thinking about field structure, focusing on national journalism cultures as they define appropriate journalistic behavior. However, globalization adds an extra layer of boundary-setting pressure that is especially important in countries on the global periphery. It affects political pressure; foreign aid dependence and a desire to present a certain image to the international community can lead to laws that look democratic and thus are internationally acceptable but are enforced erratically or not enforced at all, thus supporting journalists on paper but not in practice (Michener 2011; Tripp 2004). For instance, more than 70 countries have enacted freedom-of-information laws in the last two decades, signaling increased government transparency and, in theory, giving journalists access to information with which they can hold governments accountable. However, Greg Michener shows how a number of these laws have been passed as window dressing to appease international organizations like the UN or the World Bank. In some cases, the window-dressing laws may be harmless, but in others, they make information access harder—as, for instance, in Zimbabwe, where an FOI statute limited access to information that had previously been available (Michener 2011). This shows how pressure from a global political community can lead to legal situations that limit the work journalists can do. Global pressure can work the other way as well, giving journalists power to circumvent local pressures and publish despite restrictions. One journalist told me that "Rwanda wants to be seen well internationally," and journalists can use this international awareness to their advantage (Moon 2019, 1724).

Setting Boundaries through Stories

Along with laws, financial pressure, and other constraints imposed on journalism from outsiders, journalists themselves help define the boundaries of appropriate behavior. Even in strong-state, authoritarian contexts, journalists can often publish some critical content, thus negotiating field boundaries with sources and audiences (Moon 2023). They also define for themselves what is off-limits and what is appropriate. They do this in part by negotiating the *doxa*: the taken-for-granted foundational beliefs that set the boundaries of appropriate behavior. This shapes the playing field, within which journalists can take positions that may have different motivations and rewards but are still considered appropriate. One important way the doxa materializes is, I argue, through myths—narratives that define how things are or why they should be a certain way.

Stories are powerful. They shape collective imagination, leading to a shared understanding of history and tradition that can shape future action (Appadurai 1996). Shared stories and shared understanding of past events can shape whole societies, inspire shared loyalty, and create a sense of place. Stories inform our understanding of the world, our place in it, our fears, and our values. This influence is especially powerful today, where even in strong states with hostile policies, journalists can strategically use global networks and definitions to circumvent state restrictions.

Journalists are storytellers, and they tell stories about themselves as well as others. US journalists use stories from history—for instance, the story of investigative reporters bringing to light government misconduct in the Watergate scandal, and the story of journalists being duped into serving the government's aims during the McCarthy era—to inspire and warn each other about the role and pitfalls of the profession (Zelizer 1993). Journalists use stories to build archetypes of themselves as heroic, fearless crusaders, indispensable to democratic processes (Aldridge 1998). Aldridge shows that these stories become increasingly important to define professional boundaries when the overt rules shaping the occupation are missing or weak; I show that this happens by providing boundary structure through the power of *myth*.

I argue that stories become especially important in shaping the doxa of journalism when they become myths. I use the term *myth* to mean a statement of factual, objective reality that gives common-sense appeal to the way things are done (Boje et al. 1982). Myths can define the boundaries of appropriate behavior by explaining how something that may seem illogical to outsiders is "just the way things are" within a community. As stories that define the taken-for-granted reality, myths have the power to define legitimate behavior and rationalize work processes even if those processes do not lead to supposedly desired outcomes (Ellul et al. 1964; Meyer and Rowan 1977). In this book, I show how myths about journalism can make sense of conflicting claims and motivations and lead journalists to embrace routines and field boundaries that contradict their own professional goals.

The June panel I attended highlighted the power of myths in Rwandan journalism. While political and financial pressure made obvious appearances, the subtext extended a key myth: Rwandan journalists have immense power, and they might use it; however, they are irresponsible and cannot be trusted with it. The rest of this book unpacks this myth piece by piece, tracing where it shows up in Rwandan journalism practice and how it ultimately leads journalists to constrain themselves, gather resources, and leave the field.

Studying Rwandan Journalism

To write this book I conducted a network ethnographic study, using social network analyses, participant observation, and interviews to understand journalism practice (Howard 2002; Burrell 2012). Ethnographies have helped scholars identify journalists' attitudes and separate these from performance, expanding our understanding of not only *what* journalists do but *how* and *why* they do it (Cottle 2000; Hanitzsch and Vos 2017). Ethnography also shows us how journalists make sense of social requirements in particular contexts, revealing assumptions and newsroom practices that we had not thought to explore (Cottle 2000; Ryfe 2018). It allows researchers to explore causality and contribute to theory, often lacking in contemporary understanding of non-Western media (Gerring 2004). Classic newsroom ethnographies helped researchers better understand how reporters and editors decide which stories to pursue, how they define central professional values, and, more recently, how they react to new technology (Gans 1979; Tuchman 1972; Usher 2014). In the

African context and other Global South spaces, ethnographies are particularly useful, as they help researchers to reframe their questions in light of observed reality (Jordaan 2020). Observation and interviews help researchers better understand how and why news processes unfold in places with different constraints and incentives than those facing journalists in Global North countries that have birthed much of contemporary journalism theory. They have shown, for instance, how journalists interact with political pressure and processes in Ghana (Hasty 2005), how young people used internet cafés in the early 2000s (Burrell 2012), and how citizens of African nations incorporated the internet and other information communication technologies in their political interactions (Bailard 2014). Ethnography has also revealed nuances in how journalists incorporate new technologies (Mabweazara 2010, 2011, 2013; Moon 2022). My study continues in this vein.

Early studies on journalism education and practice on the African continent relied primarily on surveys and content analyses; however, these methods are limited in their ability to illuminate relationships, and, furthermore, they often allow the researcher to impose a particular cultural mindset on the project before data has been analyzed or even gathered (Murphy and Scotton 1987). This is a concern especially when the researcher is a cultural outsider (as, of course, I am to Rwanda). To reduce the likelihood that I would impose overly simplistic, exotic, or inaccurate interpretations on the data, I adopted a grounded theory analytical framework to center African experiences and knowledge production (Schoon et al. 2020). With this approach, I entered the field with a loose theoretical framework to guide data collection but revisited this as I analyzed my data in the field, refining my interview questions, adding research sites, and seeking out new perspectives based on what I learned (Glaser and Strauss 2017). This framework allowed me to center my research on what I observed rather than building a study around what we already know.

To collect data for this project I lived in Rwanda for seven months, from January through early August 2017. During this period, I also visited Uganda, Tanzania, and Zimbabwe, where I interviewed journalists and visited news organizations with the goal of better understanding and contextualizing the work constraints and comparative context for Rwandan journalism. I conducted interviews with 80 journalists in all, ranging from editors, publishers, and journalists in each country down through the newsroom hierarchy to include journalism students at the University of Rwanda.

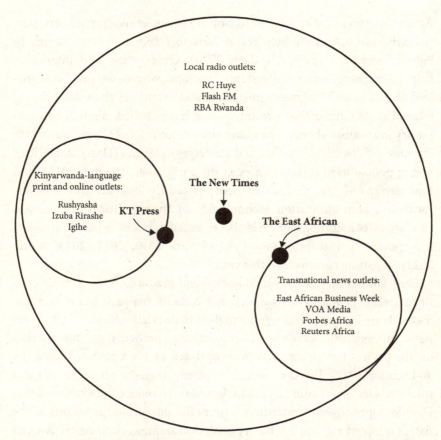

Figure 1.1 Simple visualization of communities in Rwanda's journalism field
This visualization shows the relative placement of communities within the field of journalism in Rwanda. The three newsrooms where I conducted most of my fieldwork, the *East African*, the *New Times*, and *KT Press*, are labeled and shown in reference to the communities they bridge from the *New Times*, which has the highest proportion of in-links and out-links in the network.

I conducted participant observation at three primary news sites—the *New Times*, *KT Press*, and the *East African*—which I selected from a social network analysis identifying central nodes in the Rwandan news field (see Figure 1.1). The reflexivity of participant observation as an ethnographic approach allows me to highlight the dynamic and embedded nature of cultural production and reveal the complex interactions of forces, constraints, and conventions that shape the news (Cottle 2007). I studied the Rwandan journalists' code of ethics and analyzed pre- and post-edit news articles to further understand these interactions.

I adapted data collection to the Rwandan context in a few important ways. Researchers working in Rwanda recently have reported that they were closely surveilled during their fieldwork, so I took particular care to keep my field notes and related data secure (Ingelaere 2010; Thomson 2010). I typically carried my paper field notes with me when I traveled, and when I left them behind, I locked them in a drawer and carried the key. Rwanda is well-known for its culture of secrecy and indirectness at all levels of organization; this made it challenging to begin collecting data and led me to wrap up data collection sooner than I had planned. Rwandan policy in particular is defined by "unnecessary secrecy" and "unrestrained rumour-spreading" (Booth and Golooba-Mutebi 2012, 384). This culture of secrecy shapes news production and affected my research approach. It was difficult or impossible to verify information through paper trails or other public documentation. Rwandan culture is generally private, and, while most people I met were welcoming, I suspect that editorial meetings were slow and quiet (especially at first) because of an outsider's presence. The social value of privacy combined with poor technological infrastructure made it nearly impossible to connect with people before I arrived. The infrastructure for email and other communication tools used in direct sample recruitment is often absent or poorly functioning in Global South contexts, including Rwanda (Mwizerwa et al. 2017). I could not network with journalists before I arrived in Kigali, so I spent the early weeks of fieldwork building an informal network while I waited for my research permit. I selected interview participants based on a snowball sample, starting with personal introductions to editors at the three major news organizations, who then introduced me to other participants, and so on. This sampling strategy allows researchers to establish familiarity and trust with research participants—for instance through an introduction by a trusted colleague—facilitating access to hard-to-reach participants and sensitive topics (Cohen and Arieli 2011; Dosek 2021). Finally, to protect the identities of my research subjects, I have assigned them pseudonyms and, in some cases, obscured details of their identities and workplaces, especially where there are so few employees that a workplace name and position would amount to identification. For a list of participants whose interviews are quoted in this book, see Table 1.1.

A limitation of ethnographies is that the intensive data-gathering of this approach necessitates a narrow field site—in this case, primarily elite newsrooms in Rwanda. While this allows me to draw insights along the lines noted above and to offer some insights that could apply to similar contexts

Table 1.1 Interviews Used in the Book, with Pseudonym, Organization, and Position

Name (pseudonym)	Organization	Title/Position
Gilbert	ARJ (Association Rwandaise des Journalistes)	Leadership
Caleb	East African	Reporter
Fabrice	East African	Reporter
Jean	East African	Reporter
Alphonse	KT Press	Editor
Arthur	KT Press	Editor
Claude	KT Press	Editor
Olivier	KT Press	Editor
Alice	KT Press	Reporter
Richard	KT Press	Reporter
Gabriel	KT Press	Subeditor
Peter	KT Press	Subeditor
Robert	KT Press	Subeditor
Andre	New Times	Editor
Eric	New Times	Editor
Emmanuel	New Times	Reporter
Innocent	New Times	Reporter
Jean	New Times	Reporter
Richard	New Times	Reporter
Samuel	New Times	Reporter/photographer
Gasore	New Times	Senior reporter
Maurice	Pax Press	Leadership
Auguste	Voice of America	Trainee
Bernard	Voice of America	Trainee
Philippe	Voice of America	Trainee
Fidele	Web startup	Owner/editor
Jacques	Wire service	Reporter
Lucas	Wire service	Reporter

outside Rwanda, ethnographic methods are not generalizable; they focus instead on describing and understanding a single case. Ethnographic work is also, of course, profoundly shaped by the researcher's own identity and limitations.

My identity as a white, American woman, a journalist and a graduate student, fluent only in English, influenced my interactions in the field. My status as a *mzungu*—the Swahili and Kinyarwanda word for "white foreigner"—was immediately apparent. I enrolled in Kinyarwanda lessons when I arrived in Kigali and learned enough to buy groceries and give taxi directions, but never enough to follow colloquial conversations in the language. While Rwanda has four official languages—Kinyarwanda, English, French, and Swahili—nearly 95 percent of the population speak Kinyarwanda and less than 0.1 percent speaks English (CIA 2020). However, elite journalists speak English, so I focused on English-language news outlets as my main field sites. I did this in part to avoid using an interpreter, which would have introduced interpretation challenges and a layer of surveillance into research interactions that I felt would be ethically problematic (Herod 1999). However, it means that I missed a great deal of informal conversation, most of which took place in Kinyarwanda.

As an outsider, I found it challenging to begin gathering information. My identity as a white Westerner and a former journalist also shaped my research by giving me "expert" status in some situations and making me a target of critique in others.

My background as a working journalist led me to make sense of Rwandan journalism in the context of the *Rapid City Journal*, the *Virginian-Pilot*, and other US newsrooms where I had interned or worked. This was sometimes helpful, in that it allowed me to recognize familiar routines in an unfamiliar context. It also unearthed assumptions that I had to unlearn early in my research process. In my first week of fieldwork, I was sitting in the newsroom of the *New Times* late at night, talking with an editor who was waiting for a final story to copyedit. Newsroom televisions were tuned to CNN, where Donald Trump, who had just been inaugurated, was speaking. The editor said that the relationship between the news media and the president was too antagonistic, and that journalists in the United States had an inflated and dangerous view of their own power. I was surprised that a journalist would side with Trump, who already was clearly a critic of the press. I was even more surprised by this as I continued fieldwork and saw how closely Trump's critiques of journalists paralleled the way Paul Kagame treated his own press pool. I realized I had assumed that journalists would share a global desire for autonomy and the ability to critique powerful people. Research in fact supports this, but my encounter contradicted that assumption (Waisbord 2013). This unexpected interaction has in many ways shaped the direction of my argument; it also helped me realize how grounded my own assumptions are in American journalism practice and scholarship.

Because the interviewer is a tool in qualitative interviews, my personal interviewing style affected the way I engaged with subjects and the way they disclosed information (Pezalla et al. 2012). I was concerned that interviewees would try to tell me how Rwandan journalism aligned with the US liberal democratic ideal. Some journalists did, but many instead pointed out critiques of local journalism in comparison with what they knew of American journalism. They situated Rwandan journalism in conversation with the United States and sometimes—but not always—used the comparison to highlight similarities and downplay differences. Some normalized the Rwandan situation through comparison, saying things like, "Oh, of course there are topics we cannot write about—but that is the case in every country." To avoid this normalization as much as possible, I conducted most of my interviews after a few weeks of observation and asked about newsroom routines rather than intangible concepts and values.

Another challenge I faced in the field was how to account for reactivity—the idea that people act differently when they are observed and that researcher and study participants respond to each other in a way that shapes reality through the research process (Paterson 1994). While my presence shaped the interactions I observed in some ways I noticed and others I undoubtedly did not, this is an inherent part of qualitative, especially ethnographic, research (Paterson 1994). Rather than try to attain "objectivity" (which is already impossible with observational research), I try to acknowledge my biases and patterns of communication to help the reader understand how my background might shape my interpretations (Davies 2012; Fine 1993; Paterson 1994).

I had been conducting fieldwork for less than a week when I began to see concrete ways my presence would impact the work I was observing. I was quickly put to work as an English-language expert, editing stories for the coming day's newspaper at the *New Times* and for the web at *KT Press*. In both newsrooms, I found myself occupying a position of some power relative to reporters, and in a way working for their bosses as well. After a week or two, I was asked to lead a training session on interviewing for reporters at the *New Times*. This turned into a lively and helpful discussion with reporters about the real constraints of doing interviews in Rwanda, but I felt that I had been drafted as an uninformed expert based on my Western identity, thus highlighting the power difference between my interview subjects and myself.

As one reporter pointed out to me in my first day of observation at the *New Times*, American researchers often visit Rwanda for one reason or another, but research power rarely flows in the other direction. I hope my relative power serves Rwandans by allowing me to tell the story of the complexity of journalism practice in an authoritarian state. I also hope that it paves the way for future scholars to focus on journalism in marginalized situations and perhaps empowers journalists and researchers in these contexts to tell stories from their own perspectives.

Book Outline

The rest of this book shows how and why myth is so powerful in shaping Rwandan journalism. As a window into authoritarian journalism more broadly, Rwanda shows how multiple influences converge to create a journalism field with self-reinforcing limitations in an authoritarian context. It also highlights the ways that globalization complicates and enables journalism practice. It sets ideals that are out of touch with the context, but it also provides an escape route for some journalists who have the capacity to produce journalism by the rules of a global field. Chapter 2 sketches the contours of Rwandan journalism and its political context. The journalism field is surprisingly robust in terms of size, with a similar number of journalists per capita as in nearby Kenya, whose journalism is exemplary in the region for its noisy power. However, it is characterized by low salaries and frequent turnover in both employees and organizations, signaling its transient nature. Its borders are set in part by the political environment, which has shifted from overt post-genocide restrictions on media content to looser policies that tend to be arbitrarily enforced, often at the expense of journalists. This is, in short, a context that gives extra power to narrative to define appropriate behavior.

The major myths influencing Rwandan journalism are born out of the genocide, and chapter 3 dives into these stories and their effects. This shared history shapes the journalism field from within via two myths that both constrain and guide the normative and practical possibilities of the contemporary field. The first says that journalists were responsible for the genocide; the second, that journalists might unintentionally or accidentally cause such violence again. These myths arise from shared narratives about the social role of journalists in the genocide and have become social fact, moving beyond interrogation to shape journalism today by setting the core beliefs of the field. The result is that journalists proactively limit their exploration of contentious topics rather than venturing into the space of negotiation left by political boundaries.

In chapter 4, I examine the way journalists talk about professionalism. Journalists tend to define this by skills prioritized in liberal democratic journalism, such as the ability to track down private or hidden information and use it in a story. In this sense, across news organizations and editorial hierarchies, journalists agree that they lack skill. However, Rwandan journalists exhibit another kind of skill shared by journalists across the African continent: the ability to navigate intricate social dynamics and use them to their advantage, creating routines and practices that accomplish journalists' goals in challenging situations. The persistence of Western definitions here works against journalists, as it shifts responsibility for missteps to individual journalists' lack of professionalism rather than sociopolitical challenges.

Journalists in Rwanda, like journalists and laborers everywhere, must focus on some things and avoid others to maintain paychecks and financial stability. In chapter 5, I show how business pressure leads to organizational constraints that encourage journalists to prioritize expediency and certainty in the face of opaque expectations. These intertwined influences lead journalists to develop a hierarchy of orthodox news values and routines that they can apply to obtain financial security. While in some news fields, economic pressure incentivizes journalists to find unique stories, economic pressure in Rwanda encourages isomorphic news production—news organizations mimic each other to maintain stability in the face of uncertainty, and as a result news production and story values look similar across outlets. The one exception is transnational outlets, which I explore in chapter 6. These organizations can produce unusual news because they are motivated by an audience of global, primarily non-Rwandan, subscribers, including news organizations and individuals. As a result of their global visibility, these organizations can also provide stability and security to their employees, further incentivizing news production that pushes boundaries rather than residing within them. The challenge with such organizations for Rwandan journalists is that, by working for a transnational organization, they leave the Rwandan journalism field—an act that can be interpreted as disloyalty and lead to increased scrutiny. The transnational space highlights the promise and constraints facing global journalists in locally authoritarian contexts: while they can carve out space to practice by bridging global and local fields, their bridging status means they are peripheral players in both fields with limited power in either.

These arguments have the potential to shape decisions by scholars, policymakers, and journalists. In the conclusion, I propose some ways this research can influence future scholarship, policy, and practice. My research shows how local fields can develop a variety of practices even while globalization gives journalists a mutual understanding of important values and routines. Myths grounded in local reality can shape local practice to such an extent that it overrides values often considered crucially important to professional understanding. While I show this in the case of authoritarian Rwanda, myths abound and have the potential to shape journalism's borders in a variety of contexts from democracy to autocracy and everywhere in between. For policymaking, I show how Western influences in education and training exacerbate authoritarian control rather than encouraging democratic distance and independence. Policy communities including the United States, Canada, and countries in Western Europe have treated media assistance programs as an important aspect of democracy assistance and state-building, but evaluations typically find that they have little effect on governance (Howard 2003; Karlowicz 2003). I show how local journalism is influenced by an interwoven web of myth, policy, and global influence, all of which policymakers must understand if they wish to affect the outcome of news product. Finally, this book is a story of people who practice an unpopular career in a difficult place. I show that, even amid challenges from politics and practice, Rwandan journalists exercise agency, defining their own profession in a way that currently limits their reach but that shows they have the potential to expand it.

2
Strong State, Weak Field
The Forces Shaping Journalism in Rwanda

After finishing fieldwork at the *New Times*, I often crossed the street to Meze Fresh, a Mexican restaurant, to sit in the upstairs veranda with fresh mango salsa and a margarita while I wrote up the day's field notes. The view showed off the rolling, green hills that gave Rwanda its nickname—"Land of a Thousand Hills"—and validated Kigali's reputation for being clean and organized. Just below me, a paved road came to an abrupt and awkward dead end, a few feet from another road leading to a major roundabout. Take the eastern exit and you would drive past the *New Times* on the left, followed closely by the Rwandan parliament and across the street from the National Public Prosecution Authority. The *East African*'s Rwanda bureau follows on the right, in an upper floor of an office building above Simba, an African grocery chain. A few minutes' drive away you would find Indian, Lebanese, and Korean restaurants, a yoga studio, a four-star hotel, and the roastery for Question Coffee, which distributes Rwanda-grown beans to Portland, Oregon, and other coffee hubs.

Motorcycles and vehicles follow an orderly flow of traffic down the roads; you won't spot any chickens, camels, donkeys, or other household animals mingling with the traffic, as you would in neighboring country capitals of Kampala, Uganda, or Dar es Salaam, Tanzania. You can tell traffic laws are enforced because drivers follow them; the frantic but vibrant crush of two- and four-wheel vehicles disregarding signals to cross major thoroughfares, common elsewhere in the region, is absent here. In short, Kigali's physical infrastructure makes it feel clean, orderly, and sleepy. The ideological infrastructure supporting journalism has the same effect.

The sleepy state of contemporary Rwandan journalism and the orderly flow of traffic are both outcomes of a state that encourages consensus-based decision-making, discourages rogue, individualistic behavior, and enforces strong penalties against rule-breakers. The Rwandan state today is quite strong, especially compared to its geographical neighbors and other countries in sub-Saharan Africa. This strength is evident in things like the low crime rate across the country and the state's ability to surveil everything and everyone. The strong state extends to journalists, imposing ambiguous but restrictive boundaries on news production and leaving scant protection for journalists who critique government actors. The journalism field is full of turnover, partly because journalists tend to be underpaid and poorly respected (with some exceptions, particularly in radio). Boundaries set by the political landscape signal appropriate, inappropriate, and risky behavior.

Mapping Media Outlets

While the journalism field is robust in terms of number of members, the state of financial security and general stability are dismal across news outlets and mediums. Table 2.1 lists the number of media outlets registered and legally authorized to produce content in and for Rwandan audiences and listed as such on the Media High Council's website as of December 2021. The list includes 49 newspapers, 47 broadcast outlets (35 radio stations and 12 television stations), and 32 websites. The number of registered outlets has remained fairly steady since 2017, with the exception of print outlets, which have "almost disappeared" according to the Rwandan Governance Board's 2021 Media Barometer report (Rwanda Governance Board 2021, 3). This number does, however, represent significant media industry growth over recent decades, as the media sector included only one radio station, one television station, and "a few" newspapers when the first post-genocide media law passed in 2002 (Pax Press 2017, 19).

While the MHC tracks registered news organizations on its website, the list has some discrepancies with RGB's Media Barometer. Most of the statistics I report here come from the Media Barometer; however, the MHC list in Table 2.1 provides a useful point of comparison to give a sense of turnover in the field, since I used this list to create a Twitter network before conducting fieldwork (see Methods Appendix). Between November 2016 and December 2021, 9 out of 32 registered newspapers listed on the website ceased operation, representing 40 percent of the print media scene. In 2021, 26 of 49 registered newspapers had emerged since 2016, meaning more than half (53 percent) of Rwandan newspapers available were less than five years old. The broadcast media list, on the other hand, remained more static: two outlets on the list in 2016 were missing in 2021 (the community radio station

Table 2.1 Registered Media Houses in Rwanda

Print Media	Online Media	Radio Stations	TV Stations
Imvaho Nshya (newspaper) New Times (newspaper) La Nouvelle Releve Umurinzi (newspaper) Imanzi (newspaper) Umuhuza (newspaper)	www.ruhagoyacu.com* www.umuseke.rw www.gorilla24news.com www.igihe.com www.ireme.org* www.imirasire.com* www.isange.com	RBA (Radio Rwanda and its community radios) Radio Rwanda–Inteko Radio 10 Radio1 Flash FM	RTV TV10 TV1 Flash TV
Rwanda Dispatch (magazine) Hoberwanda (magazine) Mont Jali (newspaper) Isimbi (newspaper)	www.kigalitoday.com Ktpress.rw www.hoberwandamagazine.com www.ibyamamare.com*	Contact FM City Radio Voice of America Voice of Africa RFI KT Radio	Contact TV Royal TV Family TV
Umurabyo (newspaper) Gorilla24 Ad (magazine) Ishema (newspaper) Kinyamateka (newspaper) Grands Lacs Hebdo Journal Journal Rugali	www.kigalihits.rw* www.gisenyitoday.com* www.hillywoodstar.com* www.kivu24.com www.familymag.org* www.watotosmile.com* www.makuruki.com www.urugwiro.com www.urumuri.net*	Radio Maria Rwanda Isango Star K-FM Radio Huguka Royal FM Hot FM KISS FM	AZAM TV Clouds TV Isango TV Yego TV Goodrich TV
Umusingi (newspaper) Inzobe (magazine) The Partner (magazine) Ijwi Ry'umuturage (newspaper) Hobe (magazine) (Pallotti -Presse) Angels Ubuto N'ubukuru (newspaper) Pax Press Igisabo (newspaper) Izuba Rirashe (newspaper)	www.aheza.com www.bwiza.com www.umuryango.com www.agasaro.com www.ibyishimo.com www.umukunzi.com www.rwandapaparrazzi.rw* www.inyarwanda.com* www.nonaha.com www.imvano.com www.agakiza.org www.umubavu.com www.menyanibi.com*	Authentic Radio Conseil Protestant Sana Radio (Restore Radio) Voice of Hope Radio Salus Umucyo Radio RFI Radio Amazing Grace Radio	
Intego (newspaper) Independent Publications Rwanda Focus Hope (magazine) Ihema (newspaper) Impamo (newspaper) Ingenzi (newspaper) Journal Le Reveil Indatwa (newspaper)		Isangano Community Radio Ishingiro Community Radio Izuba Community Radio Musanze Community Radio (RC Musanze) Rusizi Community Radio (RC Rusizi)	

Table 2.1 Continued

Print Media	Online Media	Radio Stations	TV Stations
Journal Imena Gasabo (newspaper) Journal Ubumwe Celes (magazine) Umuryango (newspaper) Cosmos (magazine) East African / Rwanda Today Rushyashya (newspaper)		Nyagatare Community Radio (RC Nyagatare) Huye Community Radio (RC Huye) Deutsche Well Radio Inkoramutima	
Ishya N'ihirwe (newspaper) The Diva (magazine) The Link (magazine) Panorama (newspaper) Umuseke (newspaper) Umwezi (newspaper) Urungano (magazine)			

*Many of the online news outlets mentioned above were already defunct when this book went to press in 2023; outdated links are noted with an asterisk above.
Source: Rwandan Media High Council; updated December 5, 2021.

for Rubavu in northwest Rwanda, and the BBC) and the others were still available. The broadcast market grew but experienced much less turnover than the print market over the same timeframe.

Table 2.2 lists the numbers of journalists registered to work in Rwanda under each medium (radio, television, print, online, and freelance) as reported by the 2021 Rwanda Media Barometer (Rwanda Governance Board 2021). Two things stand out about this list. First, the total number of journalists registered to work in Rwanda—1,267—works out to one journalist per 10,221 population. This is comparable to the number of journalists working in the United States (46,700 journalists, or one per 7,056 population) and Kenya (5,939 journalists, or one per 9,054 population) according to estimates from the US Bureau of Labor Statistics and the Media Council of Kenya (Media Council of Kenya 2021; US Bureau of Labor Statistics 2021). The fact that Rwanda has nearly as many working journalists per capita as a liberal democratic country with a robust and old press tradition (the United States) and a young democracy known for having the most developed

Table 2.2 Journalists Working in Rwanda in 2020

Radio	343
Freelance	323
Online	239
Television	194
Newspaper	168
Total	1267

Source: Rwanda Media Barometer 2021 (Rwanda Governance Board 2021).

media field in the East African region (Kenya) suggests that labor shortages do not constitute a major limitation in creating a strong media sector in Rwanda. However, the Media Barometer mirrors the common critique of the Rwandan media system, proclaiming that Rwanda ranks highly across four categories measuring strength of the media landscape, but falls short in "Media Development and Professional Capacity," which encompasses "financial, human, and infrastructure resources" available for news production (Rwanda Governance Board 2021, 26). In other words, official reports signal that journalists and media organizations themselves are the main source of problems related to media function in Rwanda. Second, while there are more newspapers registered than outlets in any other medium, this medium employs the fewest journalists of any—perhaps illustrating the Rwanda Governance Board finding that print outlets have declined rapidly in recent years. However, before embarking on the following summary of the Rwandan media scene, I would like to note a few caveats: it is unclear how the RGB study was conducted; the MHC and RGB lists do not add up to the same amounts of media organizations; and the survey questions are unclear, at least in English translation.

Print

While the MHC lists more registered newspapers than any other medium in the journalism field, the RGB reports that print media have suffered over recent years. Circulation has dropped and organizations closed as a result of recent growth in online network availability, leading to an audience shift to online news sources and dwindling advertising revenue (Rwanda

Governance Board 2021). This "digital disruption" led to the almost complete disappearance of newspapers from the market, according to the report, which lists eight print media outlets still operating in Rwanda in 2020. All eight outlets were privately owned, according to the report. Media consumers surveyed for the report said they had little access to print media, with 1.8 percent of citizens satisfied with their access to print media information sources (Rwanda Governance Board 2021). Very few consumers preferred or trusted print media (2.6 percent and 0.2 percent, respectively) (Rwanda Governance Board 2021). While none of these percentages add up to 100, this is the best summary available of relative trust and access to media outlets in Rwanda. This finding also coincides with recent research finding that Rwandans tend to trust state-run media more than private media; the RGB report lists all print outlets as privately owned (McIntyre and Sobel Cohen 2021).

A 2014 report on media sector challenges from the MHC notes that, based on a focus group and survey of journalists and other media workers, print journalism in particular faces financial limitations imposed by the physical constraints and requirements of publishing (Rwanda Media High Council 2014). Newspaper sales on average covered 17 percent of the operating costs of publishing houses. In fact, most print organizations spent more money printing the newspaper than they recovered in sales, with a reported budget expenditure breakdown of 29 percent on newsgathering, 24 percent on printing, 24 percent on salaries, 19 percent on office space, and 5 percent on computers and technology (Rwanda Media High Council 2014). At the same time, the average newspaper price (about 500 Rwandan francs, or 50 cents) was and remains too expensive for the average Rwandan, whose average income is about two dollars per day (World Bank 2021). As a result, newspapers are typically targeted at an audience of elite readers and distributed at office buildings around Kigali, with the *New Times* most frequently spotted in waiting rooms and offices (Rwanda Media High Council 2014). (The MHC report suggested that, to solve this pricing challenge, Rwandan journalists pool their resources to buy an in-country printing press and that the Rwandan government should install a paper factory. Neither has yet happened.)

Radio and Television

There are 47 broadcast media outlets, including radio and television stations, registered in Rwanda (again according to the MHC; the Media Barometer lists a total of 59 broadcast outlets, with 39 radio stations and 20 TV stations). Radio outlet ownership is diverse, with 15 stations privately owned, nine religiously affiliated, three community owned, one (RBA) publicly owned, one owned by a university (Radio Salus, run out of the University of Rwanda), and three internationally owned. Television ownership is similarly diverse, with 12 stations privately owned, three religious, one community owned, one public, and three internationally owned.

Radio is the most trusted and accessed news medium in Rwanda. Among respondents surveyed for the Media Barometer, 74 percent were satisfied with their ability to access radio, 94 percent preferred the radio as their information source, and 70 percent of respondents trusted radio news as a source of information (Rwanda Governance Board 2021). Television is a distant second in all of these measures: 53 percent of respondents were satisfied with their access to television news, 50 percent preferred this source of information, and 25 percent trust television news as a source of information (Rwanda Governance Board 2021).

Digital

While about one-third of Rwandans surveyed preferred Rwanda's 32 digital-only outlets as a source of information and 36 percent of respondents said they were satisfied with their ability to access digital news, trust in digital news outlets was low. Barely 3 percent of respondents trusted online publication sources of information, and 2 percent of respondents said they trust social media sources of information. All digital outlets were privately owned, according to the RGB report (Rwanda Governance Board 2021).

State Power in Rwanda

The Rwandan government contributes a set of political boundaries for journalists, defining the limits of what they can cover through legislation, surveillance, and control of dissenting voices. And, while some laws protect journalistic freedom, others define broad and ambiguous categories of off-limits content. Ambiguity and strategic silence can itself be a policy stance, as the unsaid leaves space for the more powerful actors to interpret laws to their advantage (Chibita 2010). This ambiguity provides space for journalists to negotiate expanded boundaries even in Rwanda's lopsided power distribution between politics and journalists (Moon 2023). They have the potential to help redefine ambiguous terms such as "genocide ideology" and "divisionism" narrowly to support expanded reporting frameworks and increased autonomy. However, surveillance reinforces state control, making this possibility less enticing and more dangerous.

The laws governing news production in Rwanda are an extension of the state's commitment to symbolic democracy and authoritarian enforcement. They reflect the news media's status as both an object of policy focus and a potential tool for state power in the post-genocide reconstruction project (Allen and Stremlau 2005). Rwandan laws officially provide some protections for a free press. The constitution guarantees press freedom and freedom of speech, with some supporting media laws, including one mandating information availability (Gonza 2012). Current regulatory policy, implemented in steps starting in 2003, guarantees press freedom; however, it also requires media actors to avoid defamation and discussions of ethnicity or discrimination (Bonde et al. 2015; Harber 2014; Rwandan Parliament 2009, 2013). In response to the genocide, government leaders instituted a framework of unity in a way that promoted "reconciliation and social integration," partly through strong government control over news media and other forms of information communication (Barbera and Robertson 2014; Reyntjens 2011). They made it illegal to discuss or use the ethnic labels "Tutsi" and "Hutu" and removed social references to these terms (Purdeková 2015; Straus 2015). A law prohibiting "divisionism" extends scrutiny to anyone who publicly discusses ethnic tension; critics say it defines key terms vaguely in ways that unnecessarily limit the scope of journalism practice (Harber 2014; The Economist 2019). Partly as a result of this, many journalists avoid the topic altogether (Sobel and McIntyre 2019).

Current political structures are designed to keep the ruling elite in power and prevent the return of hate media, and they accomplish this by limiting media freedom through legal sanctions and harassment (Cruikshank 2017; Fiedler and Frère 2018; Moon 2019). Media organizations in Rwanda must register with the government per a 2009 law (Kagire 2010; Shamlal 2014). A regulatory agency, the MHC, oversees media freedom, responsibility, and professionalism, and can interpret these terms in favor of or against journalists (Shamlal 2014). These political developments, of course, restrict media freedom (Freedom House 2017a; Gonza 2012). Rwandan journalists report that laws extending important freedoms for journalistic work, such as an access-to-information act, are poorly implemented, whereas others, including an anti-defamation law, are vaguely worded and tend to be enforced against journalists. In practice, officials discourage journalists from investigating politically contentious topics; one journalist reported death threats and visits from security officials after reporting on the army, corruption, and the president (Thompson 2007).

The powerful Rwandan state aggressively enforces these laws. While many African states are authoritarian with weak bureaucracy, chaotic internal politics, and lackadaisical policy enforcement, Rwanda is known for its strong and effective government (Purdeková 2015; Straus 2013). Civil servants and other government employees effectively police crime, enforce legal restrictions, and patrol social life. Crime rates are low, even in Kigali, and the majority of Rwandans—including journalists I interviewed—report feeling secure from crime in their daily lives (Goodfellow and Smith 2013). The Rwandan state swoops in to swiftly enforce legal restrictions, for instance exacting strong penalties for breaking construction codes or zoning rules, making illegal construction rare (Goodfellow 2013). As a result, streets are clean, bureaucrats are competent and available, and corruption is low (Reyntjens 2013). The Rwandan Patriotic Front regulates economics and politics to such an extent that major business interests are government-controlled, and if government employees are even suspected of corrupt behavior, they are sanctioned immediately and effectively (Booth and Golooba-Mutebi 2012). Development agencies through the 1980s found Rwanda to be a model of efficiency as an aid recipient, in spite of the country's few natural resources and unstable neighbors (Barnett 2002). These marks of power highlight the state's ability to react quickly and effectively to enforce laws.

The Rwandan government also enforces and rewards collectivity and obedience to central authority, and this is evident in uncontested national elections, executive power, and control of shared memory around the genocide. Rwanda has held regular, open presidential elections since 2003, but competition is practically nonexistent. A 2015 special election extended presidential term limits from two to five, meaning incumbent president Paul Kagame can now serve until 2034 (Associated Press 2015). He won the August 2017 presidential election against opposition candidate Frank Habineza with 99 percent of the vote (Baddorf 2017; Levitsky and Way 2002; Muvunyi 2017). In 2003 and 2008 elections, observers found evidence of ballot box fraud and reported that that voters were pressured to vote for the ruling party (Samset 2011). And, while the Rwandan parliament is staffed by proportional representation, this practice serves to support single-party rule rather than diversifying perspectives (Guariso et al. 2017; Stroh 2010). The government's development program through the first decades of the twenty-first century, "Vision 2020," relied on Kagame's individual connections, lack of political dissent, and destruction of civil society to encourage economic growth (Friedman 2012). Since 2001, the government has legally controlled the finances and projects of all NGOs in the country, pushing out opposition and independent organizations (Mwambari 2017). Through these and other measures, the Rwandan government reinforces central state power over diversity of opinion and democratic conflict.

This unified power, along with Rwanda's unique geography and linguistic context, reinforces a strong surveillance state. Rwanda is one of the world's 50 smallest countries and one of the 10 smallest in sub-Saharan Africa, and its small size reinforces government power. The larger the state, the more expensive it is to extend roads, telephone lines, and other aspects of communication and transportation infrastructure beyond major cities, and as a result, central state power is weak outside of urban spaces and toward country borders in many African countries (Herbst 2014). Rwanda is also the only African nation where almost the entire local population shares one indigenous language, Kinyarwanda; by contrast, Luganda—the official and most widely spoken indigenous language in neighboring Uganda—is only spoken by 18 percent of the local population (CIA 2020; Ssentanda and Nakayiza 2015). This shared language enhances the government's ability to consolidate power and enforce national regulations (Migdal 1988).

These things reinforce the state's ability to consistently monitor subjects across the country, and it has extended this layered oversight for centuries (Purdeková 2016). Today, the state surveils through mundane quotidian practices like community work groups (*umuganda*), identity cards, and dense administrative networks (Purdeková 2016). These regular surveillance practices have increased since the genocide, cultivating a general sense that one might be observed at any point (Purdeková 2016). Even encrypted messaging platforms like WhatsApp are subject to state surveillance, and WhatsApp conversations have been used as evidence in court cases against government critics, leading journalists to conclude that the government is listening everywhere (AT Editor 2017; Moon 2022; Srivastava and Wilson 2019). State surveillance places journalists in a state of constant visibility and encourages conformity at the expense of many journalistic routines and news values, regardless of whether the state is considered authoritarian or democratic (Munoriyarwa and Chiumbu 2019; Waters 2018). Journalists embrace the centrality of political figures, as is evident in Figure 2.1, which shows the Twitter network mapped around the central, most-followed figures (all of whom are politicians).

After the 1994 genocide, Rwandan leadership leaned into a unified, nationalistic outlook. The government discourages discussion of ethnic identities and promotes unity through neighborhood-style community organizations called *umudugudus*, education camps, and slogans like *ndi umunyarwanda*—"I am Rwandan" (Purdeková 2015). Officials and policies cultivate unity in part by controlling public retellings of the genocide. This creates a centralized process of remembering a shared history in a way that disparages blind obedience while, ironically, "demanding the very same thing from the population" (Eramian 2017, 642). The *gacaca* transitional justice program, which addresses domestic genocide crimes, has been implicated in this narrative control as a way for government authorities to silence political opposition while ostensibly acting in the interests of genocide prevention and ethnic unity (Loyle 2018). Laws criminalizing genocide ideology also reinforce a shared narrative, as people and organizations who call that narrative into question become criminals (Jessee 2011; Kelley 2017). Stories that question the provenance of the genocide, implicate Tutsis in the violence, or suggest that Hutu Rwandans died in the slaughter are likely targets of the genocide ideology accusation; the BBC, for instance, was banned from Rwanda in 2015 for a broadcast suggesting that Kagame may have played a role in triggering the genocide and that many genocide victims may have been Hutu (Baird 2015). Social understanding of the genocide is of course especially crucial in Rwandan society and is controlled more closely than many other aspects of identity. However, it provides a good illustration of the mechanics behind a generally defining feature of Rwandan society—people are reluctant to critique authority figures. News sites give the average Rwandan the ability to comment online, but commenters tend to engage minimally (Nduhura and Prieler 2017). Indeed, citizen engagement with media content in Africa is limited beyond Rwanda; a study of neighboring Uganda found that local listeners to explicitly participatory community radio programs tended to not participate for a variety of reasons, including limited access to information and communication technology and other physical barriers (Semujju 2014). Journalists from two top radio stations report that citizens are reluctant to serve as sources because they are afraid to reveal secret information that might be classified as a security risk or incriminate a powerful

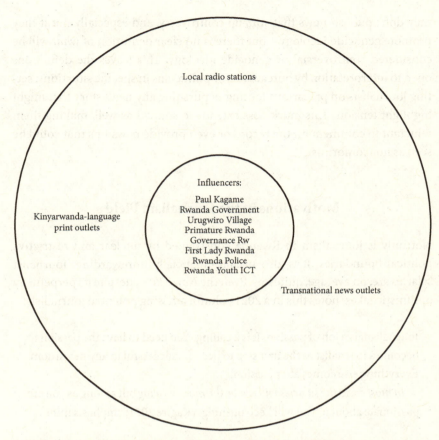

Figure 2.1 Simple visualization of Rwandan journalism influencers as measured on Twitter

This simple visualization shows the major influencers in the Rwandan journalism field, measured by eigenvector centrality—a measure of connection to other well-connected nodes. By this measure, the major influencers across all news outlets are government figures, not journalists.

individual (Nduhura and Prieler 2017). My interviews corroborated this; Philippe, a journalism trainee with Voice of America, told me that many people who might serve as critical sources "fear being seen as critics of the government." In Rwanda, the social pressure to conform extends to politics as well, and many journalists told me they struggle to find sources who will voice opposition on the record for news articles.

These things—the legal system, frequent surveillance, and pressure to conform—set up a political context for Rwandan journalists whose borders are restrictive but murky. Journalists are guaranteed freedom, but only if they don't publish news that stirs up controversy, and especially not if they promote genocide ideology—but there is no clear definition of *what* will be considered controversial or genocide ideology. This leaves the definitions open to interpretation by bureaucrats or politicians in specific situations, setting journalists on precarious footing in pursuing any news story that might highlight tension. This murkiness extends to sources as well, making them reluctant to comment on the record or even provide news tips that could be seen as nonconformist.

Motivations in the Journalism Field

Not only is journalism in Rwanda constrained by unclear and restrictive political boundaries, it is also usually financially unrewarding. Journalist salaries are, on average, quite low. Even the *New Times*, despite its perpetually optimistic takes, notes this in a 2021 column advising potential journalists:

> Journalism is a job of passion. It is a calling. You need to have the passion to become a journalist as the first step to become successful in any newsroom. Everything else comes after passion.
>
> *In most cases the salaries will not be the most enticing* but as long as you are passionate about it, you will keep pushing. (Kagire 2021; emphasis mine)

The data is thin but supports the comment that salaries are "not the most enticing." In 2014, photojournalist Sally Stapleton surveyed 100 journalists at seven highly ranked news organizations (likely including the same elite organizations I studied) and found that 43 percent of the respondents earned a monthly salary less than US$293, which was the average salary of a Kigali airport taxi driver (Stapleton 2014). In this, Rwanda resembles other countries across the continent; journalists in sub-Saharan Africa tend to be paid poorly. In many countries, they resort to brown-envelope practices of accepting bribes to compensate for inadequate paychecks. Often, this is seen as unethical but a practice for journalists to police among themselves, as scholars have explored in case studies of the Republic of the Congo, Ghana, Tanzania, Zambia, and Zimbabwe (Mabweazara 2018, Kasoma 2009, Nkie Mongo 2021). Rwandan journalists certainly also accept bribes. However, the Rwandan government's hardline approach against corruption means journalists who take brown envelopes are open to sanctions from the government as well as the profession, making this avenue for additional compensation less enticing.

In addition to the low earnings, journalists at many news organizations could not count on reliable paychecks. At the elite organizations I studied, journalists' paychecks would arrive more or less on time, but across the media sector, delayed pay is not uncommon. Delayed paychecks are not exclusively a problem of the journalism field in Rwanda: employees at the nationally subsidized University of Rwanda, for instance, experienced a several-month paycheck delay in the late spring and early summer of 2017. Thus, journalists considered it a privilege and mark of organizational success to work at a place where they would receive regular paychecks. Lucas, a wire reporter, explained that for many Rwandan journalists, this would not happen:

> The worst, and many people here are used to that, is when you will wait a month or two months to have a salary. For local journalists, it is possible ... the company doesn't have means to pay you. And journalists will keep working because they will say, "Maybe the salary will come." Maybe, maybe. And sometimes it reaches nine months without a salary.

As a result, the typical Rwandan journalist exists in financial precarity, producing news content for organizations to publish while hoping the employer will pay out a wage at the end of the month. For some, this wait stretches out for multiple months while an employer scrambles for funds to pay salaries. Many journalists, especially those working for community radio and other smaller news organizations, work for months in the hope that a paycheck might materialize down the road. And pay, of course, affects motivation; Maurice, who works in leadership with the peace journalism-oriented NGO Pax Press, said it has trouble incentivizing journalists to improve their craft. "When journalists are not paid, when journalists are not motivated financially, we cannot improve their work professionally," he said. "That's a very big problem."

In addition to low pay, I found that journalists rarely had the benefit of employment contracts—an important marker of financial stability in the Rwandan economic system. About half of employees in Rwanda who work in the formal sector—meaning they work for incorporated, registered businesses—are still informal employees, working without legal and social protection (Andersen 2021). Of course, the vast majority of Rwandan wage-earners work in the informal economy, which constituted about 90 percent of total employment in 2019 (Andersen 2021). Rwandan labor laws regulate employment in several ways, but many protections, including the right to strike and the right to collective bargaining, extend only to contractual staff (Andersen 2021). Even among journalists at the elite organizations I focused on for my study, contracts were rare beyond the highest levels of staff. Gabriel, a subeditor at *KT Press* noted, "Not many journalists here have contracts, and that is a challenge. Start with this one—you thought I had a contract? I don't. Even I don't have a contract."

A lack of contract has several implications, including precarious employment. Gabriel explained, "If they told me tomorrow I was not coming back, I would just say bye to you. . . . That's why I joke with [name omitted] and say we are mercenaries." Rwandan regulations do not extend unemployment protection to employees (Andersen 2021). In addition, employees without contracts would have a hard time obtaining bank loans for things like housing. "You may get a good salary, but if you don't have a contract, that's another problem," said Arthur, a *KT Press* editor with a contract. "Here, if you don't have a contract, you can't have a loan . . . for a journalist to get a loan for a house, you need to be married to a civil servant." Jean, a reporter at the *East African*, explained the importance of contracts to personal financial stability:

> The loan that you normally are supposed to get when you are on payroll is what they call a personal loan, and you are given that loan because you have an employer who has approved that you are a full-service member of the company. So you can keep a number of obligations, but if you don't have that contract, then the bank will not trust you.

What this means is that, without a contract, many financial benefits are unavailable to employees, who essentially cannot prove that they will be employed for any foreseeable amount of time. Thus excluded from bank loans, the majority of journalists in Rwanda are unable to purchase houses or even vehicles, which tend to be quite expensive and are themselves signals of high levels of wealth. The *New Times* was most generous with contracts among the elite organizations I studied, and even here they extended only to select editors and reporters, as well as senior editorial staff.

Rwandan employees without contracts also have limited access to health insurance. While Rwandan policy supports a comprehensive system that delivers "a minimum level of income security to all Rwandans," coverage is low and extends primarily to the richest quintile because of enrollment costs; less than 8 percent of 18- to 64-year-olds in Rwanda were covered by social security policies in 2021 (Andersen 2021, 26). This struggle to gain health insurance coverage and other benefits is a challenge for journalists (and others). In a typical Rwandan understatement, Arthur explained, "That one is the cause of many headaches in Rwanda."

Journalists have access to a trade union that, in theory, supports a minimum wage (hypothetically, as this wage had not yet been set as of 2021), contract compliance, and access to social security benefits; however, unions in Rwanda are generally fairly weak and face challenging legal restrictions (Andersen 2021). Among them, membership must include a majority of workers in the occupation, and employers may refuse workplace access to unions (US Department of State 2019). The media union is part of COTRAF, the Labor and Worker's Brotherhood Congress (Congrès du Travail et de la Fraternité au Rwanda), which, with 24,500 members, represents 10 percent of organized workers and was established in 2003 (International Trade Union Confederation 2019). However, there is no available data on how many members are actually part of the media arm of the organization (Andersen 2021). Overall, 3.6 percent of employed people in Rwanda are part of a union, and Rwanda scores 3 out of 5 (with 5 being worst) for violations of trade union rights (Andersen 2021).

To sum up: in general, Rwandan employees are not particularly well treated, and media professions tend to be on the more precarious end of the spectrum of formal employment. The ability to accrue economic capital within the field is low. As a result of this, journalists tend to prioritize building capital in ways that will transfer either horizontally, to other fields in Rwanda, or vertically, to the global journalism field. Journalists who want to be flexible across careers and remain in Rwanda focus on building up *horizontal* capital that would help them transfer to other careers in the country. These cross-field transfers within Rwanda often involved moving to careers in public relations or other types of corporate or government communication working for organizations they previously reported on as journalists. For instance, Alice, a reporter at *KT Press*, told me, "Journalism is not my dream career. My dream career is to become a motivational public speaker.... Journalism is just a way to that public speaking.... What I am doing here is just a stepping point."

On the other hand, journalists who aim for geographic flexibility or prestige within the journalism field focused on building up *vertical* capital that increased their credibility and prestige within the journalism field and would facilitate a jump from the Rwandan journalism field to the global field and, from there, could transfer to other national journalism fields in the region or beyond.

Building Capital through Networks

Social capital, in the form of organizationally facilitated relationships and personal reputation, played a crucial role in journalists' abilities to transition across fields. Organizational affiliation signaled journalists' comfort or discomfort with a state-affirming style of information-gathering and news production. Personal reputation—especially conveyed via bylines—further signaled both group membership and a reporter's personal approach to managing information flows. Both messages could build personal credibility and reputation and signal membership in a group of journalists who understood and affirmed the Rwandan state's vision of media production. They could also signal outsider status, especially to those looking to hire people with strong communication skills and critical approaches to government messaging.

This understanding of social capital extends the scholarship on journalistic capital by linking it to specific objects. Bourdieu defined social capital as the group of resources linked to a particular social network, or as the material and social benefits conferred by group membership (Bourdieu 1986). More recently, journalism scholar Kristy Hess expanded the application of social capital in journalism contexts by suggesting that journalists acquire and benefit from *mediated* social capital: "A resource of power available to traditional, commercial news media through its ability to connect people, consciously and unconsciously, across various social, economic, and cultural spaces and to link people with those in positions of power" (Hess 2013, 113; see also Hess 2015). The ability to control information flow between two parties constitutes a form of social capital, Hess argues, and journalists can build up their store of it by facilitating or blocking information flow to build up cohesion or division (Hess 2013). This approach "shifts social capital from being a societal-level resource to a resource that news outlets themselves may acquire for their own gain—and like any discussion of power—it has potential for abuse and exclusion" (Hess 2015, 483). In Rwanda, forms of social capital could be acquired from organizational affiliation or through personal reputation. This capital comes from both social network membership in Bourdieu's sense and from the journalist's reputation for facilitating or hindering particular kinds of information-sharing in Hess's sense.

Organizational Identity

Organizational identity bestowed social capital on its employees. This capital primarily signaled group membership in the Bourdieusian sense. Every news organization in Rwanda has an "editorial line" that guides what kinds of news and what angles the organization will and will not pursue and publish. The editorial line is usually unspoken and unwritten, especially when it is government aligned, but journalists used the organization's editorial line as a matter-of-fact explanation for the type of source access and audience recognition they would get. The editorial line at the *New Times* was government aligned, and the longer reporters worked there, the more they became part of that pro-government network. The editorial line at the *East African* was independent, and reporters I talked with who had worked there for a while leaned into their critical, independent identities as making them "good journalists." These stances affected how journalists saw their own identities and what kinds of networks they were added to.

Reporters at *KT Press* and the *New Times* would often hear more gossip from state officials who assumed they were "safe" confidants because those organizations would not publish very critical news. The news outlet's reputation played a stronger role in this calculus than did the individual reporter's views. One reporter at the *New Times* told me she was good personal friends with a newly appointed judge. I watched her interview him and she asked pointed questions, which he answered verbosely with the caveat that he wouldn't want them printed. This was not a foolproof way of protecting the source's interests: reporters with these relationships at the *New Times* and *KT Press* would sometimes pass along news tips to their colleagues at the *East African* and wire services when they felt a story was newsworthy but did not fit with their employer's editorial line. But sources could be confident that news that highlighted a negative element of Rwandan politics or governance would be unlikely to appear in the *New Times* or *KT Press* without their approval or the approval of another government figure; thus, they would share such information more freely than with reporters at outlets that were unconcerned with government vetting of stories.

The group affiliations signaled by organizational identity could work against journalists as well; for instance, I recommended a senior reporter at the *New Times* as a copywriter to an acquaintance looking to produce advertising materials for a new business. The acquaintance rejected my recommendation without considering the reporter's personal characteristics (which included good English writing ability and a deep understanding of Rwanda's political and social spheres) because, my friend said, this reporter worked for the *New Times* and thus would not be able to write with the appropriately neutral or critical voice that the project would demand. On the other hand, reporters affiliated with news organizations that had a pro-government editorial line would frequently be hired away to public relations positions for government organizations, in part because their employment sent a message that they understood the government's position and could support it in public communication. Within a few years of my fieldwork, one of the established reporters I interviewed at the *New Times* had moved to a program manager position for a government ministry, and a reporter from *KT Press* had taken a position at the Office of the Government Spokesperson.

In reality, journalists working for elite organizations in the news field would often move back and forth between organizations critical or supportive of government officials and policies, suggesting that not all journalists really adopted the social orientations of their employers. However, it was clear that organizational social capital conferred benefits and challenges on associated individuals. In the absence of a strong union and other signals of field leadership, organizations hold a fair amount of power to bestow capital on their employees, even as individuals build up cultural capital associated with their bylines, which are portable across organizations.

The *East African* is known for running the news "without censorship," rather than editing it to fit a pro-government editorial line. Caleb explained,

> As long as you have your facts correct, as long as you have your facts backed up on a computer somewhere or a recorder somewhere, the editor will run the story. There is no censorship, no censorship at all, you know. As long as you can demonstrate that this story is clean and all the facts are there, then you run the story, unlike many other media houses here, where even if it is right, as long as it's critical or it's a bit negative, it won't run. It won't see the daylight.

This approach contrasted with fully local news outlets in that it could be expected to run stories that criticized local and national officials and policies, even if those officials did not want the story to see the light of day.

"You get so many benefits with the *East African*—you get training, you get people trusting you as a journalist," Caleb said. To him, intangible benefits associated with the organization's independent editorial line were important along with the salary offered by the publication.

Building Capital through Personal Brand

Journalists also worked to build up individual social capital within the journalism field so that they would be known and trusted as journalists who could and would routinely produce certain types of news content. Jacques, a reporter for a wire service who had previously worked at the *New Times*, described this as "playing the game." He had come from Uganda, and described his transition this way:

> You are coming from this background where the media is independent and you are attacking government policy and corruption. Now you are coming to [the *New Times*], a newspaper which is very closed. So now what you do is you decide, are you going to go back to Kampala? If you are going to stay [in Kigali], you have to play the game. You have to write that kind of story.

Even though it frustrated this reporter that he felt a lack of real editorial freedom to pursue stories independently of government oversight or approval, he persisted in following the established editorial line because he had a vested interest in being able to pursue a career as a journalist in Rwanda. If he had decided to return to Uganda, he explained, he would feel less invested in that editorial line and would have been more likely to pursue critical stories regardless of the consequences. Another way journalists built up individual social capital was in the way they interacted with sources. Arthur, an editor at *KT Press*, explained how important this was: "When you write a story for the first time, someone has given you some information, protect him. And with time, he calls you and tells you . . . some story." The environment within which journalists operate in Rwanda is highly relational, and a substantial amount of information that is legally specified as public information is still only available to journalists who have good personal relationships with sources. Thus, maintaining and building good relationships with sources is important for journalists to find stories.

Finally, journalists measured individual social capital in terms of byline recognition and social media reach. Arthur said he felt successful when a news organization approached him to offer a job.

> It means a lot if someone approaches you, asks you, "How much will you charge us, can you join, will you please come? Can you join us?" That means my byline—when people see your byline, they feel it is a good story. My seal has always been my byline. I bring my degree as an administrative requirement, but no one asks me, "Yeah, bring your CV, this and this." No, in this country—in this career—people headhunt. You don't see people calling for applications.

A media manager at *KT Press* confirmed this, noting that he preferred to find the appropriate candidate and court that person, because publishing an open position would result in a flood of unqualified applications. Thus, building name recognition would serve journalists both at their workplace and beyond, providing them greater freedom to move around the field. Organizational backing conveyed a message about a journalist's ideological leaning to those outside the field; for instance, one small business owner rejected my suggestion of a *New Times* journalist as a copywriter because, this business owner said, anyone working for the *New Times* would have a perspective that was too pro-government. But to those within the field making hiring decisions, more personal quality metrics, such as stories written, seemed to carry more power. A number of reporters had moved at least once and sometimes more than once between organizations with vastly different and even opposing editorial lines, conveying different perspectives on what it means to be a good journalist—but no reporter mentioned encountering ideological resistance from editors when shifting across organizations in this way. Occasionally journalists were told they could not work for transnational media outlets and local outlets concurrently, but it seemed to be acceptable to switch back and forth for at least some people.

When I spent time in it, the *New Times* newsroom was located primarily on the ground floor of an office building that also housed the Star Times, a cable TV provider. It was next door to Rwanda's parliament and across the street from the Ministry of Justice, National Public Prosecution Authority, and Supreme Court. Reporters would routinely walk over to these locations to report, and guards recognized them by sight. Reporters at the *New Times* generally enjoyed high social capital, courtesy of the organization. "The *New Times* is famous," Arthur explained. "It came before us; it is an established newspaper." Because of this, sources would bring certain kinds of news tips to reporters, eager to have them investigated and sure they would be investigated in a particular way at the *New Times*.

The *New Times* is ostensibly independent, but it is common knowledge among Rwandan journalists that it is in fact a government-aligned publication. The editorial line supports the government, and stories that critique the government are unlikely to be published unless they fall within strict boundaries and investigate matters that a government official has already approved for investigation. I explore the mechanics of this process in more detail later; importantly, though, this editorial direction is never explicitly conveyed to reporters, but it is enforced through actions. Reporters who wrote stories that were "too investigative" or too critical would find those stories embroiled in multiple cycles of editing, be asked to find additional sources to make it more neutral, or just have the story disappear from the story budget—the list of stories scheduled for the next day's newspaper—without explanation near the end of the day. Editors would hear more direct instructions to refrain from publishing particular stories. Jacques, who had previously worked at the *New Times*, explained it this way:

> When I was still at the *New Times* investigation desk, we would want to run a story about corruption, for instance. Of course, you go through many sources, you call people to react. But before you publish the story, you get a call from someone telling you, "Please don't write that story."

The pro-government editorial line at the *New Times* and other local elite outlets was generally not explicitly communicated but was generally understood to exist. Editors would be penalized for letting a too-critical story appear in print, sometimes with a warning and sometimes by losing their job. Reporters generally did not face overt criticism or instruction about avoiding particular stories, but they would be penalized and instructed in other ways.

Kigali Today, like the *New Times*, had a pro-government editorial line. "*Kigali Today*, whenever they break a story, just know government has given it to them," Caleb said. "Even if it looks nice, that's nice government—they are totally government." Reporters working at *KT Press* and those working for other outlets confirmed this perception. Journalists at the *New Times* and

KT Press knew that one future career path for them would involve working in government. Many reporters referred to a pipeline from the news business to more lucrative and stable public relations work, especially between the *New Times* and government PR offices. This career path would be more likely to be available to a particular journalist if he or she had friends, not enemies, in government. Jacques summed this up by saying, "Local journalists . . . want to be nice to the state because they are trying to get a job from them, they are going to get money from them."

The Currency of Vocational Legitimacy

Journalistic credibility (often studied as cultural capital) had the most value on the vertical market.

Journalists across media organizations shared a common understanding of what they called "real" journalism. This was set in contrast to media work that was sometimes labeled "PR" and sometimes labeled development journalism.

"Real" journalism included independent investigation and stories critical of the government, especially the RPF, the majority political party. Lucas, a wire reporter, described it as harder work than its "PR" counterpart. "The real journalism is not just this kind of local journalism where you are working for someone who just tells you, 'Go and bring the story' and the story will be published," he said. "At [wire service], even though I go to this event, is it really newsworthy?" To him, real journalism involved a thought process of looking for values of newsworthiness beyond an event's occurrence. Others described real journalism as that which they felt or perceived to impact some in their community. Peter, an editor at *KT Press*, described the impact of "real journalism" he had done at a past job, contrasting it with his current job at a pro-government news outlet:

> You could do a story and you feel that this is going to shake the country, this is going to shake people. People would call even from the United States, Kenya, whatever, and say, "Wow, good story, man!" But in pro-government media, you just wait for the month to end, and you get your pay.

Part of doing real journalism also involved having an editor who would push the reporter to ask more questions and write clearly and well, Peter said:

> My boss was a PhD, and he could guide you, he could ask do this, and you find that at the end of the day you produce quality, with the right story. And he was also good at editing. So you could produce, publish this story, and when you read it you say, "Wow, I really did my job, and the editor made it look great."

This editor felt he had done real journalism when he was working as a reporter and interacting with an editor who demanded skilled reporting and writing from him, pushing him to craft what he felt was quality content.

Journalists discussed this sort of work in contrast to a type of journalism that some called development journalism and some just called "PR." The determination of who referred to this style of news as PR or as development journalism seemed to do with personal investment or alignment with the mission: those who felt they were doing important work practicing this form of journalism tended to call it "development journalism," while those who had felt more fulfilled practicing independent journalism tended to call it "PR." In this sort of *news work*, often tied to pro-government media organizations, journalists were less motivated to do investigation and legwork. Instead, one reporter said, "People are kind of relaxed because they dictate what you are supposed to publish or talk about. It's like, I do what my boss wants me to do." This kind of journalism practice also lacked analysis, another reporter said; instead of digging into the background of an issue, reporters would "just report," giving the facts of an event instead of unpacking the meaning behind it. Samuel, a *New Times* photographer and former reporter, summed up a common view of this sort of journalism, practiced at many media organizations in Rwanda:

> It's all PR. All the media houses, they await invitations from people with the conferences, the events. All our news is based on events. . . . Many people say, I know, that it's money—you can have that issue, that problem of not having enough money, but at least one article that is out, it is good. It is that one article that everyone, even journalists themselves, among themselves, they are sharing it. But we don't have them. Maybe it's because . . . owners, including the journalists, they fear that if I say this, in the way I feel I have to do, I will get troubles.

This analysis of "PR" journalism highlights the importance of gathering news—enterprise reporting—as a component of "real" journalism versus

PR. This journalist also highlights a more personal, feeling-based element that, to him, accompanies real journalism: the feeling that you have written a good story, "that one article" that everyone is sharing and talking about. To these reporters, journalism that does not at least occasionally accomplish this agenda-setting role doesn't qualify as real. It is important to note, though, that not everyone felt unfulfilled by practicing less independent journalism; one reporter told me that he felt he was doing what was best for Rwanda by writing positive stories at the *New Times*. People had seen enough hardship and sadness through the genocide and its aftermath, he said, and needed encouraging stories to come together and work to develop the country.

Conclusion

To summarize the above tensions and complications, Rwandan journalism is a high-stress and low-reward profession, where journalists face major political constraints on their freedom; common freedom indices, such as Freedom House's "Freedom in the World" report, corroborate this. Political pressure directly from these constraints and pressure channeled through friends, audiences, and other groups combine to encourage self-censorship and limit autonomy on journalists (Workneh 2020). However, even within the boundaries of authoritarian media control, journalists can negotiate flexible boundaries around off-limits topics. In Uganda, for instance, a neighboring authoritarian country with a "not free" rating, journalists use uncertainty to strategically limit their self-censorship and report on controversial topics (Moon 2023). In other words, even in unfree political contexts, journalists can exercise some autonomy.

Autonomy is central to professional fields in general and to journalism specifically, but the concept is complex, with many definitions. In the context of field theory, autonomy is, broadly, the ability of actors in a specific social area to set their own priorities with minimal outside influence (Bourdieu 1991). Social actors are always shaped to some extent by their interactions with other groups, but autonomy extends their ability to perform a different role and look different from other groups (Krause 2017). Autonomy is also generally a signal of field strength; fields with the ability to determine appropriate behavior and membership criteria among themselves are stronger, while strong mandates from outside forces or weakly defined protections tend to define weak fields (Vauchez 2011).

Among journalists and journalism scholars, autonomy gains additional layers of complexity. Journalists themselves generally prioritize autonomy, clinging to it in democratic and non-democratic contexts (Waisbord 2013). However, journalism is, by its very nature, dependent on other social actors, especially sources and audiences; so even in the most free contexts, journalists don't enjoy full autonomy (Schudson 2005). In addition, they tend to have more autonomy in full democracies and Western contexts than in authoritarian, hybrid, and otherwise non-democratic regimes (Reich and Hanitzsch 2013). Further, across the African continent, sources and audiences are conflicted about whether journalism should be free and powerful. The 2019 Afrobarometer survey conducted in 34 countries across the continent found that more Africans surveyed support governments preventing publication of harmful information than support media freedom (Conroy-Krutz and Sanny 2019).

The definition of autonomy varies across contexts. Some journalists use it to mean they can control how they develop stories, while for others it means the ability to actually publish news articles about powerful topics (Hughes et al. 2017). Journalists tend to base their own sense of autonomy on their level of freedom within an organization rather than the freedoms provided by the larger social system (Mellado and Humanes 2012). Even within the same organization, journalists can have different concepts of autonomy, focusing on it as freedom from internal organizational pressures or as freedom from external and social pressures on journalistic practices (Kotisova and Císařová 2023). And journalists don't necessarily use their autonomy to further the social service of the profession; in Zimbabwe, for instance, journalists use organizational training to resist the hostile, authoritarian media environment while also developing media "regimes" that counter ethical and professional expectations (Mano 2017).

In Rwanda, journalistic autonomy encompasses the ability to seek different kinds of rewards, but the political boundaries are narrow and the financial ceiling on the profession is low—even well-known journalists top out their pay at meager rates. Journalists can amass cultural capital, showing their peers that they are good at their craft; they can do this on two planes, either of which leads directly to another career field. Journalists who choose the Rwandan capital path learn to play effectively by the rules of Rwandan journalism and, once they have earned enough respect, tend to get poached for spokesperson roles by local NGOs or government agencies. Journalists who choose the global capital path learn to play by rules that are respected in the global journalism field, and once they are good enough, they leave for locally based positions in that global field. However, whatever path they choose, Rwandan journalists must follow the rules of a field shaped by myths rooted in the genocide, and it is to those myths that we now turn.

3
Founding Myths
Stories as Building Blocks of Journalism Practice

In early February, Gasore, a *New Times* courts reporter, invited me to accompany him to a session at parliament, which convened in an imposing, security-patrolled complex next door to the newspaper's office. We missed the hearing (which itself says something about Rwandan journalism, as I will discuss in chapter 5) but Gasore offered a tour of the grounds and building. Security guards patrol the gated entrance to the grounds, which are covered in thick, neatly trimmed grass, flowering trees, and bushes. The most imposing feature on the parliamentary grounds, aside from the building, is a memorial to the Rwandan Patriotic Front soldiers. It sits in a clearing to one side of the parliament building and depicts, larger than life, several armed RPF leaders. The grounds were mostly empty, but Gasore greeted a few media relations staff at work in their offices, and then he stopped along a second-floor veranda to show me the imposing brick and cement wall of the main building. It was riddled with pockmarks from bullets and shells—scars incurred during the genocide, jarring amid the placid beauty of the grounds. It was such a powerful visual statement that I snapped a photo (Figure 3.1). The choice to leave the wall un-renovated is intentional; the Rwandan government wanted to leave a visual reminder of the violence suffered by the building and the officials who camped out here as the genocide began, Gasore said. And, while he was only 10 during the genocide, he has his own vivid memories from that time. His family had fled to Uganda to escape building ethnic tension, but when they returned in late 1994, bodies littered the streets—a stark reminder of the horrific violence. Everything about Rwandan politics, policy, and social life since then has been shaped by a motivation to encourage and create a cohesive society in the genocide's wake.

#

While Rwanda has officially moved past post-conflict recovery, citizens still grapple on an individual and social level with the violence and

Figure 3.1 The outer walls of the Rwandan Parliament are riddled with holes from bullets and shells, left after the building was besieged during the genocide. Author photo.

division that led up to and defined the genocide (Brinkerhoff 2005; Collier et al. 2008; International Development Association 2009; EFA Global Monitoring Report Team 2011). The tour and my conversation with

Gasore highlighted the genocide's layers of influence on everything from physical infrastructure to policy and personal history in Rwanda today. The shell-marked parliament building drove home the omnipresence of genocide memory in Rwanda's public arena, especially in matters of politics and public discussion. This influence extends to journalism, where pervasive genocide myths shape the shared assumptions underlying the field.

In the last chapter, I argued that Rwandan journalism constitutes a weak field, meaning that it has fairly low autonomy relative to its peers. In this chapter, I tackle the question of *why* the field is weak. What motivations and processes reinforce a journalistic position of marginal autonomy? I argue that a major factor underlying this characteristic is the ongoing presence of powerful myths related to journalistic behavior and responsibility during the genocide. These myths in turn inform the field's doxa, which defines the normative terms by which journalists can act.

News Media and the Genocide

The genocide in Rwanda is well known and "perhaps the most clear-cut case of genocide since the Holocaust" (Yale University, n.d.). However, many of the specifics, including the cause, the exact events of the genocide, and the role of news media, have been hotly contested in dozens of books and articles, with competing interpretations gaining political overtones. To summarize, one point of tension lies between the internal, grassroots, and chaotic nature of the violence—leading many to label Rwanda a "failed state" in the genocide's aftermath—and the overwhelming evidence of a strong, well-executed state plan coordinating the genocide (Gros 1996; Hintjens 1999; Straus 2013). Another point of tension lies in identifying the messy events of the genocide itself. Scholars and observers agree that Tutsi were the primary targets and were targeted because of their ethnic and racial identities. However, the Rwandan government aggressively protects a singular narrative of Hutu perpetrators and Tutsi victimization, while most scholars and many other observers note that in fact the genocide events were much more complex, with—for instance—some moderate Hutu targeted and killed, and some Hutu helping to hide Tutsi from the violence (Kelley 2017; King 2010; Waldorf 2009). A final point of tension revolves around the role of news media. A popular narrative, and one embraced by the Rwandan government, holds that many news organizations and journalists played a significant role in spreading propaganda and drumming up support for the genocide. More precise scholarship on motivations of genocide convicts shows that a few journalists and news organizations played only a small part in exacerbating genocide violence (Kellow and Steeves 1998; Straus 2007; Waldorf 2009).

The foundations for the genocide stem in part from the racialization of ethnic Tutsi, Hutu, and Twa people who resided in the Great Lakes region of Africa. While the three groups had long-standing differences in customs and habits, they were imbued with racial identities and a corresponding hierarchy by Belgian colonists, who assigned race-based labels in censuses starting in the 1930s (Chrétien 2006; Mamdani 2001). The Belgians, aided by local leaders in the Catholic church, assigned ethnic identities based on physical features, provided Rwandans with identity cards that solidified those identities, and assigned leadership positions to the more European-looking Tutsi—thus setting the stage for increased division and turning the Hutu into a racialized "other" (Barnett 2002; Mamdani 2001). This division persisted through decolonization in 1961, when the tables turned and Hutu-identifying Rwandans claimed many positions of power. By the end of the 1980s, 500,000 or more Rwandans, many Tutsi, were refugees in neighboring countries (Prunier 1997). In 1988, the RPF (the current ruling party in Rwanda) formed in Uganda. The RPF, composed primarily of Tutsi refugees, began an attack on Rwanda in 1990, and government officials launched a propaganda campaign to label all Tutsi as RPF accomplices and all Hutu members of opposition parties as traitors (Newbury 1995). In 1993, politicians convened in Arusha, Tanzania, and officially resolved the conflict between the two groups, but extremist groups continued to plan and instigate violence (Prunier 1997). On April 6, 1994, the Rwandan president, Juvénal Habyarimana, died when a rocket attack crashed the plane he was aboard. The genocide began that night, and over the course of 100 days at least 800,000 people, primarily of Tutsi ethnicity, were killed (Prunier 1997). The genocide ended in early July when RPF forces took command of the entire country.

Popular accounts generally imply that Rwandan news organizations played a significant role in encouraging division and violence. By some accounts, many journalists and editors were also political militants, and, leading up to the genocide, most news outlets took political stances that exacerbated division (Higiro 2007). News reports built on a similar narrative, reporting that "the media became an instrument of destruction during the genocide . . . people huddled around a short-wave radio, hoping for good news but hearing only propaganda" (Barton 2001). The Genocide Memorial in Kigali reinforces the message of journalistic responsibility with an exhibit depicting how more than 20 newspapers and journals spread hate messages against the Tutsi, publishing racist cartoons and other content that deepened the perceived divide between Hutu and Tutsi.

Scholarship on the role of news media tends to focus on a few prominent outlets that formed in the early 1990s explicitly to publicize and encourage ethnic division and anti-Tutsi sentiments. In 1990, a Catholic bus driver founded the newsletter *Kangura*, infamous for its rhetoric calling Tutsi "cockroaches" (*inyenzi*) (Chrétien 2006; Mamdani 2001). Radio-Télévision Libre des Milles Collines (RTLM) formed around the same time under the influence of the Hutu Power group, an extremist movement within the ruling party (Mamdani 2001). In the months leading up the genocide, the radio station RTLM cultivated an audience through its broadcasts of "hot news" (*inkuruishushe*), which often included stories of attacks and alleged misconduct by opposition party members. The radio station relied on "excellent journalists," many recruited from newspapers, to produce these shows (Kellow and Steeves 1998, 118). After the genocide, RTLM in particular was accused of "spreading fear, rumor, and panic by using a kill-or-be-killed frame, and of relaying directives about the necessity of killing the Tutsi people as well as instructions on how to do it" (Kellow and Steeves 1998, 107). Kellow and Steeves also note that journalists were often at the top of the lists of people to be killed during the genocide, occasionally for their ethnicity but more often because of their political involvement and occupations. Observers after the genocide said that RTLM represented a powerful force for violence: those who underestimated its power committed a "lethal error," and the RTLM owners should "stand at the head of the accused" in accounting for genocide crimes (Kellow and Steeves 1998, 107, 108). However, these observations have not been supported by further research; detailed research on the motivations of those convicted of genocide crimes concluded that messages from the news media played a minimal role in inciting or exacerbating any violence during the genocide (Straus 2007, 2013).

In sum, three contested, but nevertheless important, stories about the genocide influence Rwandan journalists today. One is that the genocide stemmed from the chaos of a failed state (when in fact, research now shows that the

Rwandan state is uncharacteristically strong for the region). The second is that the violence unfolded in a black-and-white manner exclusively against Tutsi. In reality, research again shows that while Tutsi were overwhelmingly the targets, the genocide nonetheless involved acts of heroism and villainy among both Tutsi and Hutu. A final story says that the news media operated as a powerful propaganda machine promoting violence and serving as an arm of Hutu perpetrators. In reality, research supports a more minimally influential media role in the genocide. However, these three stories figure strongly into journalistic perceptions of the field's reality, role, and appropriate behavior in contemporary Rwanda.

Building Field Boundaries

The genocide has a sustained and powerful influence on daily life, politics, and other aspects of Rwandan social reality. For journalists, who have in some ways been treated as scapegoats for the prolonged and extraordinary violence, it has a singular power to define the boundaries of the contemporary field and set the rules for what constitutes appropriate ideology and practices. This happens, I argue, as genocide narratives gain the power of myth.

The concept of "myth" is rarely used in journalism studies, and when it is, it generally implies something along the lines of a fairytale—"a captivating fiction, a promise unfulfilled and perhaps unfulfillable" (Lim 2012, 72). However, other disciplines imbue the term with more power. Organizational sociology gives the concept a particularly useful meaning for this context, defining "myth" as "a structure of beliefs . . . that serves as the 'taken-for-granted' logic base" for an organization or group of laborers (Ferris et al. 1989, 85). This approach restores the power of "myth" to something that represents not just a wish or hope (though that may be part of the meaning) to something that powerfully structures reality: a story that captures a set of beliefs explaining why things are the way they are (Bowles 1989; Mills 2020, 411). A myth is a story that explains "how things are around here" (Owen 1986, 116). These stories have the power to justify potentially inefficient or otherwise questionable organizational practices and to define the reality within which the norms and routines of a slice of culture take shape at the organizational level, within organizations, or among field members (Boje et al. 1982). They socialize individuals into the values, attitudes, and forms of expression valuable in groups (Bowles 1989). Within the framework set by a myth, one can question behavior; outside that framework, one steps into the territory of the impossible, the can't-be-done or "It just won't work that way here." Myths also offer stability, as the taken-for-granted is difficult to change.

This approach accounts for the power of history and narrative to shape particular patterns and events (Bourdieu and Wacquant 1992). Cultural products are the outcome of multiple social factors, and studying the historical underpinnings of institutional practices and structures illuminates the factors that create cultural products and helps us move beyond a simplistic model of unidimensional path dependence (Hanna 2005, 168). Memories are powerful influences over decisions and behavior, whether or not they align with the "facts" of the event itself; the social world is "to a large extent what the agents make of it" (Bourdieu 1985, 209; Merton 1995). Collective memory is an especially powerful tool that journalists and audiences can use to shape their understanding of professional values and roles (Zirugo 2021a). While stories are not monolithic or unchanging, organizational narratives nevertheless tend to be persistent and valuable sources of collective identity; in addition, the various voices represented in the narratives can highlight the sources of power and privilege with the ability to shape meaning within organizations and, I argue, fields (Brown 2006). Narratives have the power to make the current state of affairs seem inevitable so that "possibilities initially discarded have become totally unthinkable" (Bourdieu and Farage 1994, 2). They also have the ability to empower change by challenging hegemonic interpretations of events (Ewick and Silbey 1995).

Another way of thinking about myths is that they are the building blocks of *doxa*—they form the unquestioned, taken-for-granted assumptions that constitute the boundaries of acceptable behavior. This is the invisible but powerful set of definitions and shared beliefs that set the field's boundaries from within by defining what is or is not up for debate. For journalists, for instance, the set of beliefs within the doxa define what is or is not a news story; while journalists might debate whether a particular story is good or not, or newsworthy enough to warrant prestigious placement in the production process, journalists most often learn quickly and then no longer debate *whether* something is news. This quality of newsworthiness is "unspoken, taken for granted, self-explaining, undisputed" (Schultz 2007, 195). Most mentions of doxa in journalism scholarship link it to an international, shared understanding of what journalism is based on survey results and analyses of professional guidelines. According to these scholars, the underpinnings of journalism include objectivity, which "assumes the news media and the journalist exist above or 'outside' society rather than embedded within it" (Hess 2013, 123). The journalistic doxa also includes a shared belief in the importance of "being a watchdog of the government, providing useful information for citizens, impartiality, detachment, keeping journalists' personal views out of reporting, verifying information, and following universal principles regardless of the circumstances" (Karlsson and Clerwall 2019, 1186). To the extent that doxa can define quality as well as defining the underlying social rules, the journalism doxa upholds products that are investigative, informative, well constructed, and time-consuming as ideal-type media content (Vos and Singer 2016, 145). The doxa of a field is important because it defines the boundaries of appropriate behavior. It sets journalists' range of possible roles (meaning their relationships to each other and to other fields) and the ways they can feasibly do their work in this social context.

The dominant actors in a social field generally have the power to set the terms of social interaction by defining its doxa. Bourdieu and other field theory scholars situate this primarily in terms of cultural dominance within national boundaries and represents the views of political elites or elites with political backing. It represents "the point of view of the dominant, when it presents and imposes itself as a universal point of view" (Bourdieu 1999, 71). Ordinary citizens and the media can contribute to the entrenchment of worldviews as doxa "by accepting and repeating the claims" (Chopra 2003, 424). The assumption that doxa can be set and maintained unquestioningly within the political, geographic, and social boundaries of a nation presupposes national autonomy and in some sense a position of global dominance, meaning the ability to either be unaware of or intentionally ignore political pressure and norms set by global power centers. This ability to ignore pressure outside national borders is itself an assumption grounded in dominant Western norms. Many countries in the world, including Rwanda, may build up their own doxa but do so within the context of awareness of global norms, which may be different. This does not erase the possibility of doxa within the Rwandan journalism scene, but it does mean that the construction of local doxa is more self-aware than Bourdieu envisioned or argued. Local journalists still must operate within the framework of the local ground rules if they want to survive in the field, but they are aware of and compare their own boundaries with those of others. The effect of globalization, then, is to render the local doxa discursive rather than taken for granted.

By the time they rise to the level of doxa, social beliefs and rules seem to have been around forever. However, they come from somewhere, and are usually born out of tension, conflict, and crisis between powerful actors. Crisis can reveal the arbitrariness of doxa and lead to explicit discussions challenging its value (Kluttz and Fligstein 2016). Particular actors can challenge it, though this is rarely effective unless they use and reproduce the "underlying 'rules of the game' on which the field is based" (Kluttz and Fligstein 2016, 198). However, the inertia of doxa is particularly open to challenge in the journalism field, which is "continually subject to disruption by both exogenous and endogenous forces" (Vos and Singer 2016, 144). One example of this is the increasing emphasis on transparency in journalism, suggesting it may be incorporated into doxa (Karlsson and Clerwall 2019). While these studies make it clear that doxa *can* change, there is not much research, especially in the journalism context, on the way this happens.

Rwandan journalism provides a window into one way that doxa originates. Foundational beliefs about journalists' social roles and responsibilities based in stories about the genocide gain mythical status as they are told and retold in metajournalistic discourse—journalists' discussions about their profession—and from there, they set important boundaries around journalism in Rwanda. Among Rwandan journalists, two stories linked to interpretations of the genocide have taken on mythical status, shaping journalists' understanding of their field and its boundaries so thoroughly that it excludes other possible interpretations. These myths limit the autonomy journalists are willing to adopt for themselves, and they also affect journalists' interactions with other social actors, which, in turn, influences the legitimacy of the journalism field.

Journalists' Genocide Myths

Two myths—both related to contentious aspects of the genocide—powerfully shape the boundaries of appropriate behavior for Rwandan journalists. The first, that journalists as a social group bear a great deal of responsibility for the events of the genocide, influences the social role journalists fill in contemporary Rwanda and leads them to accept a collective field position as objects of suspicion who deserve only limited autonomy. The second, that the genocide arose from random and unpredictable causes, fuels a sense of constant precarity and uncertainty that influences how journalists approach news selection and define newsworthiness.

Journalists see themselves as professionally responsible for personal and direct violence committed against their fellow Rwandans during the genocide. No one acknowledged a personal role in killing. The only personal stories journalists shared about the genocide involved being out of the country because parents had moved because of ethnic conflict earlier in the 1980s and 1990s, or hiding and watching others commit violent acts. However, journalists as a social group report that their occupation enabled particular abuses of power that perpetuated the genocide on a systemic level with immediate and personal effect. Journalists, along with presumably most other Rwandans in their late twenties and older, remembered vividly events surrounding the genocide. Some told me the stories in personal conversation; others recounted them in editorial meetings, including one at *KT Press* leading up to Kwibuka (genocide commemoration week). A *KT Press* editor told of how he hid inside his house and watched his 11- and 12-year-old classmates run through the streets of his village, some holding machetes and others being chased. There is a strong and inescapable personal relationship with the genocide shared by most Rwandans who are old enough to remember or have lived through the event. Eric, an editor at the *New Times*, vividly recounted this reality:

> We are part of this society ourselves. We are born of this situation. In this society, everybody is a victim. I lost my relatives, close relatives. So one way or another, that thing keeps playing on your mind. You cannot avoid it.

Shared narratives of the genocide carry weight for journalists through these two myths that permeate the field.

Myth 1: Journalists Are Responsible for the Genocide

Most of the journalists in Rwanda today were not working journalists during the genocide; of those who were working at the time, more than three dozen were killed, others fled, and still others stood trial for genocide crimes (Barton 2001; Kellow and Steeves 1998, 118). However, the narrative of media responsibility for exacerbating the violence permeates the field with far-reaching effects on the boundaries journalists set for themselves as well as the boundaries imposed on the field from outside. This myth says that journalists were directly responsible for several specific attacks and deaths during the genocide. The news media have a great deal of power to influence public opinion and behavior, and that power can lead directly to people seeking out their neighbors' hiding places to kill them. This myth highlights the responsibility of journalists and downplays, almost to invisibility, the role of political forces in providing and curating the messages to be passed along through media channels. The myth strips the complexity from the story of media's role in the genocide and gives it a straightforward meaning that places substantial blame on one set of actors who, in this narrative, had the implied power to choose what messages to convey and chose a message of violence and hate.

Journalists shared the myth in a few ways, all fitting these general contours. An editor told me that the news media were "deeply involved" in the genocide, and a reporter added that the media "played a big role in the genocide." Andre, a *New Times* editor, described how journalists during the genocide used their media platforms to spread propaganda and incite violence:

> Someone went on the radio—a normal journalist—and called on the people to start killing. And the people said, "OK, I have to do it, because they said it on the radio."

This emphasis on a *normal* journalist—not a particularly popular personality or someone well respected in the journalism community—implies that anyone could harness the power of media platforms with powerful effect. The editor drives this home with the final thought that it is the radio itself, rather than any particular charisma on the journalist's part, that commanded such respect and obedience from audiences. Others added to the myth by placing the weight of responsibility on the journalists who used news platforms to "spread the message of hate and killing." Gasore explained it as follows:

> In the genocide, we had journalists who sensitized people to kill. They were using the radio station to spread the message of hate and killing. And some people died because a journalist has told the militia where they were hiding.

While these quotations and most reports from the genocide itself primarily implicate radio for a major role in spreading propaganda and messages of violence, journalists implicated other forms of media, especially newspapers, in their myth-building. Richard, a reporter at *KT Press*, noted:

> During the genocide, radio and newspapers were really vibrant. People could just tune in and listen for directions on where they were going to attack and which roadblock should be where, what you guys should be doing at the roadblock, and things like that which were really negative. So today, I think there's a feeling of, do I really trust a newspaper?

The narrative thus builds to one of abuse of power. Regular journalists, none of them particularly powerful or popular, used their journalistic tools and platforms to spread messages of violence and hate rather than doing their part to dissipate and control the violence. The narrative does not mention the sources of propaganda or the probable consequences—often death—for disobeying orders and refusing to promote propaganda. Journalists are held fully responsible for broadcasting and publishing messages of hate. Moreover, it is not just rogue journalists who diverged from their role to take a public stance; rather, this narrative implicates all journalists, even those going about their daily routines as usual, for playing a role in the genocide. The myth says that journalists are collectively and individually responsible for genocide violence, both abstractly and in specific cases. This myth sets the stage for collective acceptance of limited autonomy and a role helping, rather than critiquing, official positions. It also lays the groundwork for a strong emphasis on personal responsibility and professional behavior, which I will discuss further in the next chapter.

Myth 2: Journalists Might Unwittingly Provoke Similar Violence Again

In spite of scholarly agreement that the genocide was orchestrated by political masterminds, journalists shared the view that it arose from an unknown set of causes. This myth sets the stage for a cautious approach to assessing newsworthiness and avoidance of contentious subjects—leading journalists to define "news" as stories that embrace the official narrative and as "not news" stories that introduce elements of chaos or uncertainty, especially around genocide-related topics but also in politics, economics, and other beats.

Because of this uncertainty around the genocide's causes, journalists tend to avoid pursuing news content that could stir up controversy or negative sentiment—in part out of concern that ideas and stories have unknown consequences that could be deadly. Philippe, an editor at KT Press, explained that controversy-avoidance became a regular part of news assessment for the average journalist because of uncertainty about what might lead to fresh conflict. In particular, he highlighted the murkiness and uncertainty leading to avoidance of "sensitive" topics. While some topics are out of bounds or explicitly must be covered in certain ways (for instance, the genocide itself), journalists tended to avoid controversy across a broader range of subjects because of this uncertainty.

> People say, "Eh, what if I say this and then spark something else?" Some people end up censoring themselves because [something] is very sensitive. Genocide is a very big thing, and it creates that confusion of differentiating what is publishable and what is not.

Alongside the motivation to promote positive change in the community, journalists are motivated by a fear of creating division and an uncertainty of what topics could lead to that division. As Eric explained:

> If there are politically charged statements, for instance, and you think, "This might fan or whip up those old ghosts, that divisive ideology," you probably are not very comfortable. So that's where you start to gauge and see. You always catch yourself with that.

He went on to give a specific example about a story he had dealt with recently regarding an advocacy group promoting social restitution for a particular ethnic group related to the Twa, who comprise a small percentage of Rwanda's population. This advocacy group had been active in the Democratic Republic of the Congo and Uganda and had received news coverage in those countries, he said, but Rwandan media had been hesitant to cover their activities. While the news story might not draw much attention in the other two countries, in Rwanda, journalists upon hearing about the story immediately follow a mental path connecting the Twa to the other ethnic groups in Rwanda—Hutu and Tutsi—and must think about whether it is worth reminding a Rwandan audience that there are ethnic divisions in the country. Rwandans have made significant effort on private and policy levels to remove reminders of ethnic division from public discourse, and a story like this one could serve as such a reminder, Eric said.

> Now in Uganda, and in Congo if you like, eh, maybe I will easily put out a story and the public will look at it and move on, no problem. It's just another story. But in our context, I may not treat it as just another story. It could be an innocent story, but then our readers here, they might look at it and they're like, oh, but I thought everybody is Rwandan?

A story that might generate no social reaction in neighboring countries could have strong effects on the Rwandan audience, raising questions of ethnicity and division and signaling reminders that there are several ethnic groups in Rwanda. In a context where government policy and social spaces are designed to signal that ethnicity is of marginal importance next to the shared Rwandan national identity, a story that reminds readers of tribal division would serve as a step backward, not forward, in development progress. And to many Rwandans, the genocide is still a recent memory, and it takes daily work to move past it in social interactions. "Twenty years is just the other day," Eric said. "The healing is a work in progress, but you wouldn't say that the costs have completely been counted." This is the kind of mental calculus based on the origin-story myth that guides story selection from the editorial perspective every day.

Doxa at Work

While doxa is primarily determined within the field, these beliefs influence how journalists interact with actors in other social fields, which in turn helps shape the field's boundaries (Bourdieu and Wacquant 1992). Journalism in particular relies strongly on relationships with actors in other fields, including politicians, sources, and audience members, to build and maintain legitimacy and authority (Carlson 2017). Studying the way journalists talk about these relationships, while of course only part of the story, provides a window into these interactions because it shows journalists' perception of their own power relative to others (Carlson and Usher 2016; Zelizer 1993). In this metajournalistic discourse, journalists usually defend their own behavior, uphold shared values, and protect the general appropriateness and value of journalism by upholding the field's role as a "powerful institution shaping public knowledge" (Aitamurto and Varma 2018; Carlson 2014, 45; Carlson and Usher 2016).

Metajournalistic discourse often centers around the importance of autonomy, which encompasses freedom from interference and regulation and the ability to criticize powerful actors (Carlson 2017; Reich 2013; Sjøvaag 2013). Journalists in many different positions hold autonomy as a core value, even when they disagree over its definition (Singer 2007). They protect this value and advocate for the journalistic profession in their discourse by drawing boundaries, upholding good journalism, and policing misbehavior by field members (Carlson 2017; Eldridge 2014). Although the reality of journalistic autonomy varies widely across political and economic contexts, studies consistently find that journalists defend their right to it, even in countries with authoritarian governance, and that it is central to their identities (Waisbord 2013). However, this impulse is, for the most part, strikingly absent from Rwandan journalists' discussions about their social role. I argue that this absence is linked directly to key doxa-setting genocide myths and, moreover, it gives metajournalistic discourse the effect of weakening, rather than strengthening, the legitimacy and authority of the field.

The Effect of Myths on Relationships

The two genocide myths I outlined above—that journalists were singularly responsible for genocide violence and that the genocide itself was unpredictable with unknowable causes—lead to a sense among journalists that they are villains or, at least, untrustworthy and in need of social rehabilitation. This shared belief permeates the way journalists talk about their interactions with sources and audiences as well, further shaping the limited autonomy of the field.

This leads to weak internal regulatory structures that tend to rely on cooperation and compromise with figures of authority in other fields rather than strong internal defenses and self-policing. This weak field-level stance in turn shapes individual journalists' work because, as one journalist said, while the regulatory commission might eventually come to the aid of a journalist accused of wrongdoing, it typically would not step in before the accusations hurt.

On a field level, this involvement shapes the way the regulatory bodies governing the field set rules for the field and protect journalists against outside critics. It also impacts the level of federal funding these organizations receive, and public reaction to journalists who get in trouble. On an individual level, it influences journalists' level of comfort pursuing stories that are independent, investigative, or critical of other fields of power, and it colors journalists' social interactions with sources. Journalists often encounter uncooperative interview subjects, many of whom say they don't want to talk to the media because of the destructive role media has played in the past.

Many journalists in Rwanda are uncertain in their ability to appropriately manage a high degree of social power, so they embrace or accept a field position of limited power. Many journalists expressed this interest in a guarded social power, and some attributed it directly to the media's role in the genocide. Two interactions illustrate this. The *New Times* newsroom is an open-concept office space with rows of desks assigned to individual reporters and editors. Two television screens hang in the center of the room, each facing half of the newsroom. When I was in the newsroom these were always on and were tuned to a news channel, often CNN's global news channel. When I began my observation period at the *New Times*, Donald Trump had just been inaugurated as US president, and he was the frequent subject of stories on CNN. Since everyone in the newsroom knew I was American and had worked as a journalist, reporters and editors frequently discussed with me their critiques of the ways US news media were covering the Trump presidency. These conversations were useful both in that they helped me build relationships within the newsroom, and also in the ways they shed light on the occupational ideology and role perceptions journalists hold at the *New Times*. An excerpt from my field notes illuminates how Eric outlined the ideal role of the media. He began by telling me that "the media should print the truth, but not be the opposition." He was telling me that CNN had recently published a piece embracing the "opposition party" role that Trump had declared the media to hold. This editor said objectivity was an important goal to meet but that actively opposing the president is taking a political position, which is not acceptable. He also said that the American media and other Western media are too strong and would get to determine Trump's legacy, which is not fair. Eric further explained,

> Yes, we are journalists, we have to be free to exercise our right to communicate, to do our job, hold everybody—but also exercise all this responsibly. If you like, there has to be that sense of accountability on our part.

In the judgment of these Rwandan journalists, it is important for journalists to exercise their power responsibly as it is for them to ensure that others are using their power responsibly.

There is a general sense that journalists are somewhat uncertain of what sources of conflict could spark violent conflict again, leading reporters to avoid seeking out or portraying overt or implied conflict in news reports. There is a contemporary reluctance to publish any content that might trigger conflict in any form. News content like updates about the stock market were far removed from the kind of conflict reporters were worried about, but stories related to political conflict would often raise concern. News stories related to ethnic division would be very unlikely to make it to publication, often because reporters were themselves uncertain whether or how such an item should be covered in light of the genocide. Political figures in turn are reluctant to trust reporters with information, as Jean, a *New Times* reporter, recounted.

> Everyone is so conscious about what they present in the paper or radio. Policymakers and leaders want to be sure: "What are you going to write?" And even journalists themselves haven't trusted themselves to, you know, to hold whoever is there accountable. There is that mistrust because of the past.

This quotation suggests that journalists are uncomfortable advocating for a powerful role in which they would hold a watchdog position. In addition, figures in power are mistrustful of journalists. Because journalists are unsure that they should fill a social role of critique and are conflict averse, they tend not to push back against mistrustful sources by demanding accountability. Instead, they are likely to take a softer approach to reporting and not push for information beyond what is offered.

This analysis suggests that journalists in Rwanda are reluctant to push for a role that exerts power to be independent of government. One of the factors informing this reluctance is that journalists have a strongly shared institutional memory of the role their predecessors played in sending messages that incited and encouraged violent ideology and behavior during the genocide. This reluctance creates some tension for reporters who wish the media would collectively advocate for a more powerful role, but most see it as unlikely to happen. "If you tried to read how other countries get independent journalism, the government didn't come and give it to them," Samuel, a *New*

Times reporter, said. "Journalists themselves fight for it—not with guns, but using the facts." However, even while acknowledging that journalists would need to fight for a more powerful position in society, many reported their fellow journalists as being personally reluctant to do so.

Along with affecting the social power journalists themselves feel comfortable claiming, the myth that journalists were deeply involved in and responsible for violence during the genocide affects the level of social support they receive, both from sources and others involved in the newsgathering process and from the public in cases when members of the journalism field are criticized for the way they reported something.

Journalists feel that the public has little faith in their ability to do their job well, and this is evident in the reluctance of most sources to give journalists information. The media's role in the genocide provides "a convenient excuse for people to start viewing the media with suspicion," one editor said. Gasore explained:

> If you are trying to interview someone in Canada, it takes two minutes. You are like, "I am [name]; I write for the *Ottawa District*. Just a quick question about this." They will tell you exactly what you want. In Rwanda, it's different. In Rwanda, the way our people think, by the time we call them about something, they are like, "What does a journalist want, why does a journalist need me?" because they don't have a good memory, or a good experience with journalists in the past.

He had worked briefly in Canada while pursuing graduate studies there and realized through this work that sources in Rwanda are relatively reluctant to talk, tending to be suspicious of journalists rather than open in sharing information. Because of this, journalists in Rwanda face a challenging level of work in writing news articles, often running into a general sense of public reluctance to engage with media outlets. Arthur, an editor at *KT Press*, said that sources often justified this reluctance by recalling journalism's role in the genocide.

> You talk to the minister and he says, "Ahh, I know you! Before you have published your story, get me the draft so I look at it." You see that type of thing. Or even a common person will say, "Ehhh, don't take it—don't take a picture of me. I can't talk." The society doesn't trust us. And it's difficult to get someone who can trust you with classified emails or a hidden agenda

from people here and there. Not that they don't know, but they have that fear of the media. They know that we denounced them, so they don't trust us.

In this quotation, an editor at *KT Press* recounts the range of sources who respond with suspicion, from a private citizen on the street refusing to let his or her photo be taken to the public official who requests to review content before it is published. Journalists find that they are rarely trusted to report on confidential or sensitive information. (They are occasionally privy to this information but are expected to keep it out of print because of organizational loyalty.) This adds an extra hurdle to the Rwandan journalist looking to report information. Before producing an article or broadcast, the journalist must first gain the trust of each source involved, building from a position of relative lack of trust in the journalism field in general.

Sources and audiences alike share the lack of trust in media outlets, leading to a further challenge for journalists: they are unlikely to receive public support when they face criticism from public officials or others in power. According to Claude, an editor at *KT Press*:

Basically, you don't have someone to fall to. In America, you know, when the government lambasts you, the public is going to say, "Good job." It's not the case here. Here, when the government lambasts you, the people will say, "Yes, they are not very good people." This is what happens. It has been said since the genocide that the media are bad people. The media are bad people; they provoked the genocide. That has created a perception in people that the media is a dangerous thing and it's not something you should trust. Because [journalists] will say things that are bad. OK? They said bad things about Tutsis, so they will say bad things about anything. Now because of that, people call here every day, some public relations officer from some office, to say, "That story, it's not a very good thing, I think you should delete that story." Some PR guy, you know. They feel they have power over you. So the government does that all the time, and ordinary people do that.

This quotation highlights several elements of the relationship between journalists and the public in Rwanda. First, based on the role journalists played in the genocide, this editor says members of the public are unlikely to trust the media over the government if they are in conflict. Instead, the first response is likely to be one of mistrust of media, and an assumption that journalists must have made a mistake somehow. If the media could report bad things about the Tutsi—the ethnic group that was targeted in the genocide—then the media can report bad things about anything, and journalists are untrustworthy. In addition to this negatively impacting public support of journalism, it also empowers sources who disapprove of content that has been published. Those sources begin to feel that they have the right and power to demand that editors remove stories published online for small reasons.

Jacques, a wire reporter who had worked in Uganda before moving to Rwanda as a journalist, reiterated the public distrust of the media in Rwanda, which he explained in comparison with the perception of journalism in Uganda.

> Say you are writing a story about corruption. Maybe money has been stolen and the money was supposed maybe to bring water to village people. You would expect that it is a good cause that people would appreciate. But here, instead, people are suspicious. When you go down and you talk to people and say, "Look here, I am doing this because this money is meant for you, not for government," they will not seem to understand. For instance, in Kampala, you write a story, eh, even when they arrest you, people generally will maybe demonstrate and say no, no, no. But here, even those who tried to speak will say, "But why are you doing this? Why are you doing this?" The society itself cannot come on the side of journalists and maybe see the good things [they do].

As this reporter explained, in other contexts where he had practiced journalism—in Uganda, a neighboring country where journalists are frequently targeted and sometimes arrested for producing content that political figures do not want—journalists would be likely to have public support in political trouble. At the least, journalists tend to be sympathetic figures in Uganda because the public is generally skeptical of government behavior and is likely to support journalists who say they are fighting for public rights against political corruption and oppression. By contrast, in Rwanda, journalists who face censure from the government are likely to also face judgment from the public, which tends not to grant the journalist the benefit of the doubt.

Throughout the early 1990s, the public was suspicious of sharing information with news media, Gasore explained.

Information was something sensitive to share because you don't know who you are giving information to and how it might affect you. That has made Rwandans very, very careful people when it comes to releasing information. As journalists, we always face challenges of even someone who has a shop selling goods and is not eager to tell you what they are doing because they don't know for what purpose you need information.

Journalists feel that the media's role in the genocide infuses the way the public interact with journalists now. To him and other reporters and editors, this serves as just a reminder that journalists must work extra hard to be "professional" and to hunt down necessary quotations and sources. But to others, this serves to excuse what they pointed out as weak points in professional practice.

In response to this public reluctance to engage with journalists, the reporters I encountered would sometimes behave in ways that they acknowledged to be ethically questionable. I watched reporters discuss a few such encounters in editorial meetings at *KT Press*, highlighting the roadblocks journalists run into and the ways those journalists respond. At this meeting, journalists were debriefing the difficulties they had encountered in reporting and writing feature stories around a genocide theme, set to run during Kwibuka (genocide commemoration week). The journalists had hoped to interview two important sources who refused, saying variations of "If you are a journalist, we cannot meet you." Both sources told the reporters that they did not trust journalists to report facts accurately and were concerned that the stories of their roles in the genocide would be misrepresented. In both cases, the reporters misrepresented themselves, saying they were not journalists. After the sources shared lengthy stories, the reporters then negotiated coverage, finding that the sources were more open to appearing in news stories once they knew what would be covered exactly. Alphonse, the editor sharing these anecdotes, acknowledged that this is a dubious ethical practice but supported it as something that was necessary to get the news coverage desired.

Everyone has their own opinion—to me, I think it was brilliant, because negotiating after is easier. You can tell the guy, "You know what, seriously, we need that story. I'm a journalist, it's a very powerful story and I want to tell it."

This and other interactions throughout my fieldwork highlighted the fact that, while Rwandan journalists are in a relatively unprivileged position in that they are generally viewed with suspicion by those in other fields of power and their desired audiences, they respond with behaviors that are perhaps exacerbating the image they wish to shed. By adopting practices like hiding their true identities and massaging quotations in translation from Kinyarwanda to English (a practice I observed several times, as many reporters, especially at *KT Press*, did not use recorders or take notes in interviews), reporters could be further solidifying their popular image as untrustworthy purveyors of information.

A reporter at the *New Times* underscores the shared feeling that the genocide has set the stage for the contemporary journalism field to be the way it is. "The media played a big role in the genocide," Innocent said. "That has undermined the profession and has caused people to feel that they should not trust the media." This feeling plays a role particularly in relationships with sources, from politicians to private citizens on the street, who journalists say mistrust the media because of the role journalists played in the genocide. "If they actually want to hide something, for example, it was so easy an excuse to say, 'You see, guys, you are known to be inflammatory, you are known to be sensational, you see what happened,'" Andre said. "A lot of excuses came up owing to what happened in '94. And of course, to a certain degree, the onus was on the journalists to prove themselves, that they are different." This presents a double challenge. Not only are journalists under heightened scrutiny from their official sources, but their readers and the citizen sources they could rely on to do more mundane reporting are also hesitant to confide in reporters. In turn, journalists respond by adopting sometimes unethical behavior by hiding their identities, which could contribute to a stronger feeling that journalists are not always trustworthy.

Innocent called this "the issue of mindset." He said:

Because most people know that a journalist is a bad man, even if you are looking for a positive comment, people will be suspicious. That is maybe changing—people have started understanding that everyone has the right to access information, and now the cooperation is improving. But you can look for a comment from someone today, and he tells you, "Can we talk after noon? Give me like two hours or three hours then you'll get it," and then he won't pick up the phone.

Because information was used as a tool to provoke dissent and conflict during the genocide, people today are reluctant to share personal histories and details with others whom they do not know well. This is broadly true across Rwandan society—Rwandans have a reputation in surrounding cultures and among the expatriate community of being private and not forthcoming. It becomes especially pertinent with journalists, who rely on information readily supplied to produce news updates. When there is a generally shared social distrust around information sharing, it has a strong effect on the ability of information workers to do their jobs. Jean confirmed this when I asked him what problems Rwandan journalists face: "The main challenge is the trust, really. Should I trust you? As a journalist, should I trust you as my source of information? Or if I'm a source of information, why should I trust you?"

Lack of trust and reluctance to share information permeate the Rwandan journalism field, affecting the ways sources and journalists interact and the way journalists think of themselves and their social role.

Conclusion

Journalists in Rwanda are confronted daily with reminders of the role news organizations and fellow journalists played in the genocide. From visual reminders like the bullet-riddled walls of parliament looming over newspaper offices, to remarks from sources and shared cultural memories, these reminders signal deep-rooted myths about who journalists are, what journalism is, and what journalism should be. These myths that bound the scope of permissible behavior by and toward journalists. Not only that, but a social pattern of conflict avoidance—for which the genocide is blamed—permeates relationships between journalists and sources and among political figures whom journalists might otherwise find to be valuable sources of conflict for news stories. As a result, the field of journalism in Rwanda is perceived by those outside and those within the field to be powerful but full of people who wield their power irresponsibly and are not worthy of trust. Partly prompted by a desire to redeem themselves from this role of villain, many individuals are driven to practice journalism in a way that they see as socially responsible and that promotes unity, development, and positive self-image within the country and to those outside.

Rwandan journalists learn the role they are socially expected to play through field-wide myths shared between journalists and communicated by sources and other members of the public. The myth that "journalists used their occupation to exacerbate the genocide" brings with it the understanding that journalists are likely to be social villains. This makes sources reluctant to trust journalists and journalists reluctant to trust themselves and leads to a field-wide role position of relative social weakness. This myth also sets up the social expectation that journalists are untrustworthy and thus likely in the wrong when they face accusations from government officials who may be unhappy with a story. The second myth stems from the first and holds that "Rwandan journalists have a responsibility to promote unity among Rwandans and present a unified picture to the outside world." This myth is generated within the field as a response to the public and personal belief in the first myth, and it sets up a role for Rwandan journalists as one of support and assistance, rather than neutral observer. Both of these myths are based in narratives about the field's rebirth after the genocide and, in several cases, are closely linked with organizational founding goals, lending them particular power in setting Rwandan journalists' role expectations and beliefs.

The journalism field in Rwanda is heavily shaped by the shared narrative of the journalism field's involvement in the 1994 genocide. This is true across news organizations, but the shaping power is particularly prevalent at the *New Times*. The *New Times* holds a unique and influential position in the field as the news outlet created to be the voice of a unified Rwanda after the genocide, and as an organization that is elite, relatively well resourced, and the first employer for most English-language journalists who go on to other publications in Rwanda. The rooted nature of these role perceptions and self-perceptions that Rwandan journalists share suggest that role perception is rooted as much in field-internal discussions, beliefs, and history as in external pressure or negotiation with other powerful forces.

Two sets of beliefs founded in this narrative have strong shaping power for the Rwandan journalism field today. The first is the message that Rwandan journalists were directly and personally responsible for increasing the atrocities and violence committed during the genocide, by using their media platforms to spread messages of violence and division and by broadcasting particular plans to congregate and kill particular people. The second is the related message that, because of the negative effect journalists had during the genocide, they today have a responsibility to contribute to rebuilding the country and presenting a positive image to observers. Both of these myths impact journalists' work and relationships. The first myth instills in journalists a reluctance to exert much power relative to other fields of power in Rwanda and creates among sources a reluctance to trust journalists with their narratives. The second leads journalists at major local publications to adopt a development-oriented role that seeks to promote an Afrocentric image of Rwanda to local and international audiences. Each of these myths serves as a "'taken-for-granted' logic base" that informs the way work is done in the Rwandan journalism field (Ferris et al. 1989, 85). In providing the foundation for journalists' work practices and ideology, these two myths support the current work of journalists and provide meaning and justification for their routines, some of which run counter to training the journalists have received in other contexts.

Rwanda is a good context in which to study the impact of myth on journalism culture because of the recency and impact of the genocide. The organizational studies literature suggests that myth plays a role in a wide variety of organizations, and my fieldwork extends this by illustrating the important shaping role myth can play in setting field boundaries as well. I also highlight the ways a myth can contribute to the discourse shaping journalism's role in a society. While the myths in Rwanda are unique to their place and time, they are rooted in the tension of a deeply felt and catastrophic conflict over race and ethnicities—a tension felt and mediated by journalists and other media actors across the continent (Mano 2015). Rwanda points to the ways that identity conflict can transform into strongly held beliefs that shape not just outlook, but professional work as well.

In Rwanda, a shared understanding of the past behavior and role of powerful individual journalists, who used their professional expertise to heighten racial tension and motivate genocide, contributes to a current understanding of contemporary journalists as powerful, untrustworthy, and possibly villains. This myth shapes the social context within which Rwandan journalists work, leading them to be socially constructed as powerful, negative social actors. This construction in turn means that Rwandan journalists are viewed with suspicion by those in positions to protect them with legislation, court decisions, or public opinion. The end result is that, in spite of a code of ethics mandating that every media professional is entitled to "an individual contract ensuring them material and moral security as well as a remuneration proportional to their social role," journalists are, for the most part, poorly paid and lacking contracts because the Association Rwandaise des Journalistes has little power to enforce that rule (Rwandan Media Fraternity

2011, 16). When journalists are taken to court, the state wins every time. And when journalists are judged in the court of public opinion, as a rule, they are found guilty.

With this perspective as a backdrop, the second myth—that journalists are responsible now for contributing to national welfare—is as much a myth built around rehabilitating the image of journalists as it is a belief that Rwandan journalists have been pushed into by external forces. The most powerful figures in the field, the editors and publishers running the biggest print news outlets, have taken this mission seriously, such that it shapes the work produced at their outlets and their missions to produce development-oriented, unifying news coverage. Some journalists practice development journalism because they believe it is the best way to improve Rwanda and serve Rwandan citizens. Others practice it out of self-preservation, because they do not have social power to advocate for a role that is more independent and critical. Within the same journalism field, and even within the same news organization, journalists have different motivations for adopting the role they do. At the roundtable discussion in June, my friend observed that the Rwandan journalism field is divided between those who want to promote the mission of the state and those who want to practice a more independent form of journalism. While the outside observer would find that much of the news produced in Rwanda is strikingly similar, the motivations of the journalists producing those news items are varied. This matters because it affects the social cohesion of the field and the extent to which field organization is likely to be possible. It also suggests that, in focusing on role perception and performance, researchers might do well to focus also on role motivations. In addition, I show that journalist role perceptions can best be understood in their specific contexts. Many journalists in Rwanda practice journalism in a development-oriented fashion, but they do so within a context where they are as much redeeming themselves as working for social development.

Myths are powerful and persistent. They tend to continue influencing an organizational culture even when many within that culture feel the myth hampers their ability to do work the way they would like. The analysis presented above supports this conceptualization and suggests that individual and shared social perceptions have an enduring power that shapes journalism work. Organizational theory suggests that organizations are capable of pushing back against external restrictions, whether those come from overtly imposed restrictions in the form of laws or other requirements, or in the form of unwritten social expectations, but that this is most easily and successfully accomplished when there is a strong internal sense that boundaries are inappropriate for some reason. When the boundaries are internalized as organizational myths, this is unlikely to happen (Hannan and Freeman 1984; Mahoney and Thelen 2009). Thus, this analysis of the routines and motivations of Rwandan journalists and media organizations has critical implications for scholarly understanding of media systems, particularly those operating in "partly-free" or "unfree" political contexts. The research presented here suggests that, even if the laws of Rwanda were to change overnight to resemble those of a "free" political environment, the journalists in Rwanda would be bound by internalized social and organizational constraints that guide them to conceptualize journalism in a certain way and to ignore certain stories and angles and prioritize others. This understanding sheds new light on the ways journalism is constructed in conversation with specific elements of local culture, and how those cultural factors can in some cases play a more powerful role than a shared global understanding of the occupational norms of journalism. As journalism studies moves to understand better the global practice of this important occupation, my study suggests that a stronger understanding of myths grounded in local narratives can illuminate the ways these journalism cultures are constructed. Myths form an important foundation for Rwandan journalism work that impact organizational and individual behaviors.

Within the space shaped for Rwandan journalists by shared history, there is still space for reporting that critiques and holds accountable authority figures—and in fact, editors at the most devoutly pro-Rwandan organization, the *New Times*, encourage "investigative" reporting. Many editors at the *New Times* and *KT Press* say they want their employees to produce more investigative reporting that holds authority figures accountable. Development journalism promotes an approach to reporting that emphasizes positive development goals of a country or community but does not preclude the possibility of strong investigative and critical reporting uncovering ways that development is not occurring or is being undermined. Thus, shared history and cultural interpretation of that history draws boundaries around what can and should be considered "good" journalism in Rwanda—but that definition of good still includes investigation and critique. However, such investigation and critique rarely occur at local news outlets, for a number of reasons.

4
Underbaked or Unrealized

"Underdevelopment" as a Journalistic Keyword

The *New Times* is the oldest newspaper in post-genocide Rwanda. It is also a central node in the social network of Rwandan journalism mapped from Twitter follower data, with the highest number of news outlet followers of any registered news outlet in the country. It is a flagship paper for Rwanda and the country's journalism field and in many ways influences media production patterns across the country. The layout, routines, and organizational structure highlight important orthodoxies—commonly agreed-upon and generally practiced routines and news values—that guide Rwandan journalists within the field boundaries imposed by political and economic constraints and reinforced by shared myths.

The newsroom at the *New Times* is highly structured, formal, and hierarchical, both spatially and psychologically. The newsroom is a classic open office, set up with many similarities to a US newsroom—most editors sit along the front wall close to the entrance, and reporters routinely sit at the same desks around the newsroom. Desks are arranged in rows and reporters are grouped roughly by area. The *New Times* does not have beat reporters but does group reporters by section of the newspaper—so news reporters sit in one area, lifestyle reporters sit in another, and so on. Workers' time is as structured as the office space. The morning begins with an editorial meeting at 8:00 a.m. every weekday, and copy is due to editors by midafternoon for the next day's edition. The organizational hierarchy is as structured as workspace and time; employees relayed rumors of how reporters who questioned the direction of senior editors would be reprimanded or let go. In editorial meetings, this was evident in the general interaction style and in the way editors assigned stories. In editorial meetings, reporters spoke quietly and rarely unless an editor called on them directly. Editors would give instructions while reporters took notes and listened. Reporters rarely critiqued or questioned editorial directives—this happened only twice during the six weeks I spent at the newsroom, and I attended nearly every morning meeting. When assigning stories, editors would give instructions at a minute level of detail, including often a list of questions to ask and instructions about how to approach events like press conferences.

These observations highlight common values and beliefs shared among Rwandan journalists. First, the field generally rewards and prioritizes hierarchy-based consensus rather than individual agency or disagreement as both a news value and a reporting routine—an important factor shaping the field and one that I will discuss more thoroughly in the next chapter. Second, the close supervision of angles, story topics, and even reporting practices highlights a shared belief that the field as a whole is characterized by a lack of professionalism. This leads editors and other leaders to focus on the need for training and other professional development tools as solutions to many problems in the field; it also reinforces a belief that, if reporters get in trouble or cause trouble, they are likely personally responsible for doing something unprofessional. Finally, the "lack of professionalism" belief is closely linked with another orthodoxy, that Rwanda's biggest need and the one journalists can fulfill is to prioritize development—leading many organizations and journalists within them to adopt a development-oriented role and associated news values of cooperation and positive development.

The Power of Professionalism

A commonly shared belief among Rwandan journalists was that journalists are not "professional" and, moreover, that this lack of professionalism leads to many of the field's current problems. In some sense, this observation pointed to reality: the contemporary field of journalism in Rwanda is young, even for Africa. The observation also captured a deeper belief shared across many in the field: that journalists are exclusively responsible when they are unable to practice journalism in the way they have learned, and that more training would enable field transformation.

While journalism practice in Rwanda dates back at least several decades, it was essentially dismantled and rebuilt after the genocide. There is very little information in English on the history of Rwandan journalism before the 1990s, but in neighboring countries—Kenya, Tanzania, and Uganda—journalism began as a colonial project. Print news outlets first appeared in the East African region in the late nineteenth and early twentieth centuries; these extensions of European news outlets carried news from home to the colonies in European settler languages (Abuoga and Mutere 1988; Musandu 2018; Scotton 1973; Sturmer 1998). Newspapers in local languages followed, focusing primarily on local conflicts through the early twentieth century. In the 1920s, Ugandan news outlets began to advocate for independence, signaling a shift to journalistic identities aligned with advocacy and political engagement in support of national interests (rather than colonial governments) (Carter 1968; Scotton 1973). In the 1950s, local universities began introducing their own journalism education programs, starting in Ghana (Murphy and Scotton 1987). As journalism practice became more grounded in local reality, the "native versus settler" tension, which extended to other aspects of social life and state development as well, set up a dichotomy between democratic liberation movements—which pushed for a democratic plurality of voices and representation—and Marxist and Africanist one-party state movements, which pushed for national unity in the face of colonial oppression (Mamdani 2001; Rønning and Kupe 2000). Rwanda joined the one-party movement, along with a dozen other African states: through the 1970s it had a legally enforced one-party political system that shaped press freedom and role (Jose 1975). By the early 1990s, policies under President Juvénal Habyarimana expanded press freedom, and there were more than 12 local newspapers and magazines available in Kigali, most of which were critical of official government stances (Mamdani 2001).

However, as I recounted in chapter 2, the genocide dismantled the media field, and it was intentionally rebuilt under strong government oversight. Importantly, this post-genocide reconstruction saw the creation of Rwanda's first in-country journalism training programs, codes of ethics, and other standardizations, which are often considered signs of field genesis (Skjerdal and Ngugi 2007; Vauchez 2008). Thus, while journalism practice in Rwanda dates back to the mid-twentieth century, the current field is young in many respects.

On an ideological level, individual responsibility for behaving appropriately (or "professionally") is a strong orthodox value among Rwandan journalists. Several editors and reporters emphasized the message that individual journalists generally have the power to report a wide range of angles and stories, if only they were professional enough. However, while I label this belief as orthodox because I found it common across the field, a few heterodox challengers invoked professionalism to prove lack of freedom. On one hand, professionalism was invoked to prove journalistic autonomy: journalists have the freedom to pursue critical angles, and where they fail to do so, it is because they lack professionalism. This belief supports a field value of individual responsibility, maintaining that professionalism is so powerful that it can protect critical journalism and that if a journalist gets in trouble for reporting a critical angle, personal flaws in his or her professionalism are mostly to blame. On the other hand, much less commonly, professionalism was invoked to prove journalistic craft: journalists have the skill to do independent, creative reporting but they are prevented from doing so because they lack the freedom.

The Complications of Professionalism and Investigation

One particular skill editors felt their staff lacked was the ability to do investigation. This generally included the ability to think beyond the routine story that is presented in media events like press conferences, and to look for another, more interesting story, through interviews or independent research. For Andre, this stemmed directly from a lack of skill among reporters in the newsroom:

> I think the main issue [with lack of investigation] is having the people with the skills and with the zeal—that drive to want to do deep investigative stories. Because we've done it. There was a time when we had a very vibrant investigative desk that was actually led, it was headed by [editor's name] when he was still a reporter. He was a reporter. And I was on it. It was very active. And we never got any problem. So I find it's an issue of skills.

While this assessment is of course not the whole story, editors across media organizations shared it, and it informed the general belief placing the responsibility on individual reporters to produce good content. Good investigative reporting can be done, and reporters and editors could point to one or two specific instances where they or someone else had produced investigative content with no problems, so it followed that the problem must be with the individual. This belief also highlights the somewhat deceptive nature of "investigative desks," and the problem with conflating investigation with independent journalism: as other reporters pointed out, much of the work done at the *New Times*' investigative desk was not necessarily independent; it might be guided by the desires of powerful figures as much as any other coverage in the newspaper.

In editorial meetings at the *New Times*, editors routinely gave very specific information to reporters about which sources should be contacted, what questions to ask them, and what angles to take. Reporters routinely checked in with their desk editor every morning when they arrived in the office, confirming which stories they should work on for the day. In one editorial meeting, a reporter mentioned that one can only ask certain questions at a press conference because the people running the conference would say that other questions were "not allowed." The editor in chief responded, "You know that even though a question is 'not allowed' doesn't mean you can't ask it. Think of other ways to ask it or ask it anyway."

This interaction highlights the minute level of oversight editorial staff took with reporters and how most of the detail-oriented instruction revolved around guiding reporters on routine tasks or responsibilities that one might expect to constitute basic, understood job responsibilities. In a private discussion, one reporter said it felt like editors at the *New Times* were sending the message that reporters couldn't be trusted to think on their own.

Reporters pointed out that the lack of training could be seen as an advantage in that it fostered the production of general assignment reporters who had not been trained in journalism ethics or appropriate behavior and thus might be more open to potentially unethical behavior such as unquestioningly positive coverage of government actors. Many people in this situation could be found working at local radio stations, said Lucas, who had himself worked in local radio before moving to a wire service job.

> You find someone finishing high school, even without having any skills, and he will just go to a radio station and start working as an intern. Later you find him going to a press conference. Maybe they don't have money to pay you, but also, they know they will get some free staff who will do what the government wants—who will not do investigative stories or bother to focus on truthfulness or the basic principles of journalism.

There is a mutually reinforcing cycle of news outlets lacking funding to pay for qualified staff and relying on free and consequently less-well-trained employees instead. This encourages observers who may in turn lack training in interviewing, writing, and ethics, but may nevertheless assume (correctly) that they can also get jobs as journalists. Thus, there is a self-perpetuating cycle that reinforces the introduction of young journalists into the field who lack the skills that would make them legitimate and credible among their peers.

The lack of training among journalists in Rwanda plays a key role in the way journalists discuss political censure of reporters. In general, the journalists I interviewed insisted that the government generally does not hamper their practice of journalism. Where journalists have been disciplined, it is because they were not trained well enough to practice "good" journalism or blatantly broke laws, for instance by attempting to bribe sources (a story one editor recounted to me in detail). Innocent noted that he has had friends arrested because of something they wrote or said, but that the arrests were clearly because "those people had no skills. They thought that journalism is something you can wake up and do.... It is something that should have basic skills before you can start." Jacques, a reporter who now works for a wire service, told me that, in past years, stories that got reporters in trouble with political authorities often were reported with no quotations, or were one-sided, or the reporter hadn't tried to find balance for the story, which he described as things an untrained journalist would do. This could lead to trouble: "So somehow there was a confrontation between journalists and the state. OK—maybe they don't want you to write the stories, but also the stories were not well researched," he said. Samuel at the *New Times* said that he thought it would be possible for reporters in Rwanda to criticize the government if they did so with well-researched and well-written stories. "We can have journalists who can ... write or publish something which I can call against the government or against what they want," he said. "If you publish it with facts with everything, they [the government] will not do anything." This belief offers both hope and constraint to the Rwandan journalist: on the one hand, if one reports a story professionally, even a critical one, it will not get the reporter in trouble. On the other hand, if one gets in trouble for reporting on a particular subject, it is probably one's own fault, because the story was unprofessional.

For journalists to produce oppositional or critical work in Rwanda, they must be able to consistently produce work that is legitimate—that is, it meets agreed-upon standards of good journalism as outlined in the code of ethics produced by the Association Rwandaise des Journalistes, both in the content produced and in the manner it was reported. If a journalist produces a critical story, it is likely to be scrutinized intensely, and any missteps in reporting or writing that story or even past work become fodder for an investigation and, in some cases, a call to remove him or her from staff. As a result, there is a commonly shared belief among journalists that journalists who do follow professional standards in reporting and writing will not be penalized or censured for writing stories that critique officials and stray from the accepted editorial line. I found this to be true in one sense: journalists who do not adhere to standard expectations of ethical behavior and professional writing are likely to face censure ranging from critique to job loss to arrest if they pursue watchdog news items. On the other hand, though, legitimacy alone does not appear sufficient to ensure that journalists can safely pursue independent angles.

Rwandan journalists contend that if one follows ethical reporting tactics and produces an article that meets accepted standards by being factual, relying on multiple sources, and including no author opinion, then one will not face political or organizational censure. Journalists tended to use one of three arguments to back up this claim. One argument was to provide examples of journalists who had been producing watchdog content and were still at work in the country. A second argument was to claim that the lack of skill in the journalism field meant there were few (or no) reporters capable of producing well-written, critical content: some had left the country in 2010, and others had left the field but remained in the country. A third argument was to point to the laws supporting freedom of the press (there are several). Each of these arguments sheds further light on the ways that "good journalism" is a necessary, but not sufficient, tool enabling a journalist to fill a watchdog role.

The prevailing belief within the Rwandan journalism field, as indicated by the evidence shared in previous pages, is that journalists tend to be untrained and not particularly good at their jobs. This leads journalists to reason that there is a relative dearth of critical, investigative, and watchdog journalism because many journalists themselves are not skilled enough to produce that journalism. When reporters are highly skilled, they tend to be tempted out of the journalism occupation by higher-paying jobs in other sectors. Journalists who are good reporters with a good grasp of English, for instance, are prime candidates for PR positions with NGOs and other international organizations looking for local staff with good communication skills. "These international organizations here, if you have a masters, they take you," one editor said. "They pay well. So the media has been like a transit to public relations. That is a challenge—someone has experience and then just look[s] for greener pastures and they leave the field. So they leave it in the hands of people, amateurs." The departure of skilled journalists for adjacent communication fields like public relations leaves the field populated with journalists who are often less well trained in necessary reporting skills like interviewing, researching, and writing. Richard, a reporter at the *New Times*, explained this from a different angle: "We don't have a lot of critics" in journalism, he said. "The people who should be, who would criticize whatever is going on, are busy doing something else. Like a friend of mine the other day was saying: the good journalists are not actually doing journalism. Good journalists are somewhere else—working for hospitals or doing something else." This feeds into a belief that many journalists left in the field are not particularly good at their jobs, which in turn provides a ready explanation—bad reporting—to take the blame and explain the result when journalists face government and public censure for attempting to do investigative reporting.

The converse of this is a belief that, if journalists do practice journalism well, they will be free to produce work that follows a watchdog counternarrative. Philippe explained the importance of professionalism, which he described as being balanced and unbiased, and basing a story in provable facts, but also as "being sure that what you are getting out is what should go out there." Grounding a story in fact, especially, is important: "It provides you security, it eliminates that fear," he said.

Journalists have observed that some in their community routinely report news that portrays officials in unflattering ways. So the assumption is that, if one follows agreed-upon standards of good journalism in reporting even a critical story, there will be no negative repercussions.

Critical stories come under intense scrutiny. Sometimes this is immediate. But when the story cannot be immediately censored by organizational forces, journalists themselves and their work history are often called into question. Jacques, a wire reporter who had previously worked at the *East African* and the *New Times*, explained how his reporting history had been scrutinized because of one critical story he wrote for the *East African*. He had written about a press conference, and a minister said she had been misquoted in the article. The reporter did not consider that story to be very critical or investigative. He said he might have slightly misquoted the minister but pointed out that it would be a poor journalistic decision to misquote a minister at a public event with many witnesses to testify to the correct quotation. However, the reporter later found out that the minister took the opportunity to call his entire work history into question, taking the confrontation straight past the editor of the newspaper to the owner of the publication. "They were so annoyed that instead of calling the editor they jumped and called Aga Khan family, complaining about the story," he said. "Later I found out that they had lined up all my stories I worked even before, so they were saying, 'You see, it is not only this story, but there is this history which means this person is doing it intentionally.'" Later, Jacques again found himself on the wrong side of the government after writing a story for the *East African*. Instead of overtly questioning the legitimacy of his work as a journalist, the editor quietly sidelined him for several years. "The government was not happy, so they told my boss not to run my stories again. My boss did not tell me, but I would see the assignments declining me. I didn't know what was causing it," he said. "I was one of the best journalists, writing good stories. I only discovered two years later that there was a directive not to run my stories." These examples illustrate ways that the articles produced by reporters practicing watchdog journalism comes under heavy scrutiny.

Reporters for wire services and the *East African*, who produce critical journalism regularly, corroborated the importance of using great care in following ethical reporting standards and producing news content that lived up to journalistic standards. Even errors that might be considered "small"—things like misspelling and misquotations, which would generally not warrant even a printed correction at the *New Times*—would provide openings for government officials and others to critique an entire body of watchdog work, Jacques said.

> When you are writing for a news agency, the risk is high since they cannot control you directly. A boss cannot tell [wire service] to stop your stories, and they know that, writing for [wire service], you are employed, and they have money. If they want to harass you, there is a way they can maybe bring up maybe charges. When you get a small problem, they can use that small problem—they will not be punishing you for that small problem, but they will be punishing you because of what you do. You have to be very smart—smart in the sense that you try to do your work properly, not to give them the chance to get you.

In some sense, then, watchdog journalism in this context is inextricable from careful sourcing, reporting, and writing, because watchdog reporters who do not exercise care in following accepted standards of news production will find their careers quite short. Only those whose stories pass a high bar of scrutiny are allowed to continue working. Careful reporting is also proactively encouraged by the organizations that tend to produce watchdog journalism. Organizational priorities and practices set higher standards of sourcing and verification for stories to be published. Jacques noted that there is some truth to the claim that journalists in Rwanda sometimes would publish poorly researched and poorly vetted "investigative" journalism that would not stand up to the scrutiny placed on news articles published for wire services or in neighboring Uganda.

> If you are writing a story maybe for the AP, or maybe for the *Uganda Monitor*, you would expect somebody to raise an issue but try to talk to all people, to balance the story. But in the past in Rwanda, you might find somebody running a story without a quote—any quote—and sometimes stories turn out not to be true. So there would be a confrontation between journalists and the state. Maybe the state doesn't want the journalist to write the stories, but also the stories were not well researched.

Reporters in general had little sympathy for their colleagues in these situations; the attitude tended to convey the idea that, if you had tried to investigate something without concrete facts or named sources to back it up, you would be asking for trouble, and you probably would know it.

Highly trained journalists able to produce watchdog stories with named sources, quotations, and facts are rare in Rwanda, but powerful. Fidele, the editor of a web start-up publication, suggested that the government tries to limit opportunities for journalists to gain more specialized skills, afraid of what a cadre of highly trained journalists could accomplish. He used the example of a well-known professor and media critic who regularly contributes to the *East African*. "The government is scared of media professionals now, I think. If you are too professional, I am scared of you. Like [name], when he writes a story—everyone is reading to know what he is going to talk about this time. So if you have like, 10 [names], you can put the government to the test." However, even skilled journalists inclined to practice watchdog journalism and write critical, investigative pieces are often prevented from doing so and trained to avoid particular topics and investigations by the pressure of newsroom routines laced with financial incentives combined with the uncertainty of knowing that an editor will likely not back up a reporter if a story backfires and draws criticism. Through the first decade of the century, Jacques said, reporters would routinely be fired from the *New Times* for stories that violated the editorial line. "There was that kind of harassment where a story was published, the government was not happy, so they decided to fire that journalist," he said. "It has happened so much at the *New Times*—so much." In other words, even journalists doing work that their peers agreed was legitimate have faced repercussions from their environment, often getting fired because they wrote something that upset a government official.

This suggests that a reporter's ability to produce critical news consistently without harm is not entirely a function of his or her level of skill. For one thing, reporters acknowledged that there had been, as recently as about 2005, many print news outlets in Rwanda that published well-reported and critical news. By the time I arrived in Rwanda, though, these had mostly shut down. One such outlet, the *Great Lakes Voice*, persisted, but published news only online without a print counterpart. Another such outlet, *The Chronicles*, had employed several editors and reporters I interviewed before it, too, was shut down after three or four years in print. Gilbert, who served on leadership with the Association of Rwandan Journalists, described this trend as a lack of "vibrancy," which he attributed to the rise in online media outlets leading to a decline in print readership and substituting the "real investigation" of print outlets with softer investigations for online organizations. "At the moment the culture is not as vibrant as it was when I joined," he said.

> When the print press was working better, before the internet dominated, there were several newspapers which were very critical. They investigated stories which we don't see these days; they could attack the government directly. It was more dramatic. But just before the presidential elections in 2010, most were banned, and the journalists had to go to exile. Of course, radios . . . continued to be dominant, online media continued to expand, but critical content decreased. It's one of the challenges we have at the moment. While the infrastructure has increased and we have many radio stations, many talk shows, and like a hundred publications online, they don't scrutinize real power.

The failure to "scrutinize real power" was a recent phenomenon, following on the heels of a glut of publications in the early 2000s whose employees had produced work critical of top government officials—and then been forced to leave the country. This source attributed the lack of current investigative work to a rise in online publications, implying that these newer outlets had pushed print publications out of business. However, Lucas, a wire reporter who had also observed this shift, discounted the business angle:

By 2009 and 2010, there were two big papers that were really good—critical of the government, investigative. Of course they lacked some journalistic skills. But still, they were giving really what Rwandans wanted. You would see, you know, when it prints, you would see copies in the morning getting finished just after one hour of distribution. And some other people would go and photocopy the paper and sell copies. That showed how print media could also do better. But the two papers were banned for six months, and later on the journalists had to flee the country. That was not good times. And the remaining journalists for print started working in fear and decided to be pro-government to survive.

It is no surprise that journalists mentioned this as a reason they self-censor today, choosing to avoid touchy subjects rather than invite the same treatment their predecessors received. But even more relevant to the current argument is the fact that this happened to journalists who, by this account of a journalism field expert, were doing good work that contributed to a "vibrant" journalism field. Thus, it seems to be the case—or at least to have been the case up until quite recently—that even several journalists doing good work investigating powerful people have faced severe repercussions and have found that career path unsustainable.

Social Roles as Orthodoxies

The drive to prioritize development goals in journalism is the second orthodoxy of the Rwandan field that this chapter deals with. This drive can be best understood as a development-oriented social role that journalists adopt, as opposed to one that is more monitorial or watchdog oriented, a role that takes the position of a dispassionate observer, or another stance (Mellado 2015). Roles align with specific social functions, and journalists see themselves filling roles as monitor, watchdog, collaborator, facilitator, or other social functions (Hanitzsch and Vos 2018).

Journalists can value multiple roles simultaneously, leading to a practice informed by multiple values and priorities—sometimes competing, especially in the Global South. For instance, journalists in Fiji and other Global South countries prioritize both a development role (typically supportive of the government) and a watchdog role (typically critical of the government), combining them into a "development journalism that sees itself as supportive of development, but wants to make sure that governments adhere to the development process" (Hanusch and Uppal 2015, 573). In many countries of sub-Saharan Africa, the journalism field is a site of tension between pressure to support a particular government or political party and pressure to reproduce journalism from a Western-style democracy, which is often critical, independent, and individualistic (Nyamnjoh 2005). Pressure to support the government comes from multiple directions, among which of course is the government itself; restrictive laws in several African nations impose boundaries around journalism, as discussed in chapter 2. However, even in legally restrictive contexts, one can see evidence of tension with journalists pushing for independent roles. One venue for this is political cartoons. After the Cold War, satirical newspapers and satirical cartoons in traditional newspapers sprang up in a number of African countries, pushing the boundaries of political restrictions commanding journalists to be "constructive and responsible" and often attracting individual and organizational repercussions (Eko 2007, 221). In Cameroon, a cartoonist fled the country after receiving threats for producing cartoons criticizing the president; he wrote an article explaining why, which was published on the first page of *Le Messager* and garnered so much negative publicity toward the government that he returned safely six months later from his exile (Eko 2010).

In sub-Saharan Africa as elsewhere, the boundaries of journalism are discursively constructed by journalists, publics, and others. In Ghana, discourse around a controversial private detective/journalist who goes undercover to expose corruption revealed both the extent to which local communities consider and debate the role of journalism and the power of global, Western journalism to legitimize local practices (Ofori-Parku and Botwe 2020). In South Africa, journalistic debate around the normative appropriateness of a particular news scandal and South African journalism ethics more broadly reveals that journalists themselves are torn between the normative demands of liberal democratic journalism and the need to develop a localized South African journalistic paradigm (Zirugo 2021b). A survey of Kenyan journalists reflects similar internal disagreement in journalists' perceptions of appropriate roles: 61 percent felt they should fill an information-provider role; 51 percent felt they should advocate for social change; 47 percent felt they should support official policies; and 35 percent felt they should act as a watchdog for the government (Ireri 2017).

These tensions have deep historical roots, as I noted earlier (83–84). Across sub-Saharan Africa, local media industries developed under colonial and post-colonial Western influences, and in many cases media systems still reflect these influences (Ndlela 2009).

While many countries, including Rwanda, now offer journalism training at local universities, the programs are often fundamentally rooted in Western practices and understanding of journalism, leaving journalists to learn the realities of local practice on the job (Ndlela 2009). In Rwanda, the local journalism program was staffed through the early 2000s by Canadian and Western European faculty (Skjerdal and Ngugi 2007). The result of these diverse influences is that journalists must negotiate between local political, religious, or social expectations and the globally shared expectations and definitions of journalism. Media actors on the continent are expected to continually negotiate liberal democratic values with inherently contradictory but equally democratic "African notions of personhood and agency" (Nyamnjoh 2005, 20). This tension leads to constant struggle for journalists, who must make sense of expectations that they will, among other things, promote democracy, save face with foreign dignitaries, and support pro-African interests—expectations that often conflict. In Cameroon, this tension leads journalists to become partisan, politicized, and militant, three attitudes that hinder, rather than help, the cause of democracy (Nyamnjoh 2005).

Development Journalism: The Orthodox Orientation

Reporters and editors, primarily at the *New Times* but also at *KT Press*, expressed a sense of obligation to promote stories that showcase unity and progress over stories of dissension and destruction. Journalists were not universally positive about this decision, but they did universally acknowledge that it is a prominent role and attributed that role to the divisive role media had played in the genocide. This affects journalists at the ideological level, in choosing to pursue development journalism at the *New Times*, and at a practical level, in emphasizing positive stories over negative stories in many cases.

Rwandan journalists feel they are responsible for encouraging unity in the post-conflict environment of Rwanda. As Emmaunel, a *New Times* reporter, said:

> Things like unity and reconciliation are so important for us in Rwanda. If we don't keep educating people it becomes an issue. And you never know what might happen, so you just have to continue to educate people. For example,

> if you get someone whose family was killed by another and they are now living together as neighbors, or forgiven, or all those kinds of stories, when we see them we have to write about them so that other people can see that we can coexist with each other.

According to this editor, Rwandan journalists have a responsibility to promote community and reconciliation, and they can best promote this goal by reporting and publishing stories that emphasize forgiveness and neighborliness, such as stories about former enemies living side by side and other events and relationships that emphasize unity as it is evident in Rwandan culture today. This editor occupied a senior role at the *New Times*, so it is reasonable to assume that his perspective on what kinds of news should be published would have a strong effect on the work produced by staff reporters and photographers. Unsurprisingly, I did find this mission repeated and shared by subeditors, reporters, and other staff at the *New Times*. Gasore said, "I find our stories a bit positive, like there is a way of trying to look for success stories . . . trying to say, 'Oh, Rwanda is great.' And I think the reason for that is the guilt feeling by the genocide and the war." He felt this motivation at work in his own decisions to pursue certain stories over others, he said.

> Instead of just keep talking about negativity—like instead of reporting how someone who lost her children hates the killer, it doesn't add up. You would rather find a story where they are trying to reconcile. So it's a natural instinct. There was so much suffering, so much violence, that people are trying to find better stories to tell, or better things to talk about, instead of just perpetuating the bad that happened.

This quotation illustrates again the ways that reporters at local news outlets tend to look for the positive over the negative. Instead of reporting on negative feelings held by someone who survived but lost family members during the genocide, reporters would look for a story of survivors who had overcome hatred and division to tell a "better story." Staff at *KT Press* and other outlets expressed a similar interest in looking for positive news and emphasizing the general development of the country.

The emphasis on stories that highlight the country's development and the ways average citizens and government policies have progressed in a positive direction since the genocide has a powerful and direct impact on the types of stories reported and the angles journalists take in approaching those stories.

While journalists are encouraged to produce investigative work, they are also encouraged to produce work that promotes socioeconomic development and shows how such development is taking place in Rwanda. Journalists are encouraged to ask critical questions, but to do so in the context of this positive movement.

Editors acknowledged that there could be a negative angle to stories but in such cases encouraged reporters to "have an open mind" to the positive as well as negative implications of policies and other issues. This occurred frequently. An interaction in one morning staff meeting at the *New Times* highlighted this process. A reporter shared a story idea about market sellers, related to how small businesses were closing down because of new, expensive government requirements. "If someone has five dresses, they can't sell them because they say the government is requiring them to have a computer to sell as a big business," she said. The editor asked her to clarify—"What is the story?" Another reporter added clarifying information. The editor responded that the real story was "a mindset issue on the part of buyers and the public generally." If everyone chooses to only purchase goods at the market, sellers will follow and set up shop in the market, in spite of the cost. To the reporter who proposed the idea, he suggested looking for people selling goods in the market. "Go ask them, are they regretting it—have they started to leave, are they seeing positive results? Then find some people selling on the streets and ask them why they are on the streets and if it is working for them. Try to look for something positive," he said. The government is waiving taxes for a year and trying to encourage them to succeed, he pointed out. He suggested a few neighborhoods where she might find good sources, including Nyabugogo, the site of a large covered market in Kigali. This interaction highlights ways an editor essentially encouraged a reporter to look away from the government watchdog story she pitched initially and turn it into a development-focused story, looking at the pros and cons of different sales techniques. While he did not discourage investigation, and in fact suggested several questions that would be worth exploring, he emphasized that the story should proceed in a direction that acknowledged the socioeconomic benefits of this new policy and the ways the government was trying to make it easier for the shopkeepers to implement the changes.

The emphasis on narratives that reinforce government messaging was also apparent in editorial meetings at *KT Press*, particularly when reporters discussed story ideas for a feature package designated to run during genocide commemoration week. During one especially long meeting, editorial staff discussed how they would portray the genocide in the stories they would run. An editor called on reporters one by one, asking them to recall where they had been and what they had seen on particular days during April, May, and June 1994. One reporter brought up a story he recalled of a Tutsi man who had begun killing Hutu people around him. Editors quickly shot down this idea, saying it would disrupt the narrative around the genocide by turning it into a civil war-like narrative with groups fighting against each other.

EDITOR 1: Was he doing it to survive or was he doing it because it was, of course there are—
REPORTER: Maybe it was power.
EDITOR 2: A Tutsi killing will not be a story.
EDITOR 1: Yeah, it cannot be a story.... The bigger picture is, the genocide is against the Tutsis. It's not—when you try to discuss it the way you want to discuss it, then it becomes war [*laughter*]. It doesn't become genocide, then it becomes war.

This quotation illustrates how reporters curated the narrative around the genocide itself, likely the most sensitive topic one could possibly cover as a journalist in Rwanda. Rather than highlight an unusual story of behavior against the status quo—a member of an oppressed group killing oppressors—editors held back on the story and turned the narrative in another direction. They were eager to avoid a murky narrative that would suggest blame on both sides or complicate the oppressor-versus-oppressed narrative of the genocide, even if such a story could shed further light on the genocide and help make events more clear. In this way, editors at *KT Press* and the *New Times* showed their interest in contributing to government narratives that would foster unity and positive change in society, rather than highlighting ways those narratives were incomplete or possibly inaccurate.

Reporters are motivated by the same myth that their role is to promote unity. Because of the legacy of the genocide in Rwanda, reporters said they are especially cautious of exercising their power in printing divisive or negative news. Gasore, the *New Times* reporter who had attended graduate school in Canada, observed that in his experience, Canadian journalists were less cautious about the news they reported because they were less aware of the power of divisive news and thus less concerned about the possible ill effects of their work.

> A journalist in Rwanda thinks more about the impact of what they write than a journalist in Canada does. A journalist in Canada is probably going to tell you this and this happened: this person is bad, this person did this. But in Rwanda before they do it, they also have to think about social responsibility, so about the impact of what you say—the impact on people's lives. Remember it's been only 22 years after the genocide, so . . . people have been thinking, "How do we not contribute to violence, how do we bring back peace in this country?" Journalists are also thinking about that. In Canada, all they want is people's attention on the screens, but that's not necessarily the case in Rwanda. In Rwanda, people think about how can our stories contribute towards making Rwanda a peaceful place.

As this quotation illustrates, Rwandan journalists are wary of reporting "just the facts," telling audiences immediately what happened and who is guilty of what, because they know that, in the past, people died because of similar facts that were reported by journalists. Journalists are cautious in an attempt to avoid creating similar situations today, and they are wary of playing a role that stirs up controversy and strife. For the Rwandan journalist, this reporter suggested, social responsibility is a more important value than timeliness and information provision—both core news values for many journalists who practice in Western democracies like Canada and the United States. While this journalist was quick to acknowledge that different contexts of journalism demand different approaches, he prioritized the importance for the Rwandan journalist of playing an active social role of contributing to peace, diminishing the value of "people's attention on the screens," a core news value he observed in Canada. To some extent this is a false dichotomy; Rwandans journalists are just as concerned with business viability as are Canadian journalists. However, it does highlight an important distinction between the focus of many journalists in Rwanda with what this reporter observed in Canada. Canadian journalists, he suggests, place critical importance on the audience and giving the audience what it wants. Rwandan journalism, on the other hand, tends to focus on providing what the audience "needs," which is determined often by political considerations and development goals. And as the above analysis illustrates, this goal is strongly informed by the genocide narrative underlying the contemporary journalism field in Rwanda.

The flip side of this ideological bent away from opposition is that several news workers embraced the role of development journalism, emphasizing the importance of partnering with those in power to lead the country in a "positive" direction. As Eric explained:

> Journalism today should be able to partner—to serve as a vehicle to better livelihoods, to educate the people about the things that directly impact them, that change their lives, that change the course of their future. ... And I think the media can play a role in that, especially in our context. ... The people's welfare, their issues, have to be seen to be improving. And then you can ensure that going forward there is reason to let everybody understand that they have a stake in consulting and making sure that they maintain and protect this peace, protect this peace that they have because they have a stake. If anything goes wrong, they lose, themselves.

A reporter explained that the *New Times* and other local outlets cover news differently from reporters from global news channels like BBC or CNN, who might come to Rwanda to expose an issue. By contrast, this reporter said, "We don't focus on negative stories." Instead, journalists in Rwanda are concerned with "constructive journalism or development journalism." The concept of development journalism, as editors explained it to me, is not necessarily positive; in fact, it involves getting "governments to really properly serve the people and invest where they should to impact the lives of the people," which can involve opposition and discord in the service of the goal of improved quality of life. However, as currently practiced—and as many on staff acknowledged—this functionally looked like positivity and a reluctance to stir up controversy, tied to memories of genocide involvement.

Motivated by Unity

Many journalists I interviewed explicitly defended an orientation toward development journalism. Reporters and editors emphasized that they feel they have a social responsibility to promote unity and positivity among Rwandans, emphasize progress, and show a good face of Rwanda to the rest of the world. Several reporters emphasized that this development journalism role is different from the more watchdog-oriented role journalists play in other countries, including Canada, the United States, and Kenya. Conversely, interview subjects stressed their responsibility to not stir up any dissent like that underpinning the genocide. "We are doing development journalism, and it's a constructive thing," Innocent told me. Many Rwandan journalists embrace a development journalism role because of concern over the negative power of divisive watchdog reporting combined with a desire to contribute to the social good and undo the negative effects their field had in the past. One strong motivation that inclines journalists to think of their work as primarily contributing to national development rather than stirring up dissent or uncovering conflict has to do with the powerful social effect of the genocide. Gabriel, an editor at *KT Press*, explained it this way. He first acknowledged that most local media houses are not strictly independent and face pressure from other angles to produce positive news and avoid critical news. However, there is also personal motivation to report this way:

> If these media houses were fully independent, they still would be doing the same kind of reporting, for one reason. You know, Rwandan society is still moving out of those genocide memories. Everyone, be it in the opposition or something else, is fully focused on rebuilding the nation. And rebuilding the nation means giving a helping hand in promoting and publishing what is mostly needed for the local communities.

Out of personal motivations linked both to the journalist's role in the genocide and to a shared cultural memory of the violence and upheaval around that event, journalists tend to share a mission of promoting local security and development. They are more interested in pursuing news coverage that builds reconciliation than in coverage that might have destructive or disruptive effects.

The *New Times* is especially grounded in a pro-development orientation. One editor explained that the *New Times* was created immediately following the genocide with a mission to unite the Rwandan diaspora. Many had fled to English-speaking countries and had learned to speak English, so the newspaper was born as an English-language publication. This language still contributes to a core identity of the newspaper; many staff were quick to remind me that it is the only English-language daily newspaper in Rwanda, and that this language choice constitutes a challenge and a mission. Related to the language as well is the unifying mission of the *New Times*: "As part of the reconciliation process, the people who had gone abroad—we needed them to come back home and help build the country . . . so they needed to know what was going on, and the language they were comfortable with was English," Emmanuel said. Eric also linked the newspaper's genesis to its mission.

You have to look at where we have come from. I would say that the *New Times* is probably a symbol of post-1994 Rwanda. It was born after the 1994 genocide with the mission to partake in the process of the rebirth of this country and to build a country that is accountable, that is of the people, that promotes reconciliation and the unity of the people, that delivers development, that commits and delivers on its commitments. The whole idea behind the *New Times* is saying, look, we can afford to do professional journalism, but also partake in propagating hope and promoting business and promoting civility and promoting a nation, a nation that wants to be there for its people, a nation that is inclusive and institutions that are inclusive but also that are accountable to the people. And I think that is our role as media in Rwanda, as the *New Times*—to be professional media, and to tell the Rwandan story, despite our challenges, using our means, and within our context. For a long, long, long time, our story, and the story of Africa, has been pretty much in the hands of someone else.

The genocide, in these journalists' retellings, comprises a compelling origin story and a raison d'être for their ongoing work. There are several factors wrapped up in this explanation of how and why the *New Times* exists the way it does in Rwanda. Some are unique to that publication, but others were echoed by editors at other news organizations, including *KT Press*. This mission combines elements of development journalism, in the commitment to promote reconciliation and unity, with elements of watchdog journalism in the idea that the government should "commit and deliver on its commitments." In articulating the mission this way, this editor positions journalism in Rwanda as a field that exists to supplement and aid the government in performing a mission of bettering the country's population. The other element of journalistic mission this editor outlines is that of "telling the story of Rwanda." This mission was echoed by journalists at *KT Press*, the *Great Lakes Voice*, and *Taarifa*. These journalists said they had a mission of presenting the story of Rwanda from a Rwandan perspective to an audience of Rwandans but also to an audience of outside observers who might only know the country from its portrayals in Western media, which primarily center around the genocide. This mission of promoting development and an Afrocentric portrayal of Rwanda, as recounted here, stems from a reaction to the powerful role journalists understand themselves to have played in escalating the genocide.

Orthodoxy and Legitimacy

For Rwandan journalists to routinely practice watchdog journalism, they must be able to consistently produce news content that meets field-level standards of good journalism. In terms of capital, the journalist must possess a high degree of cultural capital that is consistently evident across his or her body of work. Rwandan journalists typically used the term "professionalism" to capture this concept. However, the concept of professionalism in scholarly conversation is multifaceted and complex. Debate around the term is most commonly associated with boundaries around the occupation of journalism and concern with defining who is or is not a "journalist" (Singer 2003). An outdated approach to the study of professions holds that professionals are those who hold particular traits, varying but often including esoteric knowledge specific to the occupation, moral and legal authority to do work, and training (Abbott 2014; Mari 2021). Contemporary studies of professionalism in journalism tend to focus on ways journalists themselves demarcate the boundaries between what is and is not journalism and, by extension, who is and is not a journalist (Carlson and Lewis 2015; Waisbord 2013). The meaning imputed to the term in my fieldwork conversations is captured equally well by legitimacy, a concept that has been applied to journalism in a few cases and has been applied frequently in organizational studies. Legitimacy is an "assumption that the actions of an entity are desirable, proper, or appropriate within some socially constructed system of norms, values, beliefs, and definitions" (Suchman 1995, 574). Legitimacy thus captures a concept that is related to but distinct from the concept of professionalism, and useful for the present discussion.

Where professionalism tends to draw boundaries separating what is from what is not, legitimacy is more concerned with determining normative rank and status within those boundaries. One can be a bad journalist or a good journalist without leaving the ranks of the occupation per se, and legitimacy captures this distinction. This legitimacy approach thus fits well within a field theory framework in that it allows one to differentiate between different roles and practices within the field of journalism, studying within-field variation rather than focusing exclusively on defining the boundaries. In the context of journalism studies, legitimacy has been invoked typically to imagine the nature of journalistic practice. The concept has been used to explain the boundary-setting practices of journalists dealing with new forms of media content, with journalistic practices such as reliance on user-generated content becoming more and common as UGC itself becomes more common and thus legitimized (Yeo 2016). That is, edgy practices can be justified if they are seen as "legitimate," even if they are not often seen or dealt with by journalists. Legitimacy has also been invoked to explain the ways journalists sustain their occupational standing as information experts with a set social role (Tong 2018). News organizations work for legitimacy by defending their work and adopting new tools to do that work.

Legitimacy can thus be seen as a type of cultural capital. A journalist who consistently produces legitimate work has a high level of expertise in the field, which acts as a power resource facilitating access to the organizational positions at transnational organizations that will further protect and privilege the legitimate journalist in producing such work (Lareau and Lamont 1988). Journalists with high levels of cultural capital are those who possess the skills important to do the job well. In the context of news production in Rwanda, this includes the ability to consistently produce news that meets agreed-upon standards (Vandevoordt 2017). For journalists affiliated with transnational media organizations, it also includes the ability to speak and write English fluently. Legitimacy as a form of cultural capital for journalists is the ability to consistently meet the social expectations imposed on a member of the journalism field.

Among Rwandan journalists, there is a shared feeling that many journalists fail to consistently research and produce news reports that meet their field's standards of acceptable journalism narratives. The general editorial consensus is that journalists in Rwanda are poorly trained and, when they are properly trained, they tend to leave the field for other, better-respected and better-paying careers. As a result, many of those who practice journalism in the field produce material that inconsistently meets standards that editors and other field authorities deem minimally acceptable. Failure to meet those standards provides editors and officials with acceptable grounds to critique or question a journalist, and the officials and editors are likely to take that opportunity if a reporter pursues uncomfortable watchdog journalism. On the other hand, since laws in Rwanda provide some protection for journalists, a journalist who does produce content aligned with the desired standards has some protection against overt harassment.

The behaviors appropriate to the Rwandan journalist are outlined in a printed code of ethics available at the Rwandan Journalist's Association. In summary, the code of ethics provides some protections and imposes some responsibilities on Rwandan journalists. It is not legally binding, but a journalist who does not adhere to the behavior outlined in the code is likely to find him- or herself censured by the Rwandan Journalist's Association, which has the power to revoke press cards and thus bar journalists from entry to some events. According to the code, journalists are obligated to respect facts and search for truth by not suppressing essential information or distorting remarks, texts, or documents and "shall consider slander, abuse, libel and groundless accusation as the most dangerous professional faults" (Rwandan Media Fraternity 2011, 5). They are to "avoid broadcasting or publishing biased information inciting to racial, tribal, ethnic, religious hatred or hatred based on sex, age, social status, disability, or any disease or health status of the people mentioned" (Rwandan Media Fraternity 2011, 6). They must avoid publishing or broadcasting scenes of violence or obscenity and avoid sensationalism. As these examples highlight, while the code imposes some restrictions against relatively easily discernible violations such as plagiarism and acting simultaneously as a public relations officer and a journalist, many of the guidelines laid out are subject to interpretation by the authorities within and outside the field who might hold journalists accountable for them. Despite the nebulous nature of many of these guidelines, though, when journalists discuss ideal or desirable behavior within the field, they are generally referring to these. Many journalists mentioned the importance of publishing information for which they have established the origin, veracity, and accuracy (Rwandan Media Fraternity 2011, 6), not taking bribes from people seeking to influence coverage (8), avoiding sensationalism (9), and separating opinion from fact (10). The comments and analysis below reflect this.

Reporters and editors across media organizations, including some more independent organizations and some that are more state aligned, agree that overt harassment from political figures is much less common today than it was five or 10 years ago. In other words, journalists today are much less likely to be arrested, disappear, or face other retaliation for covering powerful figures critically, and there is growing acceptance of a powerful, independent, and critical role for news media. However, editors still get phone calls from officials asking to have stories pulled from the issue or the web, and reporters are still (on rare occasions) arrested. Reporters also face opposition and reluctance from the public, both as readers and as sources. These things happen, reporters and editors told me, because individual journalists lack the training, skills, and behaviors that would protect them against such backlash. Conversely, reporters and editors believe that when one reports stories in a "professional" way, even if the story is contentious, it is unlikely to result in serious censure against a journalist. Thus, professional behavior acts as an individual safeguard against retaliation for critical reporting. Reporters and editors agreed that professionalism is, in general, in short supply in the Rwandan media scene. Media professionalism is growing but is "not where we want to be," one reporter told me. Journalists are "not at their best level in terms of education and professionalism," an editor said. "I can improve my career if I can improve my professionalism," another reporter said.

This lack of training is rooted in the reality that the field in Rwanda essentially restarted after the genocide. In observations and interviews across six media organizations in Kigali, I did not encounter any Rwandan journalists older than their mid-thirties; journalists older than this were Ugandan or Kenyan and had been hired to fill specific roles at university or in the newsroom. The young average age across the field further reinforces the idea that journalism in Rwanda has "started over" since the genocide. Stories of journalism practice from 1994 or earlier are inherited secondhand rather than being recounted by the practitioners. This also means that there are few older, established reporters and editors from journalists to learn from, and fewer still who have retired to teach in journalism programs. As a result, journalism education is heavily weighted toward academic experiences, and students tend to deprioritize real-life learning experiences like internships in favor of getting good grades on classroom projects, editors said. Even attentive students with good grades have a great deal to learn once they show up to the newsroom hoping for a job and are often disappointed to hear that they need to intern or freelance before they will be offered a full-time, salaried position. Innocent described journalism in Rwanda as "something which is growing up . . . you are learning from experience, you are learning from the past, and we are trying to do our best with professionalism and ethics and the context." As several reporters and editors reminded me, the *New Times* itself began in 1995, just a year after the genocide.

However, training in the field is rare. Journalists have few opportunities to formally learn new practices or polish their current habits. At best, they may learn on the job from editor feedback, which is often indirect or communicates mixed messages. Peter, an editor at *KT Press*, explained:

> We have not worked in big media houses where there are experienced people, so there is that lack of knowing a professional story. I don't have the right words to assess it, but everyone lacks something. There is room for

improvement, and people here don't get trainings. Like since I came here, I never got any training.

Journalists tend to learn their skills on the job, often picking up here and there best practices for the occupation. Few travel outside the country for training, unless they are sponsored by the *New Times*, and during the eight months I was in Rwanda I only observed one training, for photographers at *KT Press*. This lack of formalized skills training meant journalists often felt that they were unskilled and learning by trial and error the fundamental practices of good journalists.

Peter noted a lack of experienced people in the field who could teach journalism practices to others, whether at university or on the job.

> We don't have experienced people in the media. And when you have such experience—like, have you worked in the media house? You had guys with experience and you could learn from them, right? Here in Rwanda, who do you learn from? It is like you are like an orphan trying to learn things by your own. I am telling you. Because even when you go to universities, you don't get what you need. When I left Mount Kenya University, I felt like I was cheated.

Because most news outlets and journalists in the country postdate the 1994 genocide, the field lacks a depth of experience that could be provided by those who had been working as journalists for more than 20 years. Journalists I encountered in surrounding countries, especially in Uganda and Zimbabwe, referenced this sort of newsroom learning and socialization provided by colleagues who had been in the field for decades and had long experience of how things should be done, such as where to push the boundaries and where to follow the status quo. By contrast, in Rwanda, the media organizations themselves were relatively young, and even the longest-working journalist had only been practicing the occupation in Rwanda since after the genocide. This reality, combined with the legal changes over the years, contributed to a feeling that there was a lack of experienced experts who could be expected to guide and mentor young journalists in the field.

The myth that journalists are harassed and disrespected because they are poorly trained serves to explain why many in the Rwandan journalism field come under government censure for their reporting. It is also an editorial explanation for the fact that reporters tend to not pursue creative or investigative stories at local media outlets. The shared belief and narrative is that, because the genocide destroyed the journalism field as it was, members of the field today have started from a blank slate and built to the current state over the past 22 years. Editors and staff at the *New Times*, *KT Press*, and other outlets said that media staff are constantly learning and need intensive training because they lack skills. As one editor said, "There are ... challenges that everybody in the media industry in this country faces. Skills is a general need, because this is a very young field," he said. "You get the feeling that you always are building for the future. It's always a work in progress. It's always training, day in and day out." This future-oriented approach to journalism practice both acknowledges that the journalism field in Rwanda has not reached the level of expertise that its members would like, and provides justification for the current state of affairs. There are justifiable and understandable reasons for why journalists are not occupational experts, and there is a goal editors and reporters are trying to reach that has not yet been achieved. The subtext is that, once that goal has been achieved, reporters will be able to take a stronger social role that includes investigation of power.

Conclusion

This chapter shows how a belief in underdevelopment—both of Rwanda as a country and of journalism as a local field—shapes orthodox values and practices in the field. For journalism as a field, the orthodoxies stemming from underdevelopment hold that journalists are inadequately trained to tackle big stories that involve investigation and creative insight. Journalists' belief in underdevelopment in Rwanda as a country leads to a primary field orientation toward a development journalism role, which tends to support government interventions and promote collaborative and cooperative news values over critique and conflict. The authoritarian-development role orientation is not unique to Rwanda; it has been or is practiced in many places across the African continent, including Kenya in the 1980s (Ireri 2015). This chapter adds to our understanding of the implementation and practice of development journalism by highlighting in particular how journalists describe the practice and how they feel they can best justify it in light of global norms—increasingly inescapable—that tend to promote more distant and critical roles for journalists.

5
Money Matters
The News Values of Business Pressure

Routines in news organizations lead journalists to prioritize certain kinds of news over others, defining a hierarchy of news values and sending messages, directly and indirectly, about what types of stories should be pursued and which should be bypassed. How does this happen in the Rwandan journalism field? At first glance, Rwandan news organizations send a variety of competing messages about good newsroom behavior and news judgment. Editors say they value both straightforward news and creative angles; they are interested in enterprise reporting that involves many sources and investigation, but they also want finished stories filed daily. These mixed messages were often apparent in editorial meetings like the one I attended at *KT Press* in early April.

Editors and reporters had gathered for a routine meeting to debrief the past week's content and plan the week ahead. The 100-day genocide memorial period had just begun, and staff were discussing the previous week's coverage—which had primarily focused on genocide-related stories in honor of *Kwibuka*, genocide commemoration week—and upcoming coverage. As usual, most of the newsroom reporting staff were there, seated around a large table. The meeting began when a senior editor asked for summaries of last week from reporters around the room, asking his staff how many stories they had written since the previous meeting.

The editor asked one reporter, "You are not contributing—why not?" The disgruntled reporter responded forcefully, "Last week I was on a team covering the president. I don't like teamwork. It destroys my own creativity and angles. I found an angle we liked, and we didn't use it. It feels like a waste of time to be working together on something like that."

The editor dismissed the reporter's frustration: "This is a standing order," he said. "If the president speaks at any event, we write everything he says. We don't pick out one thing. That is how we cover the president at *KT Press*. . . .

The rule is, we always cover everything. It's not like we go on Twitter and pick a few things. Go on SoundCloud, find the recording, and cover everything."

After discussing the past week's productivity, the editor turned to the coming week. "We need stories," he said. "All of you have an agreement with the company to produce a certain number of stories. Are you guys sick? [Editor] is saying I'm not doing my part because we don't have enough stories."

Several reporters responded to this prompt with story ideas. One pitched a story about a youth gathering the previous week; the editor dismissed the idea as "too old." The same reporter pitched another story about reconciliation: a Hutu man who killed people during the genocide later married the daughter of a Tutsi man he had killed. "There are so many cases of that—so many," the editor responded. "What makes this a story? There are so many cases. Just marrying someone from a certain family does not—is not news."

Another reporter pitched a feature story about a person who, during the genocide, shuttled Tutsi refugees across the Kagera River to Tanzania. The reporter had photos and had already interviewed the person; the editor responded, "I have heard that story." The team had already posted a video of an interview with the person, he said, and a story would not contribute enough. "There is nothing new in it."

The editor followed up with a general directive to the reporters: "The way you present your stories is not attractive. You should always find a way of convincing us." He assigned reporters to cover a few events, including a parliamentary hearing, and dismissed the group.

The editor leading this meeting conveyed all the major messages about news values and newsroom priorities that I observed in Rwandan newsrooms. Certain stories could only be told if the reporter conducted enterprise reporting and found a creative angle; others would only be acceptable if they followed a standard formula. Reporters were responsible for pitching stories that were new and "attractive," but were also assigned to cover routine events and expected to regularly meet an assigned content quota, per company agreement. Reporters, editors, and other staff reconcile these contradictory messages through a financial logic: they pursue creativity and enterprise where it is least likely to impede financial stability. This means that, while enterprise and creativity are encouraged across beats and angles, editors are more likely to enforce and reward these values and reporters are more likely to pursue them when the story involves figures with low levels of financial and political power.

Reporters and editors develop routines and news values in the context of financial pressure that leads them to integrate professional values like creativity and enterprise in storytelling about low-power figures, while adopting standardized frames and approaches to news stories that involve figures wielding financial power over the organization. In short, in the face of uncertainty, journalists prioritize producing news in a way that will get them paid, and they learn what kind of news this is through the spoken and nonverbal routine interactions of newsroom norms.

KT Press in the Field

KT Press was less hierarchical and more collegial than the *New Times*, but similarly government oriented. When I was there, this newsroom was in a residential neighborhood in Kigali, with offices in two large houses that had been repurposed into office space. Broadcast reporters primarily worked in one building and text-based reporters worked primarily in the other. Rooms throughout the house had been transformed into work spaces, with small groups of desks scattered in each. The *KT Press* investigative web team worked out of one room on the ground floor of a building in the back of the gated compound, when they worked from the office. On any given day, two or three reporters and editors worked remotely. The newsroom routines were more individualized than those at the *New Times*. Reporters met with subeditors and the chief editor on Monday mornings to critique what had been published the week before in a postmortem and discuss ideas for the week ahead. After this meeting, individual editors and reporters conversed in the newsroom about stories and deadlines. The head editor stopped in occasionally but more often would send updates or questions by WhatsApp to the entire group. Editors would proofread stories as they were submitted and post them to the web platform, which had a WordPress-like blog interface. Reporters at *KT Press* routinely expressed of their frustration with editors; one reporter spent nearly 30 minutes arguing directly with her editor in a group meeting called because reporters were not meeting deadlines. They were more subdued when interacting with the head editor, but several reporters vocally disagreed with him or grumbled in frustration at editorial decisions during Monday meetings. Editors tended not to list specific questions for reporters to ask in interviews but would give detailed instructions on angles to cover and to avoid.

Linking Government Control and Business Pressure

Journalists around the world face pressure from powerful sources to produce the news in flattering ways. In restrictive political environments where the state is strong, this pressure tends to be even more pronounced. Government actors in particular pressure journalists to produce coverage that supports official goals and to avoid critiquing, probing, or investigating official versions of events and programs. Their methods of control have changed over time. Historically, government actors often controlled media coverage by censoring it, overseeing the content production process to approve or revise particular items so they aligned with official values and goals. This overt censorship was sometimes enshrined in law. Through the late twentieth century, a number of African countries formally instituted the government's right to review news content and ban anything considered objectionable (Jose 1975). In other places, including many countries in Central and South America, government actors used threats of violence and even death to reinforce the censorship norm and incentivize journalists to withhold politically sensitive content from publication (Hughes 2003; Smith 1997).

Contemporary states tend to rely on less overt, more subversive tactics to ensure that media actors cooperate with state goals. Global power flows influence state tactics. Countries with high levels of global power and capital or little need to project a democratic image have little incentive to avoid overt censorship. The Chinese government, for instance, routinely censors mass and social media content using internet police, monitors, and social media censors (King et al. 2013). Chinese journalists are subject to a number of policies, including overt censorship, which ensure that they operate as government partners rather than independent observers (Repnikova 2017).

However, there is a global trend away from clientelistic economic control of the media and toward commercialization; governments increasingly control the media through financial pressure and other surreptitious means (Hallin 2009). This is especially true in countries that rely on global goodwill—often smaller states with large aid inflows—where media control strategies are often enacted under the cover of freedom-of-information acts and other laws ostensibly protecting media freedom (Dukalskis 2021; Michener 2011). In Malaysia and Singapore, ownership and licensing restrictions and laws against publishing sedition or secrets resulted in journalism that generally avoids government critique (Means 1996). The Turkish government instituted surveillance of journalists through the early twenty-first century, leading journalists to avoid potentially critical stories (Yesil 2014).

On top of this legal pressure to self-censor by avoiding controversial or negative subject matter, journalists in many places are in financially precarious positions. Salaries are low and jobs are scarce, making journalists more willing to ignore or give up certain stories in exchange for regular paychecks. Across sub-Saharan Africa, news organizations struggle to make a profit, and journalists are poorly compensated. Journalists in francophone Africa—a group of 17 countries, including Rwanda, that share French as an official language and have conflict or post-conflict contexts and successful semiauthoritarian governance—encounter a variety of "democratically acceptable" risks (Frère 2014, 185; 2015). These include financial harassment via exorbitant taxes and licensing fees and withholding or bestowing advertising funds to encourage media allegiance and discourage critique (Frère 2014). The financial risks are exacerbated by small and precarious media markets, high production costs, and low newspaper circulation (Frère 2015). Among Rwanda's immediate and near neighbors in the Great Lakes region, financial precarity manifests among journalists in a number of ways. Ethiopian and Tanzanian journalists' low levels of compensation lead them to take "brown envelope" bribes to cover certain topics or adopt positive angles (Skjerdal 2010). Kenyan journalists reported that they were satisfied with their jobs in general but not satisfied with their salaries and that journalism is one of the "least well-compensated professions in Kenya" (Ireri 2016, 182).

These pressures can be summed up as a "financial logic." Journalists learn that, in order to stay financially stable, they need to produce certain kinds of news and avoid others. The financial logic is nearly ubiquitous, but it gains extra strength when the surrounding environment is so financially precarious.

The Incentive of Financial Stability

Reporters and editors alike are motivated to prioritize financial stability by the precarious nature of journalism practice in Rwanda. Reporters, whose paychecks often depend on meeting strictly enforced story quotas, are motivated to avoid complex enterprise stories whose publication is uncertain. Editors, who are responsible for maintaining the economic viability of news organizations, are motivated to avoid angles and stories that jeopardize the organization's financial stability by angering or frustrating advertisers, while still upholding professional news values.

Editors are motivated to pursue a financial logic by witnessing news organizations go out of business and by threats from advertisers to withhold advertisements or payment. It is a process of isomorphism—a process by which organizations with similar social roles and in similar environmental conditions come to resemble each other (DiMaggio and Powell 1983). Two types of isomorphism are particularly relevant to the financial logic of the Rwandan journalism field. Mimetic isomorphism, in which organizations and people within them are motivated to mimic each other as a response to environmental uncertainty or ambiguity, is evident in the ways that editors learn about and respond to financial pressure from outside the field. This process, along with normative isomorphism, where professionalization—work conditions, methods, and other things defined by members of an occupation—legitimates certain behaviors over others, characterizes the process by which Rwandan journalists learn what kinds of news content they are and are not expected to produce. Isomorphism has been used to explain how journalists construct subfields (Davidson 2013), how they partner across news mediums (Lowrey 2005), and how they respond to economic uncertainty (Li and Lee 2010). In older newsroom studies, this process is called newsroom socialization or "learning the ropes" (Breed 1955); a narrower instance of this is the process of indexing, where news organizations choose a selection of appropriate voices to represent ideological debates, leading to similar news coverage of politics across a range of geographies and mediums (Bennett 1990). The process of socialization or isomorphism instills a particular logic in Rwandan journalists, uniting seemingly disconnected routines to send a powerful message about the interpretation of news values in story production.

The Rwandan journalism field exists in a state of financial uncertainty. For editors, this is most strongly communicated through messages and experiences of news organizations' financial precarity; for staff, including reporters, photographers, and low-level editors, this is felt most strongly in individual uncertainty around paychecks and job stability. A common story in the Rwandan journalism field is that of the organization that started with a mission of providing independent, critical news, only to go out of business a short time later because advertisers would not support the goal. An editor at the *New Times*—the largest and best-known English-language newspaper in Rwanda—observed:

> A very big number of newspapers are off the street already. They have closed shop here because of the business aspect. If you cannot fund your operations, what will happen is that you cannot even pay your reporters ... you cannot do the basics. (Personal communication, February 22, 2017)

The director of the Rwandan Journalists' Association said many news organizations had started and then gone out of business over the previous decade because they could not find funding. The result is that news organizations mimic each other. They may have different audiences and areas of coverage, but they tend to produce news with similar content and similar, non-critical editorial styles. This process is visible across forms of media, observers say. "We report the same way," one reporter said. "It's like many radios, many newspapers, from one place—from one mother. Some media houses started and we thought, we will get *news* from these guys. But at the end of the day, they also became like the others" (personal communication, May 4, 2017). News organizations formed with ambitious goals to be different from the others in the Rwandan journalism field either go out of business quickly or shift behavior and publication style to align with the more established players in the field, ensuring financial success by adopting an accepted style of positive journalism that does not scrape below the surface on subjects that are touchy to major sources of advertising funds.

Advertising is scarce in Rwanda, as in the rest of sub-Saharan Africa (Africa Media Index 2019), but editors rely on advertising for a major portion of their operating budgets (for instance, the editor of the *New Times* told me about three-quarters of his annual budget was funded by advertisements). In 2017, except for a few telecommunications companies—MTN and Airtel—government agencies had the biggest advertising budgets in the country, editors said. Many smaller organizations did not advertise; an editor at *KT Press* said that about two dozen organizations produced most of the country's advertisements. "It's very difficult to get people to come and advertise," Robert, an editor, said. Government organizations and organizations with strong government links dominate advertising. "The government, they want to sensitize, they have policies they want people to know, they have institutions, and they have a budget for communication," Robert said. As a result, editors are reluctant to lose the country's few, lucrative, often government-affiliated advertisers. The link between advertiser funding and flattering news coverage is discussed across multiple levels of the organization and field. Jacques described the pressure of advertisement funding as the "government ... trying to win all media organizations on their side by giving them adverts and offices, such that they write good stories." Samuel concurred: "One of the ways to make money is being a friend with the government, because the government is like the only person who has money in the country," he said. "They do everything—business, politics, leadership—everything, they are there."

The limited nature of advertising in Rwanda can be seen in a glance at a newspaper. For instance, the April 5, 2017, edition of the *New Times*—published around the same time period as that alluded to in the opening vignette—included about six and one-quarter pages of ads over the first 20 pages of content. Of those ads, two pages were dedicated to government agencies (the National Institute of Statistics, the Rwanda Revenue Authority, the Rwanda Energy Group, and the Rwanda Housing Authority); one and one-quarter pages consisted of ads promoting nonprofit or corporate organizations (German nonprofit GIZ, Indian telecommunications company Airtel, and Oshen Health Care Rwanda Limited, a local agency branch of an Angolan management company); and three pages consisted of ads from organizations with close links to government agencies (import/export controller Magerwa and the Institute of Certified Public Accountants of Rwanda). With most advertising coming from government and para-governmental organizations, editors prefer to negotiate or capitulate rather than refuse to accommodate advertisers when they make requests (or demands) about news content.

The scarcity and importance of advertising to news organizations motivates editors to temper their news judgments and accommodate advertisers. Gilbert said he had heard numerous stories of editors changing content under pressure from advertisers, afraid they would lose a major chunk of revenue if they refused:

> Most of it has to do with the economic structure of the country. It will not be somebody threatening to jail you or beat you or do whatever, but to cut the ads. And we understand. If you are running a business, you have to work; at the end of the month, you have to pay taxes, you have to pay dues. And you also have to pay yourself as an owner. Business matters.

The financial logic thus entails making decisions that shift or neglect news values for an organization in order to accommodate financial needs and, as a side effect, benefit politicians and business leaders.

Editors aim to avoid conflict with advertisers by preemptively cutting items from story budgets that are likely to result in unpleasant encounters. "We have tried to be very careful," Olivier, an editor at *KT Press*, said—meaning he requires thorough reporting from his staff and considers whether stories are likely to bring criticism. Even then, he said, "We find ourselves not running certain stories, and we have to throw them away." The result is a cycle where editors learn which topics are likely to be controversial: "Next time something like that happens, you'll tell yourself not to publish it. You know this is a no-go area." These off-limits topics included anything that officials deemed a national security risk, as well as articles likely to show prominent government officials or major corporate advertisers in a bad light. (In reality, as Booth and Golooba-Mutebi [2012] show, government officials and major corporate advertisers are often closely linked, as members of the Rwandan Patriotic Front hold majority shares in many of Rwanda's major private enterprises.) Another way editors negotiated the boundaries around news content was by meeting with advertising staff within the organization. Senior editors at *KT Press* would call strategy meetings with the advertising department and subeditors to determine what content they should and should not pursue, to determine where reporters could reasonably push the boundaries of investigation without attracting criticism from powerful advertisers. Olivier explained,

> The advertisers are our biggest problem. They are our biggest problem and our biggest solution because they give us money. We always have to think very hard about how we will balance letting the journalists do their work and maintaining an income so they can be paid.

Identifying the "No-Go Areas"

The messages about what is and is not appropriate to publish start at the levels of organizational management, with editors (and sometimes publishers) fielding requests and demands from advertisers who want to have news stories withheld from publication. News organizations rely on funding from a limited number of advertisers, and as a result editors and publishers tend to prefer bargaining over issuing ultimatums or ignoring advertiser content requests. In addition, the Rwandan context, where journalists are more likely to find social and political support in the soft power of persuasion rather than in political protection or positive public opinion, encourages editors to engage with such requests, often on a case-by-case basis. Three general categories of content are particularly troublesome. They are news stories that critiques business practices of big organizations, stories about misgovernance on a large scale or involving highly placed officials, and stories aimed at middle management and others with only moderate social power, when the story or the journalist behind it could be called into question for an ethical breach or another professional error.

Stories investigating the largest corporate advertisers in Rwanda would inevitably draw censure. In the late spring of 2017, *Taarifa*, a relatively new online-only publication founded by a former *New Times* reporter with a mission to produce investigative news coverage, reported a story on a local scandal involving MTN, one of the largest telecommunication companies in Rwanda and one of the most prolific advertisers in local media outlets outside of government organizations. MTN was being fined by the Rwandan government, and rumor had it that the company was surreptitiously skimming customer accounts to pay the fine. Officials and journalists took *Taarifa* to task for producing an article that, they said, did not contain enough knowledgeable sources. Caleb, a reporter at the *East African*, a transnational news outlet with a bureau in Kigali, said:

> Even in the media industry they are being criticized, you know: "Why are you doing these things, you don't even verify, you are attacking MTN." Everyone, including journalists who were against them, were like, "You guys, you can't do this to MTN, you are lying, you only interviewed yourselves."

This backlash against *Taarifa* demonstrates the way that Rwandan journalists and officials pressure journalists who publish unpopular stories by calling out perceived instances where the journalists in question did not meet standards of good journalism.

Investigation of government errors, particularly when they involved whole ministries or prominent mistakes, would also attract attention and criticism, often partnered with threats to withdraw advertisements and funding. For instance, Olivier recounted how the Ministry of Health—a major advertiser, with a budget of nearly $100,000 to promote health messaging—was caught off guard by a resurgence of malaria in 2016, and *KT Press* reported on the number of people hospitalized with the disease.

The minister was furious. "We're going to cancel your contract," that kind of thing. So you see—balancing that is not very easy.... We are in a situation where the institutions that are causing trouble are paying you for ads.

Leaders at the Rwandan Journalists' Association told me how editors and publishers at newspapers and broadcast media outlets would receive phone calls or visits from officials threatening to cut advertising from the outlet if some critical story were to run. In addition to this preemptive threat, news outlets that run critical content would often find themselves the subject of smear campaigns where officials would send messages over social media calling the organization unprofessional and would prod other news outlets to produce more flattering stories about the government. Olivier shared another example, this one a story involving the Rwandan Stock Exchange, a major advertiser. In early 2017 the Rwandan Stock Index dropped dramatically—by 60 percent—and a reporter wrote a story on it for *KT Press*. As soon as the story posted, the CEO called a marketing executive and then posted to Twitter calling out *KT Press* for being "unprofessional."

When we released the story about the stock market, there was a story in the *New Times* saying that's not true, the stock market failed because of blah blah blah—they don't refute the fact that it failed, but they are giving other dynamics. Then they are all over other radio stations explaining. Basically, they try to make you look like you didn't know what you were reporting and kill or damage your credibility.

By appealing to public mistrust of journalists and journalism and to commonly shared beliefs about good journalism, instilled because of the association of journalists with the genocide, officials who are unhappy with stories can undermine journalists' credibility with public criticism of reporting that they feel does not portray a news item appropriately. In the case of the *KT Press* story, officials appealed to a journalistic standard that news should consist of a full picture of the facts as much as possible, outlined in the Rwandan media code of ethics. According to that document, journalists shall in no way "suppress essential information or distort any kind of remarks, texts and documents" (Rwandan Media Fraternity 2011, 5).

Attempts to investigate mid-level managers or others with moderate social power would be scrutinized closely, and if journalists failed to follow ethical codes or other professional standards, they would face repercussions. Andre at the *New Times* recounted one such encounter where a reporter had allegedly tried to blackmail a powerful source, alleging that the source, a hotel owner, had sexually harassed his staff.

> The hotel owner called the managing editor at the time and said, "There's a man here who came and said you guys have a story on me about me harassing my female waitresses, but it is absolutely, like really, really, not true. It is outrageous, and I have not even been given a chance to hear those facts that the journalist has." The managing editor told the other person, "You know what, you play along, show him that you bought into his blackmail, and then we're going to come—the police—and arrest him." And that's what happened.

In other words, a reporter attempted to bribe an important figure—a hotel owner—to pay him to keep quiet about a story of this hotel owner's alleged sexual misconduct. The hotel owner took the story to the reporter's superiors, who then worked with the hotel owner to have the reporter arrested for attempting the bribe. On one hand, seen through the eyes of a mid-level editor, this story reinforces the ethical standards to which journalists in Rwanda are held. On the other hand, it highlights the stories that are likely to get editorial scrutiny: investigations of people with some level of power. It also highlights the fact that news organizations and editors are likely to refer cases of unethical behavior or misconduct to government officials rather than handling them within the organization or field. Journalists working for transnational organizations, who routinely produce critical reports, said they were always careful to hold their work to high professional standards, including fact-checking and citing sources, because any critical story would be scrutinized and a breach in professional standards would create space for criticism.

In general, the strategies employed by editors and advertisers aim to prevent the publication of certain stories. When critical stories slipped through to the printed or web page, the strategies shifted and repercussions became clear. Organizations would ask *KT Press* editors to remove stories from the internet; occasionally, editors would comply—particularly if the request involved an appeal to national security. More often, they would update part of the story to reflect requested changes. Alternatively, editors might assign a story with a positive angle to balance the negative coverage and satisfy the frustrated advertiser. Where those strategies were ineffective, editors and reporters could be fired or removed from rotations (as Jacques recounted in chapter 4). Other reporters also told stories of editors who had been called into management offices and fired for letting particularly critical stories get to publication. In general, stakes were higher once articles had been published; because of this, editors use several strategies to prevent problematic stories from reaching publication.

Communicating a Contradiction

The rules around which angles and stories should be pursued are usually not communicated directly to reporters (with the exception of a few specific rules, such as the one about presidential coverage editors communicated in the newsroom meeting). Indeed, reporters often noticed that their colleagues would discuss investigative ideas in staff meetings and editors would encourage the projects, but the stories would never appear in print or online. In newsrooms, editors and policies encourage investigation, but little content that is critical or investigative shows up in publication. Published editorial policies, even at news outlets known to produce primarily government-aligned news such as the *New Times* and *KT Press*, condemn self-censorship and call for independent reporting. In fact, "No one will ever tell you" that self-censorship is expected, Caleb explained. "There is an editorial policy that looks clean." Even a newspaper aiming to be truly independent of government control might borrow the editorial policy of the *New Times*, because it looks "OK." "They look like they are following journalistic standards. But that's all on paper." The major newsrooms in Rwanda—*Kigali Today*, the *New Times*, and others—are, officially, independent news organizations, with editorial lines—that is, mission statements—supporting those goals. Emmanuel pointed out that the official mission of the *New Times* was to "inform, educate, and entertain... like any other newspaper." At what point, then, does the message change from one supporting independent, enterprise reporting, to one that narrows the limits of reporting? How are the acceptable limits of information, education, and entertainment communicated to newsroom staff?

For the most part, reporters do not encounter the same direct requests to remove content or face loss of advertisements as their superiors. Instead, organizational expectations around appropriate news content were communicated through editing interactions and enforced through routines around time constraints and pay. Reporters learn appropriate behavior through a process that incorporates elements of mimetic and normative isomorphism. They face financial uncertainty because most lack contracts and those contracts that do exist stipulate story quotas, or minimums, that must be met for a paycheck to be issued. In addition, reporters face pressure to produce news content that meets fast-paced deadlines maintained by the organization. Both of these routines encourage certain styles of news production and discourage others.

Reporters who do not meet their story quotas or who fail to produce content regularly for the publication are seen as non-productive and are either reprimanded, suspended, or demoted. To avoid these repercussions, reporters observe their peers and learn from their own mistakes to develop routines of rapid story production, often covering same-day events to meet deadlines for the next production cycle and neglecting enterprise or innovative angles because those types of stories tend to take more time to produce and have more uncertain outcomes, often never making it to publication. Thus, reporters model mimetic isomorphism in responds to the financial uncertainty of not having guaranteed paychecks by adopting behaviors that they can see lead to financially stable and predictable results, rather than taking chances on behavior that they are ideologically inclined to practice but would lead to financial uncertainty. They are also motivated by the normative pressure to meet professional standards of deadlines and quotas.

The expectation that a reporter will self-censor to produce stories that are not negative or critical of the government tends to be communicated on a case-by-case basis, rather than directly as editorial policy. "Of course, they cannot use those words, 'These are the stories we *don't* publish'—we publish everything," Samuel said. "But I know some stories—reporters have written a story, and then the story goes on the website, and then within the next hour, it's not there." If a clearly controversial or contentious topic was pitched, an editor might tell a reporter directly to drop a story right when he or she pitched it, Caleb said. In other cases, and in most cases reporters recounted to me, the message is communicated more obliquely. Caleb explained:

> First of all, if a journalist pitched a story, a very strong story about some weird corruption going on in government, they will tell him, "Drop it." Or they will somehow find a way to disincentivize it and discourage him against doing it. And then they will pressure him: "Don't do this," something like that. Journalists find themselves having to stick to the normal stories.

This reporter recounted the way he learned at the *New Times* that critical news stories would not run. The typical process, he said, would be something like this: a reporter would find a lead and begin investigating a story, conduct several interviews with sources who corroborated the wrongdoing, and then write the story. "Somehow the story doesn't run," Caleb said.

> Then they give you a reason—"This might cause a few problems," maybe, "It's not factual," maybe, "You didn't do this," maybe, "Do this—get more voices"—and you're frustrated. You don't follow it up again. Because you know eventually they won't run the story. It happens once, twice, thrice—you know that means they won't run the story. So you stick to stories that are hopeful and optimistic.

This reporter found that the expectation of self-censorship was not communicated directly and was only invoked obliquely after he had produced a story and submitted it to his editor for review.

Samuel recounted how he learned the expectations of his news organization. When he was a new reporter, he wrote a finance story where he investigated a building project that was supposedly underway with massive amounts of funding but had never broken ground. He interviewed several officials and wrote a story that his editor said would run on the front page. But the story never ran. "I spent my time on that. And I was thinking this is a very, very good story," he said. "Everyone would be calling me asking, 'Hey, how did you get these guys, how did you get the contacts?'" He was proud of the story and knew it was good journalism, but then his editor cut the story from the front page and substituted a different story that this reporter had not written but using his byline. When he asked the editor why his story was cut, the editor had a vague response about "some issues," this reporter said. He didn't push the matter further but surmised that "some issues" meant an official had requested that the story not run.

Jacques, who had worked as an investigative reporter at the *New Times* before he shifted to working as a stringer for a wire agency, explained how the self-censorship rule was communicated to the investigative team. "Of course, you go through many sources. You call people to react. But before you publish a story, then you get a call," he said.

> They would call, like, my boss, the primary boss. Because they know as a reporter you don't have power. They call somebody, then somebody comes

and they say, "I have heard you are following A, B, C, D. We think that story might cause us problems." So, kind of negotiating with you, but indirectly.

These anecdotes illustrate the process by which reporters learn the expectations around self-censorship. It is communicated through norms around what makes something a quality story, thus subjecting the reporters to cultural pressure and aligning the expectation of self-censorship with expectations of appropriate organizational behavior. After a few experiences like those outlined above, reporters pointed out, they learn to not fight for things that will not happen anyway. As Jean explained, "We want to dare, but we don't know if daring is good. We want to try something different, but we are not encouraged to try something different. Even when you try, they will encourage you, and then all the sudden they will trash your story."

Quotas, Deadlines, and Beats

Several newsroom routines reinforce these practices into a financial logic. One major factor influencing this decision to go with the flow is that reporters are paid on a quota system, where they must produce a certain number of published stories every month to get a paycheck. No matter how much a journalist might want to serve the public, he or she can only do so if employed and financially stable—which means that many journalists, even though they have been trained in journalism school to ask "tough questions" and investigate official narratives, in the end resort to covering events and other non-confrontational stories. Samuel explained,

> A media house will tell you, "We want 45 stories per month, or 37." And that is how you will get paid. So you want to like the public the way you like yourself, but you have to like yourself first and then you like the others. Every month you have to pay your bills, your rent, your food, your everything—so you will do what the editors want. You go to the events, you cover the events, you come back.

Even at the best-known and wealthy news outlets, very few journalists below the level of senior editors have contracts guaranteeing employment, and reporters are often paid on story quota systems that penalize them for failing to produce some quantity of stories in a given month.

Across local news organizations, story quotas were enforced regularly, and editors typically did not consider story length or complexity in accounting for each reporter's productivity. Jean explained:

> We have to produce on a daily basis. . . . If I'm following up on a story for four days—maybe it's an investigative piece or a feature piece—that means I will be rendered unproductive in the company. It doesn't matter if I bring a 2,000-word story that is well researched—they will still say you are not productive.

Story quota expectations could and would be enforced by pay cuts, and newsroom staff knew this. One editor at the *New Times* recounted that he was demoted and his pay cut for an entire year when he failed to meet a quota soon after he was hired. At the time, general assignment reporters at the *New Times* made around 120,000 Rwandan francs per month (around US$150). His story count had "really, really nosedived," he said, but no one had discussed the reasons with him before docking his pay. After a year with lower pay, he was reinstated at his previous level of pay. "Someone felt, I think, that I had been unfairly treated," he said.

Norms around productivity were also communicated in editorial meetings, like one I observed at the *New Times*. As was typical in morning meetings, an editor was calling on reporters around the room to share story ideas and generate a list of the content that would go into tomorrow's newspaper. A reporter was curious why a particular policy was not being implemented well, and in the morning meeting, she pitched the idea as a story she wanted to pursue for publication in tomorrow's newspaper or a few days from now. She explained that a county official had followed the wrong procedures to perform an audit and had escalated the audit, perhaps unnecessarily, to take a case to court. She wanted to explore the proper procedures and see if the auditor had done anything wrong. The editor did not reject this idea but did suggest a caution, saying that perhaps the government was taking measures to improve matters, and that the reporter should "approach it with an open mind." He said there were many parties involved with this story and listed several names of people who would need to be interviewed, including the Rwandan attorney general. Before he moved to the next reporter, he added a cautioning reminder: this reporter could cover the investigative story she had pitched, but not at the expense of her regular coverage—she would still need to cover the next day's parliamentary session, but could pursue this story on the side.

This scene captures several elements of the process by which editors and other senior staff at the *New Times* discourage investigative, "creative," and non-routine news coverage by relying on standard routines, rather than explicitly forbidding it. This reporter—one of the most senior at the *New Times*—pitched an idea that could yield interesting results but would involve investigation and had an uncertain outcome: there might be some corruption or some mismanagement involved in how a particular type of audit was being performed. She explained how she would pursue this story to find out if anything indeed went wrong. The editor cautioned that the story was a big one, hinting that many sources, including some high-up government officials, would be required to make it publishable. He further suggested that the critical angle be toned down, at least at first, by acknowledging the probable complexity of the problem. He concluded by allowing pursuit of this story, but not at the expense of regular productivity. This message explicitly allowed the story while implicitly discouraging it by including several constraints on the story itself and no concessions to the demands of investigative reporting.

The deadline-based nature of journalism featured prominently in newsroom routines and often served to prevent or discourage reporters from pursuing a longer story, more nuance, or additional quotations. Instead, reporters at the *KT Press* and the *New Times* often turned in shorter stories with overt angles and quotations from few sources in order to meet short deadlines. Editors consistently included in their meetings messages about the importance of meeting deadlines and producing a certain number of stories per week, and also reminded individual reporters of deadlines throughout the day. For the most part, reporters seemed to follow a routine of producing one or more stories per day, with the majority beginning a story in the morning to finish it by afternoon for publication on the web or in the next day's newspaper. The occasional story or set of stories took longer than a day to produce, but none took longer than a week. Deadlines at the *East African* were equally important, but often incorporated a longer cycle from idea generation to story completion, given the publication's weekly print production schedule.

Editors also routinely emphasized the importance of deadlines in editorial meetings. Once the managing director at the *New Times* wrapped up the meeting with just a one-word reminder—"deadlines." The other editors concurred, adding, "Yes, deadlines." The context implied a reminder: "Please remember your deadlines, and keep them." The editors fleshed out their concern over deadlines in an editors' meeting after that newsroom meeting, with news editors expressing frustration that reporters turned in news late in the day, in turn keeping them at their desks until late at night to produce the newspaper. The concerns expressed align with standard norms of timeliness, but the proposed solution (more prepackaged features and fewer news events) further discourages creativity and enterprise reporting:

> There is no reason why news should keep us here until midnight, says the managing editor. Let's finish it by 6:00 p.m. Do more features if you have to and cover fewer news events. It is not sustainable or healthy to stay past 9:00 p.m. every day. You can't think of new story ideas, and it is dangerous because you miss things that you wouldn't miss if you were well rested. What happens now is that reporters come in and check social media, then eat lunch, and file their first stories at 3:00 p.m. We need to be tougher and make them get stories in earlier, he says. (Field notes, February 2017)

At *KT Press*, editors similarly emphasized frequent deadlines and fast-paced reporting, oriented around web production deadlines. On one occasion an editor called around the room for status updates on stories, noting that he needed to publish 10 stories today and was waiting on a story from one woman in particular. When another reporter entered the room, coming from an assignment, the editor informed him, "You are late. You have 30 minutes" (field notes, March 2017). Demanding daily stories by deadline was a common part of the routine at both *KT Press* and the *New Times* and led to reliance on events and other coverage that reporters knew would result in publishable stories.

News events, such as press conferences, tended to be lengthy and formal, structured and scheduled in a way that discouraged enterprise reporting or non-official angles. In February 2017, I accompanied a reporter at the *New Times* to a ribbon-cutting event for 35 new cross-country buses that would replace decades-old buses in driving routes connecting Kigali with communities in the periphery of Rwanda. The event was scheduled to start at 2:30 p.m. and wrap up after a few hours, but the transportation minister—the guest of honor—spoke 20 minutes longer than he was supposed to, pushing back any opportunity for unstructured interview questions to later in the afternoon. By the time journalists lined up to ask questions, it was after

4:30 p.m.; the reporter had missed a 3:00 p.m. deadline for the next day's paper and said he would aim for the 7:00 p.m. late deadline instead. We—the reporter, the *New Times* photographer, and I—waited 10 minutes or so for an opportunity to interview the press secretary directly. The reporter exchanged a few words with someone else in line, then told me he did not think it would be worthwhile to wait because he probably wouldn't learn anything he had not already heard in the speeches. At around 5:00 p.m. we left. The reporter said he would write up the story quickly when he returned to the newsroom and file it by 7:00 p.m. for the late deadline. I attended many other press conferences with journalists, and they followed a similar pattern. The events tended to start late, run longer than scheduled, and incorporate a number of official speakers and presentations with little time allocated to unstructured questions and answers or private interviews. At many, the norm was for each reporter to ask at most one question.

Deadlines are a deeply embedded routine of news production, and timeliness is a standard deeply valued by reporters across space and time (Waisbord 2013). However, this value can also curtail the production of news that accomplishes other core goals that professionalization in Rwanda demands. In the situation outlined above and in many others I observed, the pressure of meeting a deadline to produce timely news demanded that the reporter table any inclination to pursue a more in-depth narrative around the new buses. Talking with me on the way to the event, the reporter shared how the new buses would be important to poorer women in rural Rwanda because they might now be able to transport more goods to Kigali and other big cities to sell on a regular basis, thus increasing their family incomes. The reporter could have expanded the story to touch on this angle, talking with women about how helpful the bus might be (or not), asking the officials how much more cargo could be stored, asking if fares on the new buses would be more expensive, and so on. None of this made it into the final article, which was a short narrative focused on the ribbon-cutting event, featuring official voices. In this case, a long, afternoon event coupled with a short deadline curtailed the time for creativity and seeking alternate angles. The reporter had a deadline to meet and, because the event took longer than scheduled, he ran out of time to pursue any deeper angles, instead returning to the newsroom with two hours' worth of official, public narrative to write about for the next day's paper.

Journalists in Rwanda generally learn the financial logic obliquely, through comments tied to story quality. Those expectations are then reinforced with newsroom routines around timeliness and deadlines alongside the quota-based paycheck system, which combine to send the message that journalists should not rock the boat, encouraging routine behavior and events coverage rather than creative and edgy reporting. The logic is strongest in organizations that are more financially dependent on local advertising for financial sustainability. As Caleb explained, being a journalist in Rwanda is "a bit tricky—there are so many land mines you don't want to step on, you know? You have to know what you're doing" (personal communication, June 8, 2017). These findings highlight the ways behavior journalists consider to contradict "good journalism" can be institutionalized and enforced through commonplace newsroom routines. "We used to get arrested, right?" Caleb said. "There was a period in which at least every month you would hear of a journalist in Rwanda being arrested. But now, they only threaten you or find a way to cut you off your job or taint your name."

Solidifying Orthodox News Values

The result of the financial logic described here is a sliding scale of news values that treats possible news targets differently depending on their level of economic power. Organizations and people with high levels of advertising power, from the president's office and other government ministries to major telecommunications companies, are covered in ways that emphasize news values of standardization and event-based narrative; they tend to report strictly what happened in documentary fashion and avoid analysis or reportorial emphasis. On the other hand, stories involving organizations and people with low levels of power, including average citizens, street vendors, and health professionals, are discussed and covered in ways that emphasize values of creativity, deviance, and novelty.

Journalists pursue news values of standardization and event-based narrative, avoiding controversy and investigation, in their coverage of powerful figures. Editors encourage these values. Gilbert emphasized this approach in a conversation about the biggest challenges facing journalists in Rwanda, saying that journalists tend to only investigate "low- and mid-level" officials.

> The people who are in power, the president, the army, the minister of finance, the ruling party secretariat, and the big corporations—those are the actual people who exercise power in this country—they are not scrutinized.

Journalists only report on what the government has said. "The minister of finance has said they will spend this much on the road." No one says, "This money is from where? Why this amount? Last year you said it's this; we don't see this. Why has public debt reached 40 percent of GDP?" That scrutiny of people who actually hold power is absent.

These news values were occasionally explicitly described in newsrooms, especially when reporters and editors discussed coverage of the president. One instance is recounted in the field notes that open this chapter, where a *KT Press* reporter who tried to break the norm and report a creative angle on Paul Kagame's recent speech was reprimanded by his editor, who said that there was a "standing order" to cover everything the president says at an event. "The rule is, we always cover everything . . . find the recording, and cover everything," he said. Jean, who was assigned to cover the presidential family for the *New Times*, said editors at that newspaper enforced a similar news value.

The editors want you to say—if the president went here, just say, "He went here," full stop. Write what he did, what he said, and that's it—instead of focusing on his message and what he is trying to explain."

The news value here is communicated clearly: focus on chronological facts, not on analysis or creative angles that would impose a reporter's news judgment over the event.

Below the most powerful officials in the country, the values of standardization and event-based narrative would usually be communicated in routine and practice, rather than direct instruction, as outlined above. However, the result would be the same. Caleb explained: "When you get to the real practice, whether you are at RBA [the biggest radio station in the country] or Igihe [a well-known outlet that produces written news in Kinyarwanda] . . . as long as a piece is critical and it is going to cause some chaos, it won't run." This reporter listed the two factors that together determine whether a topic would be treated with the standardization and event-based news values or with the values of creativity, deviance, and novelty: criticism and chaos. Critical pieces would be encouraged with low-power sources because they are unlikely to cause chaos; with high-power sources, who do have the ability to cause financial chaos, criticism is unwelcome.

In contrast, news values of creativity and enterprise were encouraged and evident in news coverage of topics involving lower levels of power—the "mid-level" officials and organizations mentioned by the Rwandan Journalists' Association's director. When stories with angles critical of the government were approved for publication, reporters often found that the government had approved the investigation because the critiques were aimed at a program, person, or problem officials wished to change already. "If you are going to write something about the challenges facing some center, you will get it out, as long as it is something that is just shallow, it is not so deep and involving government," Caleb explained. Investigation is encouraged, but only within carefully patrolled boundaries that do not question upper levels of political power. Jacques explained the same thing:

> When I was heading the investigations desk, it was not an investigations desk like in the US sense. It was, like, maybe people come and give you stories—especially government people would come and give you stories. But later on when you try to investigate, you find out that they have given you a story about somebody who has already fallen out.

Conclusion: Business Pressure at Work

Organizational routines influence journalists' behavior and affect the application of news values to potential stories. Reporters and editors at news organizations are guided by financial logics that, for editors, encourage mimetic isomorphism as an appropriate adaptation to an uncertain financial environment and, for reporters, photographers, and other employees, encourage mimetic and normative isomorphism through professional routines imposing the financial logic as a filter over news values.

In many ways, journalists in Rwanda are motivated by pressures similar to those shaping the news industry in the United States and elsewhere around the globe. As news organizations became profit-driven in the United States, they became increasingly susceptible to what Michael Schudson calls "market-driven censorship" (2011, 112). While the profit motivation is often countered in the United States by individual journalists' news judgment and overcome by professional values, in the case of Rwanda, this financial logic is often a driving factor in news production.

Common journalism routines can create an environment where journalists have substantial incentive to produce news that does not align with normative values instilled by leaders of professionalism within the field. Reporters themselves—the people in a news organization who do most of the work to produce content every day—are, for the most part, not directly coerced or pressured by unethical demands from advertisers or editors. This happens occasionally, but relatively rarely. Instead, they are encouraged by innocuous organizational routines to pursue news stories that perpetuate a trusting, non-critical narrative of public events by powerful figures, rather than news stories that are investigative and skeptical, as demanded by professional norms. In fact, these routines are not just innocuous; they are considered integral to journalism practice around the world. Timeliness is a component of newsworthiness around the world (Shoemaker and Cohen 2006). Journalists value rapid story production (Picard 1998). And in all journalism fields, creativity is somewhat at odds with rapid, prolific content production. But the Rwandan case illustrates the extent to which these standard norms can discourage an important type of news production, especially in a journalism field where journalists mistrust themselves and are distrusted by others, making it easy to accept the status quo and not critique official narratives. Considering Rwandan journalists' weak social position, the financial logic gains traction and, in combination with logic of individual responsibility, leads journalists to play it safe most of the time.

I have also illustrated how professional routines can enforce an institutional logic that counters the professional logic and undermines organizational control (Oliver 1991). Because editors and reporters must navigate between professionally enforced norms on one hand and organizationally necessary norms on the other hand, both groups spend a great deal of time translating messages from one language to another. Editors must translate messages of coercion from advertisers to messages of preference and suggestion for their subordinates. Reporters must in turn translate those messages of preference to correspond with organizational routines and financial incentives, resulting in the production of news content that often serves a financial logic rather than a professional logic.

6
Bridging Worlds
Working Global While Living Local

Toward the end of June—near the close of Kwibuka and the beginning of election campaign season—I joined the *East African*'s newsroom, a three-minute walk down the road from the *New Times*, on the sixth floor of an office complex whose first level was occupied by Simba, a Kenyan grocery chain with outlets across Kigali. We met for the Monday editorial meeting in a glass-walled conference room facing the newsroom and next to the editor's office—also glass-walled and easily accessible, in contrast to the many flights of stairs and closed doors I had to navigate to the find the head editors at the *New Times* or *KT Press*. In the newsroom itself, two rows of desks held computers, laptops, and other electronic equipment for reporter workspaces; about eight reporters, some freelance and some on staff, worked regularly from the office, along with a freelance photographer.

The *East African*—a weekly regional paper printed in Nairobi—had a small but vibrant newsroom. About a dozen staff worked in an office suite above Simba. The *East African*'s office was close enough to the *New Times* that reporters would often run into each other eating lunch or shopping at Simba or would catch rides with each other to field events. Despite the social and geographic proximity to the *New Times*, though, several factors from this editorial meeting suggested it belongs to a different journalism field altogether.

This meeting began like others I had attended at *KT Press* and the *New Times*. The editor introduced me and my research then moved on to the regular agenda, calling on reporters around the room to share their story ideas. Someone explained to me that each reporter was expected to come to the meeting with three ideas to pursue for the week (though not everyone did). Reporters shared a few story ideas, including one about a pan-African grant that a Rwandan had just received, and then discussion turned to the upcoming election, scheduled for August 4. The three-week campaign period was set to begin, and the editor wanted story ideas.

One reporter mentioned Diane Rwigara, a woman attempting to garner the 600 signatures required by the Rwandan Election Commission to enter the campaign for the presidency. She had a press conference planned for that day because the REC had invalidated some of the signatures on the forms she submitted, making her ineligible to enter the race. Someone else chimed in to say that the manifests containing the signatures might exist, and the reporter should try to find copies. The editor responded, "OK, capture contrasting views. We need to start aggressive campaign coverage next week." He then brought up another candidate, Frank Habineza. Habineza, he said, was an adversary in exile and was then "rehabilitated" by the government. Two reporters interjected here, and one mentioned an online poll that favored Kagame over Habineza. The editor was unfazed. He said the majority of people on Twitter are pro-RPF, and public opposition voices run into trouble, sharing how in November, a woman who tweeted something critical of Kagame was mobbed. The Twitter poll, then, did not represent true public opinion. He added guidance for the story, saying, "We need to bring out the details of how the landscape has changed. Did we have a woman before? Get information ready to go for candidate profiles."

Moving on from election coverage, another reporter pitched an idea about fire management. The government wanted to control building material for fire resistance, but there was no way to check fire ratings in Rwanda since there were no labs in the country equipped to appropriately test materials. The editor asked how he knew and listed some questions to ask in the story. He told the reporter to look into the *East African*'s archives to find past coverage of fires as a starting point for this new story. This reporter shared another pitch about "problems with tourism." The tourism board had recently begun targeting luxury tourists, more than doubling prices to visit the mountain gorillas from US$700 to US$1500 and eliminating the local discount, which had previously steeply reduced the price to less than US$100 for Rwandan citizens. A source had come to this reporter listing the problems with this approach. The editor said, "Good, something about this is a story the *New Times* won't publish." In response to this, the reporter suggested that he get a response from the Rwandan Development Board and another person "to soften it." The editor responded, "No, we don't need to soften it. A story is a story. He went to the *New Times* and the *New Times* as usual skirted the issue. That's why he came here. We should run it."

While this editorial meeting had a structure similar to the others I observed, it felt different on a few levels. These reporters brought more ideas to the meeting than most did at the *New Times* or *KT Press*; not everyone had three ideas to share, but everyone had at least one. The focus on opposition candidates campaigning for president was also unusual in that it signaled an interest in finding controversy and presenting alternate viewpoints. Editors and reporters at *KT Press* and the *New Times* had previously dismissed the presidential race with comments about how Kagame would, of course, win. This was apparent to all observers of the election, but the *East African* appeared to take the opposition candidates more seriously. This openness to exploring unpopular candidates rather than focusing on the incumbent and shoo-in candidate Paul Kagame revealed a comfort level with investigating authority that was not apparent at the other news outlets. The instruction to the reporter writing about fire codes to read past coverage of the topic was also unusual. I heard very few references to past coverage at the other two news outlets; editors frequently chided reporters at *New Times* editorial meetings for not even reading yesterday's newspaper before coming to the meeting. The final admonition to the reporter with the tourism story drove home the *East African*'s interest in finding angles of critique, with the editor's explicit command to not "soften" the story or skirt the issue, but publish it. Finally, the editor's oppositional position relative to the *New Times* was another cue that the *East African* belongs in a global field: the stance directly contradicts the doxic value of togetherness emphasized in the local field.

The *East African* is one of a handful of transnational news organizations in the Rwandan journalism field. As this editorial meeting illustrates, journalists at these organizations have the permission and, in some cases, the mandate to play by different news production rules than their counterparts working for local organizations. In this chapter, I argue that the differences are best explained by the unique field position these organizations and, thus, their employees hold as bridging agents between local and global journalism fields. In Rwanda, the local and global journalism fields intertwine most clearly in the spaces represented by transnational news organizations. As a result, reporters working in these spaces have unique opportunities and challenges. While they cannot escape local journalism norms entirely (nor do many wish to), they also face the pressure and responsibility of producing work that meets the expectations of a global journalism field, which are in many ways quite different from those of the local scene.

Finding the Global Field

Transnational news organizations in Rwanda and elsewhere provide a unique opportunity for their employees to bridge national and global journalism fields. These organizations are situated in local spaces, and employees must maintain relationships with local sources, journalists, and authorities, yet they produce and distribute news products for audiences spanning national borders (Moon 2019). Historically, these organizations represented primarily outposts of their own local fields situated in parallel but not overlapping with local journalism practice in the host countries. They were overwhelmingly representative of the Global North, with news produced by Western European and North American journalists for news outlets in their home countries, to be consumed primarily by audiences in those countries (Silberstein-Loeb 2014). However, economic demands, global power shifts, and other factors are increasingly de-nationalizing and, to some extent, de-Westernizing this form of news production. News is produced for audiences who are presumed to cross national borders. Organizations such as Al Jazeera and the humanitarian-focused news outlet IRIN intentionally seek out non-Western angles and news stories, and employees of even traditionally Western-focused news wire services are increasingly hired from the local community (Mitra and Paterson 2019; Scott et al. 2017). As a result, transnational news organizations and the staff working in them increasingly straddle two fields and face the challenge of playing the journalism game in the global field while also remaining qualified and accepted in the local field.

Situating transnational organizations in a global rather than national journalism field means that, though they have some motivations and definitions in common with nationally bounded journalism practice, these are not inherent and should not be taken for granted; in fact, members may face entirely different sets of rules in the global version of the field versus the same occupational field at the national or local level (Buchholz 2016). Research suggests that this is the case for transnational news organizations, whose rules and expectations—while strongly influenced by Western imperialism—nevertheless vary somewhat from news production in both their local contexts and their home countries. In fact, transnational organizations have merged more and more into a global field over the past century.

Transnational organizations initially produced news content explicitly for and by Western voices, filling positions more resembling foreign outposts of particular countries' journalism fields than truly cosmopolitan or global field members. Wire services, such as Reuters, Agence France-Presse, and the Associated Press, are prime examples of this kind of transnational journalism, as they came into existence primarily to create news content that could be publishable by local news organizations across broad geographic distances (but still primarily targeting audiences in the Global North). To accomplish this goal, these organizations tended to require news content produced to meet Western standards of reporting and writing that emphasized values of neutrality, impartiality, and objectivity and relied on demonstrably correct factual information (Fenby 1986). These organizations' business models reinforce the need for reporting that meets Western journalism standards; wire services in particular, including the Associated Press, Reuters, Agence France-Presse, and others, are built on a business model that provides global news coverage to subscribers, primarily other journalists and news outlets, on the assumption that those subscribers are often unable to report directly from countries and regions that are nonetheless of interest to readers in the United States, United Kingdom, and other parts of the world (Fenby 1986; Putnis 2004). Meeting these standards ensures that subscribers as diverse as partisan presses in Great Britain, relatively young democratic or development-oriented news outlets in Kenya, and small-town daily newspapers in the United States can use provided material alongside their own reporting for local readers. While the standard style ensures accessibility across countries, transnational news organizations based in the West, such as the BBC and CNN, tend to select news topics and produce content for Global North audiences (Atad 2017). Of course, there are a few notable Global South exceptions, such as Al Jazeera and Inter Press Service (Giffard 1984).

Historically, much of the international content for transnational outlets was produced in bureaus staffed with international correspondents (Fenby 1986; Silberstein-Loeb 2014). Throughout its early history, Reuters relied on "correspondents" from trading companies along with the occasional local journalist for most of its international coverage (Silberstein-Loeb 2014). In the early twentieth century, the position of foreign correspondent gained more prestige, and the organization shifted to relying primarily on trained British journalists stationed in countries around the world for its international wire content (Silberstein-Loeb 2014). Transnational news production today looks quite a bit different. The "man in gray flannels" who reported on foreign affairs for his counterparts back home has largely disappeared, due in part to budget constraints that have reduced foreign news holes and also to changes in information availability making locally produced content about foreign affairs more accessible and economical (Hamilton and Jenner 2004, 301; Hamilton 2010). Instead, news for transnational organizations is now produced by people from a broad range of backgrounds and positions, including parachute journalists who drop in to cover particular events rather than staying in-country; amateur or citizen journalists; and the focus of this chapter, foreign nationals who produce news about their home country for outlets outside of it (Hamilton and Jenner 2004). By the 1980s, news agency journalists were primarily recruited from local talent, though they were usually overseen by bureau chiefs who were nationals of the agency's home country (Boyd-Barrett 1980; Bunce 2010). The staffing hierarchy perpetuates the dominance of Western values and lenses in news coverage (Bunce 2010).

As a result, local nationals who work for transnational news organizations occupy an unusual position where they must understand and respond to the rules, boundaries, and expectations of multiple fields of practice (Hellmueller 2017). This makes them both precarious and invaluable, as new scholarship makes increasingly apparent (Arjomand 2022). On one hand, they are embedded in and part of the local environment in a way that traditional foreign correspondents, parachute journalists, and other content creators are not. On the other hand, they must produce news content in a way that satisfies the predominantly Western and, in any case, non-local norms of their employers in the global field—something their local counterparts need not do. In some ways, these news workers occupy particularly precarious positions because of their bridging status; they tend to be under appreciated and under-supported in the global field while taking riskier positions in the local field than their fully local counterparts (Mitra et al. 2022; Palmer 2019).

In Rwanda, the unique position of transnational organizations poses both a benefit and an inhibition to the local journalism field. On one hand, it allows members to occupy a position they could not otherwise hold—one of opposition and critique of the status quo. On the other hand, these organizations' membership in the global field means that their employees' position in the local field is inherently peripheral. While journalists working for transnational organizations repeatedly emphasized how empowered they felt at being able to critique power and expand the borders of their autonomy, they are, I suggest, unlikely to transform the local journalism field. Rather than contributing to change in the local field's doxa, journalists working for transnational organizations are accruing capital in the global field. As a result, their work might be personally fulfilling, but their power is limited, as they occupy peripheral roles in both global and local fields. For individual journalists, this trade-off can be worth it to attain vertical capital with the potential of transferring fully into the global field. However, for the local field, it ensures that opposition journalism is inherently "other," which has ramifications for the long-term potential of the field to change from within.

Gaining and Losing: Capital Crossing Borders

Local reporters working for transnational organizations gain and lose capital by virtue of their field position. They gain capital in the form of vocational legitimacy—these reporters were the most likely to say they felt they were doing "real" journalism and making a difference—and this capital is closely linked to cultural capital within the global journalism field, making it possible though not necessarily likely that a journalist could transfer from the Rwandan field to another geographic location in the global field. On the other hand, they lose social capital in the local field, reporting that it is more challenging to find sources, they are more closely surveilled, and they face accusations of disloyalty because of their field-straddling positions.

Conferring Vocational Legitimacy

Reporters working for transnational organizations shared a high level of vocational legitimacy (one of the forms of vertical capital I introduced in chapter 2). This form of capital has some unusual characteristics but is nevertheless a powerful motivator for journalists in this field position. In short, this form of capital is best described as a personal feeling of validation and fulfillment based on one's ability to produce news that meets standards of "news" as defined by the global field and by local journalism education (both heavily influenced by Western models, as I have discussed throughout the book). This form of capital is more personal than tradable, but it is still conferred in relationship, based on field position relative to other players, and motivates journalists to behave in certain ways.

The ability to produce the news content that accrues vocational legitimacy is both ensured and mandated by transnational employers, in contrast to organizations in the local field. One Rwandan wire reporter, who often reports news that aims a critical lens at powerful government figures, including the president, members of Paul Kagame's cabinet, military leaders, and others, explained the reasons he could consistently report this type of coverage.

> I don't think the government would want to arrest somebody who is working for [wire service], because this country, much as they try to harass people, they want their image to be very, very positive, every time. Arresting somebody working for AFP or Reuters, they think maybe it will cause problems. And of course, by the time a story passes and it goes on the wire, it has been edited properly and describes exactly what is on the ground. There is no way you can file a story for [wire service] when it is half-baked, when you don't have enough information.

This explanation incorporates the range of factors that enable journalists in Rwanda to consistently report news that deviates from the status quo of positive journalism. The first factor the journalist mentions relates to the relative power that wire service and other multinational news organizations hold in Rwanda. Wire organizations are funded primarily by subscriptions rather than by advertising, and they likely place higher value on appearing independent on a global stage than on appeasing capricious advertisers in Rwanda. In addition, the lack of dependence on advertising means they are financially independent from Rwandan power sources. The *East African* is primarily advertising funded, but advertisements come from across the East African region, and editorial decisions made in Rwanda must be justified as "good" journalistic decisions to head editors based in Nairobi, Kenya, where the strength of Rwandan advertising income is diluted by advertising funds from Tanzania, Uganda, and Kenya. Thus, for a variety of reasons, this group of organizations is willing to publicize retaliation against their employees, threatening to write or actually writing stories when a reporter is harassed or arrested for a particular story he or she has written. The second factor has to do with the *legitimacy* of the story itself—norms of the news organization ensure that articles undergo a rigorous editing process so that when a story is published, it contains a narrative built on verifiable facts and quotations, rather than personal opinion and rumor. But legitimacy in printed content is only one element of the legitimacy needed to ensure that a reporter can safely produce critical journalism. He or she must also use legitimate practices to obtain the information. As this reporter went on to point out, the only thing that would really place him in danger would be unethical behavior, because it would lead the news organization to cut ties with him. If he were to take money from a source—or even appear to do so—it would be simple for a government official to accuse him of being "unprofessional," and the wire service would be unlikely to support the reporter in that case.

This narrative provides important insights into the nature of the production of counternarratives in Rwanda and other journalism fields. My findings suggest that, while individual and organizational attributes are both necessary, a combination of the two is key in the continued production of news content that departs from social and political expectations. This narrative and others like it suggest that there are institutional and field factors that enable the pursuit and production of oppositional news in a journalism field like that in Rwanda, where organizations encourage the practice of self-censorship and social pressure encourages the practice of positive and nonconfrontational journalism. To further explain how this happens, I proceed by explaining the concept of legitimacy and its application to journalism, the factors that allow organizations to oppose institutional regulations, and the process by which these are both implemented in Rwanda.

Wire service reporters shared a similarly independent editorial line with the *East African* but had more independent work environments. None of the wire services whose staff I interviewed had bureaus in Kigali, so the reporters affiliated with the services had freedom to choose where they would work and, to some extent, freedom to structure their daily routines. Some wire reporters worked from home, where they would listen to and read the news for the day and do much reporting from home offices. Others worked from a state-owned work space that served both as the office for the Association Rwandaise des Journalistes—a union-like organization that represented Rwandan journalists' working rights—and as an office space for journalists whose employers didn't have separate office space in the city. In this office, about 15 desks were set up in a narrow, open room, and reporters worked at those desks on desktop or laptop computers. Wire service reporters also had the freedom to write stories critical of the government. They generally wrote fewer stories on a more sporadic schedule than any of the other outlets, as they were dependent on global news norms and competing with a larger pool of newsworthy stories. The wire service reporters I interviewed were paid on some variation of a monthly retainer and a per-story fee.

Lucas worked from home and said his daily routine was widely varied, depending on whether he heard of a story that he thought would be newsworthy for his employers. Much of his job consisted of listening from his home office to what others were reporting:

> I go to my office, look at the stories that are there, then say this is not good for me. Then I wait for when there is a big story. But I will be listening to radio stations, monitoring whatever is going on, talking to local journalists, because I do not have a local job.

Transnational news organizations provided a cushion of stability for their staff. One wire service reporter said his regional editors were aware of the sensitive and sometimes risky nature of newsgathering in Rwanda and would check in with him before publishing stories to ask whether a particular story was too sensitive and would bring trouble. "Because of the kind of stories they write, they make sure that the stories are well researched, especially in countries like this," Jacques said. "They understand the context here, the fragility—they understand. Sometimes they even ask, 'This story, don't you think it will maybe cause you problems?'"

International organizations also occasionally insert their authority into local situations, when staff reporters seem to be in danger. Lucas told me how he had been harassed online after researching a story for a local radio station, where he worked briefly while also freelancing for a wire service. He had been researching the members of a commission created to investigate allegedly genocide-denying broadcasts by BBC Rwanda (which had been banned because of those broadcasts). He wanted to find out what connections each commissioner had to verify government claims that the board was neutral and independent of the government. He produced and aired a broadcast story about the independence of the commission, and within days became the subject of a smear campaign by unnamed social media accounts that he attributes to the government. In detailed and lengthy statements, phantom Facebook and Twitter accounts called him a "genocide denier," an accusation that, if proven, carries a strong penalty in Rwanda.

> I know the situation was not good. So I kept quiet. And I told [wire service] because they were giving all my background. They were saying he now feels more powerful since he works for [wire service]. It was terrible. After two days, [wire service] was like, "OK, if you find it is going further, tell us and we will call the government." The bureau chief in Nairobi told me, "We can call the government and ask them to look it up, because they can use their cybersecurity whatever and know who exactly is doing that." [Wire service] said they would do it if it went on for more days. Then it stopped.

In this case, the intervention of the organization was unnecessary in the end, but the organization was ready to question authorities to protect its employee—and it was willing to do so even for a story the reporter had written for a different news outlet. This behavior is a marked contrast with the organizational behavior reported of Rwandan media houses, where managers under critical pressure tend to sacrifice employees lower on the totem pole. Another employee of a transnational media house had been arrested the previous year for a critical story, but the arrest lasted only hours, because the organization immediately threatened to run a story about the arrest—something that no local media house would have done, reporters said.

By contrast, local media organizations have a reputation for not supporting employees whose stories catch criticism, Lucas said.

> It is dangerous for the organization or for the journalist who has done the story. It will not be like the manager will say we are answerable for that content; no, they will say, "The journalist is accountable for that. Ask the journalist"—which is very dangerous. The editor would say, "Ask the journalist who did the story," yet we discussed the story in the newsroom.

Journalists who attempt to produce critical content in a local newsroom tend to do so on their own initiative and often risk organizational censure, whereas journalists doing the same for a transnational outlet are rewarded for that work and protected by the organization from some forms of penalty.

While transnational organizations clearly are willing to support their employees for critical stories they have run, reporters also noted that they face less criticism, in general, when producing news for transnational organizations than when they work for local organizations. Jacques, who joined a wire service after first working for the *New Times*' investigative bureau for several years, explained that, while he had been regularly hassled about critical stories at the *New Times*, no one questioned his wire service work. He attributed the lack of overt critique to two things: knowledge that wire services are less susceptible to local pressure, and knowledge that employees are less likely to be won over by financial offers.

> From the day I started working for [wire service], I haven't gotten any calls from anyone telling me, "We don't want those stories." I think maybe they know they cannot control AP. They cannot control Reuters. And the

international media pay well. When you are working for international media, you feel like you are empowered. Your bosses, you feel they are protecting you. So you try to write in pure journalism.

In addition to the protection they can offer, transnational organizations tend to demand reporting from their employees that is critical, investigative, and independent—news values prioritized in the global field and downplayed in the Rwandan field. "There is a big difference" between news produced for local outlets and that produced for international organizations, Jacques said.

> *New Times* is going to write only the PR stories. So that is the difference. Reuters, AP, will try to probe. If people are being evicted, the *New Times* is going to say people are being evicted for the good of all. Maybe they are settled in wetlands, but they are not going to tell you that 20 people were evicted, but not given alternative housing. The government has taken the land but it does not compensate them. For us, we are going to say that government is not compensating those guys. *New Times* is going to say they are evicting them because they are in wetlands, and government is evicting them for the good of these families. So that is the difference.

But the editors who demand that investigation into the alternate explanations for events will also demand that those explanations be provided by credible, named sources, with verifiable facts—key elements that protect a journalist's *legitimacy*. Jacques said:

> The people at AP, they are going to write, like, OK, Kagame has done A, B, C, and D; there is also this other side according to Human Rights Watch or the UN. When you read the story, there is no way you can burn the journalist, the writer.

By imposing these standards of reporting and research on employees, wire services like the Associated Press, Reuters, and Agence France-Presse and international outlets like the *East African* buttress their own reputations as factual news sources, but they also protect the employees working for them by guarding against content that could merit criticism.

Lucas told a similar story from his days reporting at a local news outlet, before he shifted to wire work.

When I was working at [local radio station], we just did a very simple commentary one day and I went home. I worked Saturday with the youth program. I was really controversial. A few weeks later, I was on leave when someone told me, "Man, things are hot here—apparently one of your programs has created problems with the government, with the president's office." When I went back, the boss told me, "Come in my office with your colleague." They told us, "Your program is anti-government and we have to suspend it, I've been told." But you see, at [wire service], that cannot happen. It's only when I commit an ethical mistake or do something wrong that they can say, "Eh, you are no longer part of us because you are not meeting our rules and regulations." But here when you are working for local media, anything can happen, anytime, which is bad.

In other words, local news organizations would often not hesitate to sacrifice reporters, while international organizations would be more likely to protect their reporters and stand behind their work unless the reporter had done something overtly unethical.

Many of the international news organizations represented in Rwanda did not have editors or bureau chiefs stationed in the country. As a result, I have few firsthand interviews with these sources. However, it seems clear that at least one element affording these organizations the power to both demand a particular quality of news reporting and then protect the employees who deliver it resides in the organization's financial independence from the Rwandan business environment. With less pressure from local advertisers, editors do not adopt the expectation of self-censorship that is internalized and then passed on down the hierarchy at organizations that depend on local advertising to fund ongoing business. Source interviews suggest this to be the case. Thus it seems that, by virtue of being financially independent and possessing a high degree of economic capital, international news organizations are able to resist the prevailing institutional pressure in a manner more overt and direct than that practiced by most news organizations in Rwanda. They pass this freedom along to reporters, providing necessary protection for those inclined to practice watchdog journalism.

In Rwanda, the *East African* occupies a somewhat similar position. While it is dependent on advertising, the magazine's readership stretches across East Africa, so writers are compelled to provide content that will be easily understood by readers in Kenya, Uganda, Tanzania, and Rwanda. So for these outlets, the goals of producing watchdog journalism coincide with the business model rather than contradicting it as with local outlets. Jacques pointed this out:

> Most newspapers tend to be nice to the state because they want to get funding through adverts. If you were at the *East African* there is a way they can maybe talk to your boss—we are supposed to cooperate, we are supposed to do this and this. But international media is a bit freer. Now there is a bit of space, and I think the state is understanding that maybe the media is not their enemy and we have to work together.

However, the *East African* conferred some social capital drawbacks along with some benefits. Government sources would often be reluctant to talk with reporters from the *East African*, a point the editor brought up in editorial meetings. But sources who were unhappy with the status quo would be more likely to bring their woes to this newspaper over the *New Times* or *KT Press*, expecting these reporters to have more leeway to pursue and publish a critical angle. One reporter used this point to his advantage in an editorial meeting; he brought up a story idea and noted that the source who brought the idea was fed up with a bureaucratic process. The editor responded with a pleased smile, noting that these are the kinds of stories the *East African* could and should run, because the other outlets would not. In addition, reporters at the *East African* could experience the viral nature of social media when they published critical stories. Caleb noted that the reach of his tweets would often spread—"in the thousands and tens of thousands actually if it's a critical story," he said. "The *New Times*, they don't get that. So, I feel like this is satisfactory, in a way. I don't earn much, but I feel like journalism satisfies me."

Social capital within Rwanda tended to be weak for wire service reporters. Lucas went so far as to say that one challenge of working for a wire service was that "many will say if you are working for international people, you are betraying the country." The government would send this message in meetings, he said, particularly in training sessions it held for Rwandan journalists.

Threats to Social Capital

A final factor differentiating watchdog journalists from the rest of the Rwandan journalism field lies in their distinct interpretation of national loyalty or patriotism and the way journalism should support that loyalty. For most Rwandan journalists, the practice of journalism should be positive and promote a unified image of Rwanda inside the country and on the international stage. Most watchdog reporters told me that a goal of their work was to make Rwanda a better country, but the best way to do so was by practicing social distance between themselves and powerful leaders and providing information to audiences to make better-informed decisions. In other words, the choice to practice watchdog journalism accompanied a shift from viewing journalism as a somewhat paternalistic tool of development to viewing journalism as a more neutral tool for providing information. This makes sense, as these different views of journalism align with the actual goals and orientations of the respective styles of journalism practice. I found, though, that most watchdog journalists along with the rest of the Rwandan journalism field prioritized a patriotic, loyal goal of making Rwanda a better country, though they disagreed on the best form of journalism to accomplish this. In adopting a watchdog role, journalists choose to exercise a power that is somewhat removed from the Rwandan journalism field, with one foot in the local field and one foot in the international journalism world.

Watchdog journalism in Rwanda is not widespread but does have an influence on the field. As noted above, the journalism produced by international outlets like wire services and the *East African* is held up across the field as proof of the fact that journalists can produce critical work without facing exile or prison. What many observers fail to note is the importance of the organization itself in enabling and encouraging that work. As a result, many journalists attempt to produce watchdog journalism in local organizations before realizing that it is practically impossible to routinely function as a watchdog within the organizational structure of local media outlets. It is an open question whether the watchdog function of international media organizations will influence the rest of the Rwandan field to normalize the practice, as the practice has spread in some other regions (Smith 1997; Waisbord 2000). After all, wire services are predominately aimed at telling stories to an international, largely Western, audience. However, reporters for wire services and the *East African* were partly motivated to continue in their jobs because of the impact they felt their work had on the local community. This was most apparent in the reaction to their work journalists would see published by colleagues at local news organizations. Lucas gave an example:

> There was a time the European Community issued a statement on the human rights situation in Rwanda, and I did a story and asked the minister, "What's your comment on that?" He said it. But he was not happy with the interview, so afterward, he was like, "Please, put that there is freedom in Rwanda. Because even you, you are free—you do whatever you want. I always read your stories." And I was like, "No, I cannot just write a story about me. This is not autobiography." He gave me a very strong statement. I put it in the story. Then in the morning I saw a story in the *New Times* commenting on the [wire service] story about the EU statement.

This reporter was assigned to write a story on an international community's negative assessment of human rights in Rwanda. The local minister he interviewed suggested that the reporter write that the country is free, based on the reporter's personal experience—"even you . . . you do whatever you want." The reporter refused, insisting that he must stick to accepted standards of newswriting rather than writing a first-person narrative account of his own experience. The story that he produced about that human rights rating stirred up enough interest that local outlets, including the *New Times*, reported on the way he had reported on the story—a metastory, but nevertheless a story about human rights that otherwise likely would not have been published in a local news outlet. Through this and similar occurrences, wire reporters were convinced that, even though they were writing to an international audience, their work had an effect on local discussions by introducing dynamics of independence that local media had to contend with and interact with. At least occasionally, the news produced by local journalists for wire services would thus introduce new discussion topics to the local press, who could report on the news by reporting what their colleagues had published for transnational outlets.

Of course, wire services and other international news outlets also seek specific angles and reject stories that do not meet standards of newsworthiness or timeliness. The reporters I interviewed had practice pitching stories and discussing angles before they began reporting, as they knew that some things just would not make international news. Some wire reporters would only write two or three stories per month, and sometimes no content at all, but would wait on a retainer for news that merited international attention. But at its best, reporters felt they had a local influence as well as an international influence. Lucas explained this as a "social role." It was more limited with a wire service, though he had pitched feature stories like one about street beggars being put in prison (something a Human Rights Watch report claimed was happening, but local officials denied). Some feature stories would still make the cut, but they would have to be "very big," he said. However, for him, the trade-off was worth it. "I know I can do a political story and be able to interview all sides, not only the pro-government but also the opposition, and get away with it," he said. "Local media, they will not publish that story. They will say remove that part. So it's still good to be a journalist."

Wire reporters pointed out that the wire services, with their largely international audiences, could actually have a great impact on policy changes in Rwanda, which is heavily dependent on donor money and has a good reputation to maintain in the donor community. "Rwanda is a country that wants to be seen well internationally, so they will change if you write a story that is true," Lucas said. "It may be fake change, like provisional change, maybe to show the international community, which is huge in this country, that something has changed—but it will be there."

The implication in this quotation is that, while lasting change is slow to come, the Rwandan government is swayed by international opinion. News coverage that is factually accurate and portrays Rwanda is an unflattering light for something that can be corrected by some sort of policy change is likely to impact discussions and lead to such a change so that government officials can look proactive and positive to the international community living in Rwanda and onlookers outside the country.

Journalists face some social pressure for doing watchdog journalism, and it tends to be aimed at their organizational affiliations, rather than the work itself (though individual reporters also find their reporting the subject of investigations). One reporter noted that reporters working for wire services were occasionally told by government officials that, by working for international employers, they were "betraying the country." Many reporters in Rwanda attend a several-week government education training where they learn about the history and culture of Rwanda. Lucas, who had not attended, called it "brainwashing" and said officials spread messages at those events that working for international outlets was unpatriotic.

> They will be telling them no, don't work for those international media. Those are people who want negative things from us, nothing positive. That is total bullshit, because when I am working for [wire service] I cover some positive stories—economic growth, investment, investors coming around. Is that negative? But some people when they are training them say look at

BBC, look at CNN, look at Al Jazeera—have they, have you ever seen them criticizing their own governments? Why can't you just work like them in Rwanda?

For this reporter and others practicing watchdog journalism, these questions set up a false dichotomy—for him and others, they practiced critical journalism as a form of loyalty to the country and their fellow citizens. Fabrice explained that he was a genocide survivor—a Tutsi—and was grateful to the government for feeding and clothing him and others, but still wanted to raise questions about how to improve governance:

> There are always some issues which are not clear cut, and I don't think it's wrong to raise them. I don't think it's wrong to tell the people involved, "Look, this is not good. Can we do it better? Is there a way it can be done better?" There is nothing wrong in holding whoever is doing nothing accountable. Accountability is a must. I am very grateful to what this current government did to my family, to me, but I don't think I should be restrained from telling them, "Look, this is not good."

This reporter thus calls into question the conflation of loyalty with unquestioningly positive coverage that reporters feel is demanded by local organizations and taught in training sessions like the one led by government officials. But even in critiquing this conflation, the reporter is acknowledging its existence. On some level, watchdog journalists in Rwanda face an ongoing critique that they are disloyal because they question best practices and probe dysfunctional government practices.

While watchdog journalists tend to face social pressure in the form of critical assessment of their loyalty to Rwanda, they also enjoy the benefit of higher social capital, afforded to them by virtue of their work. Producing the watchdog content allowed and required from an independent news outlet places reporters under scrutiny, but it also lends them some respect from audiences looking to find news that differs from that routinely produced by Rwandan journalists. As Caleb explained,

> With the *East African*, you get trainings, you know, and you get people trusting you as a journalist. At the *New Times*, even people with the *New Times* think it's a joke. You get? But then when you start getting out these critical stories, you go on Twitter and check the reach—it's in the thousands

and tens of thousands if it's a critical story. The *New Times*, they don't get that. So I feel like this is satisfactory, in a way.

Other journalists echoed this feeling of satisfaction from knowing they were producing news that would be read by a wide audience including Rwandans and international readers or listeners. They felt they gained social capital in the form of name recognition and respect in their roles as journalists from audiences interested in reading an alternate perspective shaped less by local economic pressure. Caleb noted that he had heard from many readers who appreciated the perspective the *East African* offered. "I've listened to quite a number of people and they appreciate our role in Rwanda," he said.

> They believe that we offer an alternative in most situations. If, for example, the head of RwandAir is fired, we are going to find reasons why they fired him—point blank, he was fired, and this is what they say about it. So I believe that most people find us an alternative for information, like to find their way through the right information.

In general, watchdog journalists enjoyed the feeling that they were able to provide a different perspective on current events than their counterparts at local news outlets, and they felt that readers appreciated this perspective as well.

Of course, one characteristic of most wire services, at least the ones featuring most prominently in the Rwandan journalism field, is that they have Western roots. Agence France-Presse is based in France, Reuters in Great Britain, and the Associated Press in the United States, and all have associated normatively Western values and expectations of news reporting. Some journalists find that this suits them and provides an outlet for the kinds of watchdog reporting they want to do; others do not. A few journalists in Rwanda are fed up with both the local approach to journalism and the wire service alternative and are attempting to build purely local and independent news outlets. One, an editor for the web start-up *Taarifa*, said he felt there was a need for a different kind of reporting than that produced by journalists at local outlets or by wire reporters. However, both *Taarifa* and *Great Lakes Voice* were, when I visited, relatively small newsrooms funded by the owner, and it remained to be seen if they would have long-term, sustainable business models.

Conclusion

The *East African* editorial meeting highlights the unusual field position of transnational news organizations in Rwanda. As members of a global rather than national field of journalism, editors are motivated to produce content that appeals to news values and audiences spanning national borders; even within the East African region, this means emphasizing conflict, drama, and exclusivity rather than the national field's news values of cooperation, consensus, and development.

Transnational organizations, including wire services and global and regional publications like the *East African*, are agents of the global field embedded in local contexts. Because of this, they provide unique promise and challenges to local reporters working for them. On one hand, they enable reporters to fulfill vocational mandates and accrue global journalistic legitimacy while benefiting from greater levels of autonomy. This leads to potential vertical capital, though local reporters were not particularly interested in cashing it in to leave Rwanda for other jobs in journalism. On the other hand, the position of these organizations limits the amount of local social capital that reporters can accrue. This not only has the potential to hinder horizontal transfers to other fields in Rwanda, but ensures that journalists with higher levels of autonomy also occupy only peripheral positions with limited power in the local journalism field.

This analysis highlights the potential value of transnational employment opportunities for local journalists. It also suggests that—based on some of the contrasts between journalists who produce critical, watchdog news coverage on a regular basis and those who do not, instead producing content that is encouraged by field myths and organizational routines—both individual and organizational factors are necessary to enable reporting outside the box. The individual must be able to produce news that is legitimate and does not break with field standards in the reporting process or the technique present in the final content produced. He or she must also prioritize loyalty to the profession of journalism or its mission as stated in the code of ethics and training materials, either holding them to be more valuable than loyalty to Rwanda or seeing them as a more desirable form of patriotism than the loyalty to Rwandan unity most journalists prioritize. Finally, he or she must be employed by an organization that has financial capital outside Rwanda and is rooted in a global or transnational journalism field. My observations show that each of these conditions is necessary but not sufficient on its own;

as long as all three coexist, they ensure that a journalist can practice critical, creative, and independent journalism in Rwanda.

The journalists who produce this content consistently are employed by transnational news outlets with bureaus or stringers stationed in Rwanda; these include the *East African* and many wire services. These journalists tend to talk less about journalistic roles during the genocide; they are more inclined to think optimistically about the power of journalism, rather than highlighting the negative social role journalists have played. They have strong grasp of reporting skills valued in English-language, transnational wire reporting, including the ability to write fact-based narratives that are "objective" and rely on quotations from named sources, and strong English writing skills. In addition, an equally important factor enabling these journalists to produce work that breaks from field expectations is that they are employed by organizations that exist with some buffer from the economic realities constraining news organizations based in Rwanda.

I argue that three factors—financial independence, that is, a high level of economic capital at the organizational level that is independent of field resources; a perception of patriotism that prioritizes independent thinking and free information in service to country stability; and legitimacy, that is, the ability to consistently produce news content that meets field-generated expectations of quality—enable journalists to practice watchdog journalism in Rwanda. Watchdog journalism is not necessarily critical or oppositional, and it is not necessarily produced by any particular method, but is independent from political influence so that journalists feel obligated and empowered to investigate government statements and actions regardless of whether particular state actors approve. In Rwanda specifically, I find that the field actors consistently practicing watchdog journalism are highly skilled and are employed by transnational organizations, including wire services and regional publications such as the Associated Press, Agence France-Presse, Bloomberg, Deutsche Welle, the *East African*, Reuters, and Voice of America. The journalists working for these outlets produce news for an audience that includes some elite Rwandans but also includes many international readers or listeners. While they face some criticism from local officials for working for "international media," they feel that they are part of the local journalism field, partly because many of them are Rwandan citizens with families in the country and a strong desire to remain in the country. Thus, they are somewhat different from the transnational journalists profiled in recent research who have a cultural and political alignment with a country other than that where they are reporting. Instead, the Rwandan journalist working for a transnational organization finds in that organization an outlet to pursue the reporting that he feels is in the best interests of Rwandan politics and society. Transnational organizations like newswires thus provide an opportunity for local journalists to produce journalism that falls outside the prevailing local culture of self-censorship and positivity while not abdicating their desire to remain in the country.

These findings highlight the ways different forms of capital can enable particular behaviors in a journalism field and show that economic and cultural capital may not always be in tension but could work in parallel to enable journalists to accomplish particular goals. My findings complicate the expression of economic capital by suggesting that the source of capital relative to the field in question can be an important element of consideration. Some organizations within the Rwandan journalism field, notably the *New Times* and *KT Press*, possess a high degree of economic capital, in that they are financially stable, retain staff of several dozen employees, possess functioning equipment, and pay employees on time at expected intervals. Within the context of Rwandan employment, these are symbols of stability. However, this financial capital is inextricably linked with the interests of the organizations providing capital in the form of advertisements. Thus, the high degree of economic capital these organizations possess essentially bars their employees from pursuing independent journalism. On the other hand, transnational organizations also possess high degrees of economic capital, but the capital is linked with a motivation for journalists to produce news that meets standards of independence and factuality that ensure a watchdog approach to newsgathering. The possession or pursuit of economic capital as such does not preclude the practice of any specific kind of journalism or the pursuit or prioritization of cultural capital. What matters is the source of, and motivations attached to, that financial capital. Where it is tied to interests contrary to the pursuit of strong watchdog journalism, it prevents this type of journalism from occurring. But where it is tied to interests that encourage watchdog journalism, this type of journalism flourishes. The motivations behind economic capital are important in determining how it will interact with other forms of capital.

This argument provides a compelling starting point for future research on both local and transnational journalism cultures. While transnational outlets have a problematic history of perpetuating Western hegemony, my fieldwork experience highlighted the importance of their existence to enable local journalists to remain in the local field while practicing journalism that does not align with status quo expectations. Individual factors are also important in that journalists must be able to consistently produce highly legitimate content, but the organizational protection afforded by transnational organizations without strong financial dependence on the Rwandan advertising sector is critical in enabling journalists to sustain careers of watchdog journalism in a society that rather encourages "puppet journalism," as one source called local journalism in Rwanda. A next step in this research could be to examine the ways that this watchdog journalism does or does not spread through journalism culture to become adopted by local organizations. Past research suggests that, under certain circumstances, a norm of watchdog journalism can start with a small group of practitioners and spread to be adopted by a substantial portion of the field (Smith 1997; Waisbord 2000). However, it is unclear whether this could happen in a context where the only practitioners of watchdog journalism are employed by transnational organizations and the financial situation of local organizations prevents their encouragement of the practice.

Rwandan journalists make strategic decisions to pursue particular kinds of journalism based on the resources available and protection afforded them. Empowering local journalists to be watchdogs is not a matter of enabling one or two brave individuals but effecting structural change on many levels. While my analysis is confined to the Rwandan context, I predict that a similar combination of circumstances is needed in any situation where journalists are interested in practicing their occupation in a way that is neither encouraged by routines within the field nor well tolerated by powerful forces outside the field.

Conclusion
What Is Weak Journalism Good For?
The Power and Potential of Peripheral Practice

As Caleb and I predicted in the anecdote that opens this book, incumbent president Paul Kagame won Rwanda's August 2017 presidential election with nearly 100 percent of the vote. There were, likewise, few surprises in the ways Rwandan news outlets covered the campaign and the re-election. The *New Times* reported that the presidential elections were "free, fair, and transparent," while the *New York Times* reported that the "lopsided re-election" was seen as a sign of oppression (Lacey 2003; Muvunyi 2017). Two days before the election, the *East African* ran an Agence France-Presse story with the headline "Kagame Set for Sweeping Victory in Rwanda Election" and a succinct story summary noting that the incumbent faced "two little-known candidates who were given only three weeks to campaign against the incumbent, who has kept a tight hold on power since his rebel army ended the 1994 genocide" (Agence France-Presse 2017). Several people told me that three journalists who had tried to publicly question the RPF's official narrative of the campaign season, including turnout at campaign rallies and other events, had been fired or suspended from their jobs without pay. In short, it turned out to have been business as usual. Journalists who played the game by official rules had reported on a relatively peaceful campaign season leading to an election confirming the incumbent's power. The few journalists who broke the unwritten rules in trying to live up to normative expectations faced financial consequences. And most journalists covering the campaign did not attempt to pursue such "creative" stories.

Samuel, speaking with me shortly before the campaigns started, succinctly summarized the set of challenges facing Rwandan journalists:

> Some challenges are in ourselves, the people doing the journalism. Other challenges are where we are working from and our bosses, but if you read how other countries get independent journalism, the government didn't come and give it to them. Journalists themselves fight for it. You don't have

guns, you don't have whatever; just use the facts. Let's say you are going to cover the election. Everyone knows Kagame will win. But now the question could be how many points he will have. Will he have 98 percent? 99? 90-something? 80-something? If we can now start working on *how*, you follow them and you see how they will get that number.

Journalists are constrained from within and without: they face pressure to report in certain ways because of their own uncertain social position, bounded by myths—especially myths about the role of media in the genocide. They are pressured by employers with important relationships and financial interests to protect. And they also face the challenge of reporting in a place where much traditional news about political conflict is replaced by foregone conclusion: there's not much of a horse race to report when everyone knows the incumbent candidate will win the presidential election by a landslide. Of course, there are still creative, insightful ways to report a routine election campaign with a foregone conclusion, as Samuel pointed out—following campaign officials to find out how they drummed up a 99 percent vote for Kagame would certainly be a creative angle, and likely an engaging one. However, no reporter told that story.

Rwandan journalists operate within a paradoxical set of pressures that on one hand encourage skepticism, independence, and power while on the other hand sending the message that journalists are untrustworthy, unskilled, and better off choosing routine over creativity and enterprise. These competing constraints shape the journalism field by signaling how journalists can and should think of their own social roles, how others should perceive them, what journalists should do, and how they actually behave. And while this book presents a detailed exploration of the journalism field in one case, it offers lessons applicable to journalism in many other contexts and sets the stage for future research on journalism fields around the world.

Doing Journalism in Rwanda

Journalism serves a valuable social and political role in a variety of democratic and non-democratic regimes. News produced by journalists can provide an important social role by routinely informing the public of official events and other items of public interest (Cook 1998; Ryfe 2006). It can influence political culture and political engagement across different regime types (Mattes and Bratton 2007; Paluck and Green 2009). Journalists can shape transitional justice processes through news coverage, which can bridge opposing communities, break down stereotypes, and cultivate empathy (Laplante and Phenicie 2009). Journalism can encourage or discourage peace amid conflict situations (Bläsi 2004; Hanitzsch 2004; Shaw et al. 2011). It also plays an important role in constructing a shared community around citizenship and information (Anderson 2006; Höhne 2008). Even where the media are strongly controlled by hegemonic forces, as with television in apartheid-era South Africa, they communicate powerful social messages that can undermine official narratives and change the framework of social engagement (Krabill 2010). We also know that news production is shaped in myriad ways by the context in which journalists work and by their own motivations and goals. And yet there is a surprising lack of research approaching the construction of journalism fields and the motivations of individual journalists from an inductive perspective. As a result, scholarship and popular perspectives on media actors in a variety of non-democratic contexts miss out on a realm of nuance and rich information that can help us better understand how and why journalists act in particular ways. In this book, I set out to enrich our understanding of journalism in post-conflict, authoritarian contexts by exploring the ways that myths about journalism can help journalists make sense of their worlds and embrace boundaries that otherwise seem contradictory.

The political context of Rwandan journalism sets the stage for practice. Consensus-oriented authoritarianism means that journalists are motivated and controlled by a political system that discourages dissent. Not only does this political system affect the kinds of stories most journalists have access to—often bland and missing the narrative tension that makes political intrigue such a topic of discussion in US journalism—but it also shapes the reward system of the journalism field by permeating and defining the forms of capital available to journalists. Within this context, journalism is shaped by a powerful myth rooted in shared conflict history: journalists are untrustworthy instigators of violence who cannot be counted on to act thoughtfully or de-escalate conflict situations. From this belief comes a reliance on the concept of "underdevelopment," which reinforces the idea that journalism is a young profession, full of unskilled laborers who need constant attention and supervision. Finally, the boundaries of journalism are shaped by organizations, which use the routines of quotas, deadlines, and sourcing requirements to reinforce corporate priorities. Local organizations enforce news production that does not rock the boat and stabilizes the status quo, while transnational organizations enforce news production values that invoke drama, high stakes, and global interest.

This book shows on a concrete level how many of the most powerful pressures on journalists come not from overt restraints imposed by political laws or organizational rules but, instead, are learned through myth and narrative—stories about the way things are and the way things should be. Some of these myths are rooted in the political and organizational environments but are communicated in ways that bypass overt regulation to instead form a reality within which unacceptable forms of behavior are not only unacceptable, but also unthinkable. Journalists are individually responsible for integrating these messages into a coherent framework for playing, and winning, the game of journalism. To do this, they sort and combine lessons about journalism into different ways of playing the game, with three major frameworks for justifying behavior. On one hand, journalists can choose to play the game in a way that gains capital within the Rwandan nation-state, which entails following formal rules of journalistic content production but subjecting news values to those of the Rwandan state and business world: consensus and positivity, with some elements of calculated dissent. On the other hand, journalists can choose to play the game in a way that gains capital within the global journalistic community; this path entails prioritizing news values of conflict and global-scale drama, emphasized to gain global readers and to achieve placement in tight news holes around the world.

There are three main narratives journalists use to make sense of their behavior. For journalists at local organizations, it makes sense that they would try to enhance Rwandan governance and development by partnering with the state to message unity and collaboration. In essence, these journalists say, "We need to make Rwanda better and uniting the power of the press with the power of the state is the way to achieve that goal." Journalists at transnational organizations are motivated by a feeling of duty to the profession, and they explain this by upholding independent journalism that meets global field standards of quality as an intrinsic good. To these journalists, producing good investigative journalism is inherently rewarding; they might explain it in terms of gaining social capital or just enjoying the feel of the game, but in either case, the reward comes from producing the work. As an additional bonus, these journalists would sometimes see their work influence national politics, further enforcing their feeling of accomplishment and power. The journalist with a global mindset working at a local organization was the most resigned of the lot. This journalist tended to be motivated either by the possibility that his journalism career could translate to a good career in a different profession—government messaging or private PR, or another communication field—or by the stable salary. "It's PR, but I have to buy groceries," was the essence of this explanation. Such journalists didn't feel they were doing the journalism they had trained for, but they were resigned to their jobs for another reason (often to do with financial capital). This utilitarian approach to journalism meant they might leave for another field or critique the field privately, but they would learn the rules and cooperate with the expectations of the local field.

This research not only highlights the ways myth informs journalistic action, but it also shows how journalists situated in a local field encounter global power in their daily work. In Rwanda, a country on the global power periphery, journalists encounter mixed messages from the beginning of their training, which is rooted primarily in Western norms of liberal democratic journalism practice, through their entry to newsrooms that are situated in spaces defined by local politics and social reality. The result is a set of perspectives that universally see "professional" behavior as a rarely attainable goal, such that journalists often attribute social and political censure to failures of individual professional behavior in a way that hobbles experimentation and innovative journalism. On the other hand, the global power available to journalists allows some individuals with a global outlook and affiliation to bypass some local restriction and produce more critical and independent journalism than is encouraged in local organizations. These are just two complications globalization introduces to the journalism field, but they are both important.

In Rwanda, journalists who have the perceived freedom to produce critical or independent news and yet rely on event coverage and official news presented by official voices are themselves criticized for lacking the capacity to "think critically." This is evident in how expatriates talk about local journalists and also in the forms of humanitarian intervention I saw implemented during my fieldwork. The assumptions tended to be that, because journalists were not actively critiquing or investigating authorities, they did not know how or had not even considered the possibility. In fact, it takes a great deal of intellectual work to be a journalist in Rwanda, whichever mindset the journalist inhabits. This research highlights the ways that journalists in a strong, restrictive political context negotiate and navigate many layers of pressure and messages about what journalism is and should be while they construct individual identities and rules for success in the field.

In this book, I rely on and extend field theory to understand journalism practice. I suggest that field theory concepts should be reconsidered and redefined to be most useful in non-Western journalism contexts. This is less a shortfall inherent to field theory than a function of how it has been applied in journalism up to this point; this study illustrates how some underutilized and undertheorized concepts, especially those of doxa and field scales, can be examined and brought to bear on the study of journalism, especially in peripheral countries, in a globalizing world. Scholars of journalism fields in several different countries recognize the importance of political systems, organizations, and global journalism communities in shaping journalism praxis, and my focus on myth as a guiding structure illustrates how these concepts coalesce in a non-Western, non-democratic journalism field. In so doing, scholars can move away from explicit or assumed bias toward observable factors like laws and policies and toward a stronger understanding of how narrative and myth form a third dimension of power that underlies and bounds journalism practice beyond explicit laws.

My study points to the importance of treating capital as a flexible concept whose useful dimensions might change across contexts. The categories of capital that Bourdieu defined relative to the journalism field in France and that have been applied to journalism in other contexts, particularly in Western Europe and the United States, do not translate directly to the Rwandan field because of the close relationship between the economy, social capital, and political engagement. Rwanda reinforces the importance of overtly questioning Bourdieu's categories before applying them in a new context. This book also expands our understanding of field construction by examining the mechanisms by which Rwandan journalists come to understand the acceptable ways to practice journalism. In other words, even as they are legally bound to practice journalism in particular ways and financially motivated to narrow their interpretation still further, journalists might have important additional motivations and justifications for their behavior, as this book illustrates. Focusing on the construction of field boundaries allows scholars to push beyond "objective" national spaces defined by politics and into the ways that journalism is constructed individually and collectively by narrative and myth.

Changing a Field

In this book I primarily aim to understand the complexity and contradictions of journalism practice in Rwanda as an example of a contemporary authoritarian state—not to make predictions about the future. However, my analysis of the journalism field and actors within it can inform some hypotheses about the future of journalism practice in Rwanda and similar countries.

I have argued that a defining feature of Rwandan journalism is the field's internalization of a lack of autonomy as an appropriate position, setting doxic boundaries for the field based on myths about the role of journalism in the genocide. This myth informs the field's orthodox news values of cooperation, consensus, and development, which are reinforced by the fact that advertisers are scarce and the major funding sources—government and corporate advertisers—routinely threaten to withdraw their financial agreements over critical news content. Boundary-pushing content such as investigative reporting is made challenging by inadequate training and tools and is further disincentivized by legal and rhetorical strategic maneuvers that place responsibility for this heterodox behavior and any associated missteps exclusively on the individual. The journalists who do have license to routinely practice heterodox behavior do so by way of their position straddling the global and local fields working in transnational organizations—a position that empowers them to follow more globally accepted standards of practice but also pushes them to the margins of the local field.

Changing a field is challenging; it is always more likely that stability and the status quo will prevail (Fligstein and McAdam 2012). However, sometimes fields adapt to or adopt new norms, and journalism in particular is subject to change via influences from existing social relationships (de Burgh 2003; Yuezhi 2000). When change does occur, it happens in one of two ways (Fligstein and McAdam 2012). A field may evolve incrementally, a process often led by powerful members pushing for more prestige or power in terms of some form of capital. The field could also change suddenly and dramatically in moments of social upheaval. This generally occurs under the guidance and pressure of entrepreneurs, who are skilled social actors with powerful roles who are able to negotiate of multiple sets of expectations, embedding ideal organizational goals in existing problems or debates (Clemens and Cook 1999). As the language of entrepreneurialism suggests, these actors work by exploiting existing values or organizational forms, especially making use of changes in the social or political climate to accomplish new or previously unpopular goals. In either case, powerful actors in strategic positions are important elements of change and, if no sources of capital reinforce or reward the new behavior, it will not persist.

Journalism practice has evolved following both paths at various points in time. Some practices have been incorporated gradually. The interview, for example, became a standard element of news production over a decade or so, spreading as it "excited sensation" along with outrage and indignation among reporters and observers (Schudson 1994, 570). At other times, the rules and boundaries of the field change dramatically and suddenly. As Fligstein and McAdam predict, this tends to happen during moments of social upheaval. For instance, in Mexico, institutional entrepreneurs within news organizations took advantage of democratization and economic liberalization in the 1980s and 1990s to transform journalism from a generally government-aligned field to one with several different motivations and models (Hughes 2003). Similar changes occurred in other Latin and South American countries, where individual journalists took advantage of institutional chaos and contradictory guidelines to promote watchdog journalism. It spread across the field in the 1980s and 1990s, protected by constitutional changes and spurred on by marketing success (Smith 1997; Waisbord 2000).

When journalists do adopt new practices and persist in them, they do so because the behavior is rewarded in some way. Investigative journalism, for instance, becomes a routine (though limited) practice in authoritarian countries like China when it brings in greater revenue because of its popularity or when it becomes an important element of journalistic identity, increasing economic capital in the first case and increasing cultural capital in the second (Tong and Sparks 2009). When truth-seeking journalism in Russia ceased to be economically rewarding, journalists tended to revert to reporting practices aligned with government propaganda and less likely to attract negative political attention (Roudakova 2017).

Journalism in Rwanda faces two major factors, then, reinforcing the status quo. The pressures from external local fields, in the form of political stances and profit models, all reinforce the current field position of limited autonomy and its attendant news values. While journalists were quick to offer anecdotes of splashy investigative journalism raising newsstand sales and otherwise increasing audiences, the few organizations practicing this in the local field were small and seemed to be just scraping by when I visited. This suggests that attempts to change field boundaries or challenge orthodox news values are likely to be met with strong opposition and little encouragement, thus reinforcing the status quo.

At the same time, the weakness of the field means that actors who might become powerful enough to advocate effectively for change tend to leave rather than do so. Actors within the local field who might advocate for change based on their skill and status in the field tend to leave quickly rather than stick around long enough to do so. The actors who are motivated to practice heterodox journalism have the most financial, physical, and psychological support in doing so if they are employed at transnational organizations located in the global, rather than the local, field. Taking this position relegates these actors to peripheral positions in the local field, as they sacrifice local social capital the longer they work for transnational rather than Rwandan news organizations. The actors who stay in the field and are best positioned ideologically to advocate for change are pushed by their heterodox values to the periphery, where they are unlikely to wield enough power to actually effect change.

This is not to say that journalism in Rwanda will be static indefinitely; this is unlikely in any field, as social groups constantly negotiate their boundaries and priorities incrementally in relationship with each other. However, it does suggest that significant changes are unlikely unless Rwanda experiences major changes in governance or funding models at the same time that powerful actors fully within the local journalism field advocate for changes in the field's doxa and values.

Situating Rwanda in the World

Rwanda is an example of a modern semiauthoritarian state—one of many countries with seemingly benign, development-focused authoritarian governments where life is, as political scientist Thomas Pepinsky describes, "boring and tolerable" (2009, 2017). This form of governance is in many cases replacing the traditional model of authoritarian dictatorship, a manner of governance defined by a state media monopoly controlled by formal censorship, a closed economy, lack of civil society organizations, and prevalent state exercise of force to control disputational counternarratives, which is falling out of favor around the world (Freedom House 2017b). Instead, in Rwanda as in many semiauthoritarian countries, laws protect journalists' freedom of speech while at the same time economic incentives encourage self-censorship, enforcing government alignment through bureaucracy rather than direct force.

Since the genocide, elections inclusive of multiple political parties have occurred in Rwanda at regular, seven-year intervals, with the most recent in August 2017 (Baddorf 2017; Gettleman 2010; Lacey 2003). The elections have been, for the most part, peaceful, and multiple parties have been represented on each ballot. However, Kagame, the incumbent, successfully campaigned in 2015 to extend presidential term limits so he could continue to run for office (Baird 2015). Critics have noted that the heavily controlled campaign process serves to silence some contenders and favor the incumbent (Human Rights Watch 2010, 2017). Rwandan policy has grown increasingly favorable to international trade (Heritage Foundation 2021). Most news organizations are, ostensibly, privately owned and market regulated; as a result, journalists report that the primary source of direct external pressure shaping media content comes from advertisers threatening loss of revenue, rather than state threats of jail or other legal sanctions (Rwanda Governance Board). This shift in media control has parallels in many countries, including Turkey, Hong Kong, and Indonesia (Ngok 2007; Tapsell 2012; Yesil 2014). In Rwanda, nongovernmental organizations like Pax Press exist to support the development of civil society by promoting independent media and critical reporting, but these organizations are functionally at the mercy of state authorities, who provide most of the funding needed to facilitate training programs and grants to journalists (author interview). A close examination of the Rwandan journalism field highlights the ways that journalists and media organizations are persuaded on moral and practical grounds to partner with ruling authorities. These noncoercive methods might parallel those practiced in other states with contemporary authoritarian governments.

A growing number of countries lean toward authoritarianism. Global watchdog organizations including Freedom House and the Economist Intelligence Unit documented decreasing levels of respect for and practice of democratic institutions over the past decade. Freedom House data documents the spread of authoritarian practices from authoritarian regimes to partly democratic countries. These practices include election practices unfairly weighted toward ruling parties and the suppression or discouragement of dissenting voices in the public sphere (Puddington 2017). Overall, over the past decade, democratic practices have been gaining ground less quickly than authoritarian practices for the first time in 40 years (Puddington 2017). The Economist Intelligence Unit documented a similar trend, measuring a move to more democratic practices for only 27 countries, while 89 countries shifted to more authoritarian behavior (Economist Intelligence Unit 2020). The latter notes that roughly one-third of the global population lives in authoritarian regimes. Along political dimensions, Rwanda shares similarities with many countries across sub-Saharan Africa, the Middle East, and Southeast Asia. In its categorization as moderately authoritarian, Rwanda falls in with Congo (Brazzaville), Cuba, Egypt, Ethiopia, Algeria, Cameroon, Cambodia, Myanmar, Venezuela, Hungary, Ecuador, Russia, Ukraine, and Afghanistan. Comparison across specific indicators highlights possible points of comparison. Over recent decades, referenda and special elections have extended presidential term limits in many countries, including Bolivia, Russia, Kazakhstan, Uzbekistan, Azerbaijan, Belarus, Venezuela, Cameroon, Algeria, Uganda, and Burundi (Dahir 2018; Guliyev 2009; Puddington 2017). Some other countries, like Turkey, have more heavily democratic institutions but are shifting toward authoritarianism. These countries appear to be adopting similar practices of media control, and the Rwandan example sheds light on how this might occur.

Not only is Rwanda exemplary of many countries governed by a contemporary authoritarian regime, but it is an important country to understand because it occupies a role of power and leadership on the African continent. Rwanda is a bellwether for governance across sub-Saharan Africa. In July 2017, Kagame was elected president of the African Union for the year 2018, chosen to lead the 55 heads of African states in a process of reform, fighting corruption to create a "sustainable path to Africa's transformation" (African Union 2018). Rwanda is considered a prime model of efficient development policy, exhibiting rapid growth over the past two decades in gross national income and per capita income, decline in poverty rate, and a rise through the rankings in the United Nations' Human Development Index (Molt 2017). It is touted for its high degree of gender parity in salaries and in political representation (Thomson 2017). The strength and durability of Rwanda's model of authoritarianism is likely to serve as an example to other African rulers, proving that it is possible to cultivate economic development through foreign investment while also suppressing political dissent and preventing the development of strong civil society spaces (Matfess 2015).

Rwanda also invites parallels with other countries that have experienced conflict, especially where journalists are seen as instigators or promoters of that conflict. A unique element of the Rwandan journalism field, at least in scope and extremity, is the social and historical role the genocide takes in shaping the contemporary mythology of the field. However, even here parallels can be drawn. As information is increasingly highlighted as a tool for various political ends, the Rwandan case shows how the instrumental use of media organizations can affect the field itself. The countries within former Yugoslavia exhibit strong parallels to this element of the Rwandan story; across the ethnically divided republics of Bosnia and Herzegovina, Croatia, Montenegro, Macedonia, Serbia, and Slovenia, media organizations published messages of distrust in the other republics, setting the stage for the ethnic violence of the 1990s (Oberschall 2000; Pejic 1996). This book highlights through the case of Rwanda how a journalism field can be shaped persistently and for long periods of time by its perceived or actual role in a civil or cross-national conflict, and how that perceived role can shape and limit the social role journalists are able to fill in the future. More broadly, a study of Rwandan journalism reveals the ways that journalists rebuild their occupational field after it is essentially decimated in a conflict; on this level, Rwanda has parallels with other post-conflict countries like Afghanistan, Iraq, East Timor, and Kosovo, all of which have received substantial amounts of foreign media assistance on the grounds that journalism has great power to reduce or inflame political tensions immediately following conflict (Kumar 2006).

Rethinking Policy Approaches

My findings have value for policymakers interested in assisting journalism work in their own countries or abroad. Rwanda has been an ongoing recipient of media assistance programs aimed at improving various aspects of the journalism field with an end goal of strengthening and promoting democratic institutions. These programs often aim to promote independent and professional media, with the assumption that a strong, independent, and professional media field will lead to democratization by "facilitating the free flow of information, transparency, accountability in the government, and economic growth" (Kumar 2006, 652). These interventions are motivated by the assessment of local journalism fields as "poorly equipped, inadequately trained, and largely controlled or owned by the state or dominant political and/or economic elites" (de Zeeuw 2015, 493). Media assistance aims to reduce the degree to which media outlets and individual journalists withhold useful information from the public due to censorship or self-censorship, instead creating a media system that encourages debate and discussion around public policy and other political issues. The amount of aid earmarked for media assistance grew through the 1980s and 1990s and was seen as an important tool for democratization in countries like Rwanda, former Yugoslavia, and many other countries across Eastern Europe and Latin America (Cary and D'Amour 2013; Kumar 2006, 652). More recently, media assistance has been deployed to countries in the Middle East, including Afghanistan and Iraq (Al-Rawi 2013; Barker 2008). USAID has awarded hundreds of millions of dollars in aid to Rwanda since the genocide in 1994, with one goal being to develop the governance structures in the country, partly by professionalizing the media sector. In 2017, USAID planned to spend $137.2 million in the country. As part of this assistance, from 2009 to 2011 a media assistance program was implemented by the Millennium Challenge Corporation on behalf of USAID with an objective of promoting "free, responsible media in Rwanda" by building the capacity of professional media associations and skills of individual journalists (Cary and D'Amour 2013). This study provides the opportunity to examine the complexity of a local journalism field that has been the target of substantial international media support and, importantly, the ways current media assistance policy falls short of its goals.

The first lesson, which seems obvious but is not reflected in the bulk of media assistance programming at present, is that journalists have diverse motivations and constraints. Even in a small country with a correspondingly small journalism field, journalists are motivated by several different pressures, with some prioritizing the identity of "global journalist" while others prioritize the identity of "Rwandan citizen" in their decisions about how to act. Moreover, even within a particular identity alignment, journalists act differently depending on the values and economic constraints of the organization they work for, with local and transnational organizations enforcing and rewarding different news values and production schedules. As a result, any effective media assistance program must be designed to accommodate a range of motivations and constraints among local journalists in the target country—a range that should ideally be identified in conversation with actual journalists at a variety of publications and editorial levels in that country. This book also shows that media assistance programs may meet their immediate goal—generally to increase the skillset and operating capacity of journalists—while failing in the ultimate goal of promoting democratization. In Rwanda, several highly educated journalists who had received graduate training in Western journalism programs and had also benefited from in-country media assistance programming persuasively articulated a goal of promoting and assisting the Rwandan government, rather than a more democratically aligned goal (and presumably the goal of media assistance programming) of improving free flows of information or government transparency and accountability. The assumption that empowered and autonomous journalism inherently leads to support for democracy is rooted in Western values and understanding of the journalistic occupation and tends to break down on the ground, as shown in this book and in other recent studies, including Natalia Roudakova's account of Russian journalism through recent history and Maria Repnikova's account of critical journalism in China (Repnikova 2017; Roudakova 2017).

A second lesson is that, in order to have any hope of being effective, media assistance policy must examine and encompass business practices and economic realities as well as capacity-building for individual journalists and professional organizations. Not all journalists in Rwanda are motivated to critique the government, and some who are so motivated are already doing so under the auspices of transnational organizations. However, there is a group of journalists who are interested in producing critical journalism but have decided not to do so because of the financial and social penalty they would incur for pursuing such work at a locally based organization. For these journalists, the path to resistance or independence is blocked not primarily by lack of individual training or tools but by organizational structures, which are themselves enforced by the economic realities of doing business in a small country where government and business interests are intertwined. A fruitful focus for media assistance policy, then, would be on organizational models and leadership aimed at developing financially independent business models for media organizations in such countries.

Lessons for Journalists and the Public

Finally, I hope this book offers useful lessons to readers who are journalists and interested observers or supporters. This book argues that journalism in peripheral semiauthoritarian contexts is complex work, undertaken from a variety of motivations, and that even in a small, strong-state context like that of Rwanda, journalists cannot and should not be reduced to a unidimensional understanding. I hope the description and argument I have developed here contributes to greater understanding and compassion for the difficult work being undertaken in these situations. The Rwandan journalism field also offers two critical lessons that can be useful in shaping the space of journalism across political contexts.

The orthodoxies and heterodoxies of Rwandan journalism combined with divergent organizational financial logics lead to two types of news production. On one hand, journalists working at local organizations pursue the orthodox values of cooperative news production that primarily promotes and defends government activity, out of a motivation to improve the country for those with a national orientation and out of a motivation to get a paycheck for those with a global orientation. On the other hand, journalists with a global orientation working at transnational news organization are motivated to produce news that is of global interest, which often means it focuses on national-level conflict, scandal, or other dramatic events that are relevant to a global community outside Rwanda's borders. Both paths miss a category of news coverage that would focus on major challenges to Rwandan development or Rwandan people but that may not have audience interest or news value outside the country. For journalists working at local organizations, negative or critical coverage of large private or government organizations is likely to result in loss of advertising and potentially job loss. For journalists working at transnational organizations, stories that are highly relevant inside Rwanda's borders are nonetheless unlikely to capture the attention of global audiences and thus are not likely to be picked up by an editor.

Both approaches miss out on the chance to produce deep, critical analyses of issues that are important to the Rwandan community and citizens but are too conflict-laden to be pursued by journalists occupying the nationally oriented journalist and too locally bound to be pursued by globally oriented journalists. This is an important space. It grows out of the monitorial role of keeping an eye on public figures, which journalists uphold across countries (Hanitzsch 2019), and is also important for journalists who are oriented toward collaboration in the vein of development journalism or solutions journalism. Rwandan journalists, operating in the context of contemporary semiauthoritarian governance, shaped by genocide history, and working amid strong distrust from within and outside the field, cannot practice journalism in the same way as journalists in the liberal democracies of North America and Western Europe. What might be possible, though, is for entrepreneurial local journalists with a global orientation and the assistance of international financial support to begin operating in this space. A few small organizations in Rwanda have tried or are trying to produce this work

(*Great Lakes Voice* and *The Chronicles* are two examples), but they face major barriers from financial and political forces. Here, my second lesson may be helpful.

This study makes it apparent that journalism is enabled and restricted as much by narrative and belief as by policy and regulation (a fact supported by other scholars, including Matt Carlson in his 2017 book on journalistic authority). In Rwanda, this power is particularly strong, for a variety of reasons outlined throughout this book. At present, the force of narrative serves to limit and constrain the Rwandan journalism field. However, the discursive nature of narrative means that it can be changed and, perhaps, new myths be fashioned. Journalists in Rwanda and other countries facing similar narratives of constraint should consider whether and how they can begin to perpetuate competing narratives about the value of journalism. This work can start within the journalistic community: in Rwanda, the two major communities of journalists, defined by their global or national orientations, could benefit from a discussion overseen by the Association Rwandaise des Journalistes to identify points of solidarity and overlapping missions. Journalists united and committed to spreading a few self-determined stories about journalism's power and potential might be able to claim space to produce national reporting that serves both the national interest and the interests of individual, disenfranchised citizens.

The power of myth conveyed through narrative in constructing journalistic identity does not stop at the Rwandan border or in the realm of semiauthoritarian or peripheral states. It extends around the world, even to places like the United States, where journalists have traditionally benefited from government policy that extends a great deal of institutional protection to their work. This power suggests that, even in such places, journalists' power can be challenged and diminished by the stories they tell about themselves and the stories others tell about them. Of course, the power of myth rests partly in its subconscious construction and application. However, there is always space for reflective consideration of prominent narratives and especially for attending to what stories journalists tell about themselves and what sort of public interpretation is offered for their behavior. Journalists have the responsibility and power to act in a way that invites public trust and support, using behavior to influence changes in narrative; they also can consider the stories they tell about themselves, to consider what blind spots they might have about themselves, and how narrative blinders might lead to neglect and oversight of important audience communities or missions. This is a call for journalists both to be aware that their power is constrained by narrative even in places where they enjoy significant legal protections, and to consider how their own narratives might limit their effectiveness in their stated goals. Structural power rooted in legal protection and laws is important, to be sure, but myth and narrative also matter, both in shaping individual journalistic behavior and, by extension, in forming a field.

APPENDIX

Note on Methods

This study is informed by a desire to both "observe what people do" and understand the motivations for those actions (Gans 1999, 540). I adopted a network ethnographic approach, which uses a social network analysis to identify core sites for on-ground observation and interviews (Howard 2002). Because this approach integrates physical and virtual spaces, it is an especially useful way to study news production, which incorporates information and virtual platforms with physical workspaces (Anderson 2009, 2013; Boyles 2016, 2017). It is also particularly appropriate for African newsrooms and other sites of knowledge production, because these processes on the African continent are influenced by virtual networks but still centered primarily in physical production spaces (Mabweazara 2010; Mabweazara and Mare 2017). In general, site-selection processes encompassing multiple methods and field sites are a good way to better understand contemporary news production, as journalists are members of a distributed community, often gathering information in decentralized ways, and yet still reliant on physical spaces like newsrooms (Lewis 2010; Mari 2021; Reese 2016; Shoemaker and Reese 2013).

Social network analysis aims to conceptualize and quantify the way the social world is structured, often by producing a graphic map and quantified measurements of network connectedness (Scott and Carrington 2011). Social network analysis capitalizes on the ideas that there are several possible kinds of ties between people or things; that those ties and an individual's location in a network determine the individual's power and potential outcome; and that network ties and tie formation are important to study (Borgatti 1995, Borgatti et al. 2009). Research using social networks has shed light on the ways people share information, spread diseases, and interact in other ways (Barabási 2016; Christakis and Fowler 2009; Granovetter 1973). Social network analysis provides a way to capture networks of news production and identify nodes for in-depth study (Anderson 2013; Boyles 2016). The network ethnography strategy's iterative mapping of the news ecosystem allows for the possibility that the boundary of a news ecosystem is no longer confined to traditional media (i.e., newspapers, radio, and television). Important work happens and routines are negotiated within newsrooms, and these were my primary sites of observation. However, media messages are shared back and forth across many channels, some of which are traditional newsrooms and some of which might not be immediately recognized as such. Thus, the boundary of a journalistic ecosystem can extend beyond the newsroom to include traditional journalists and editors, along with activists and bloggers (Anderson 2013). Expanding the boundaries of my study through an ecosystem approach allowed me to capture the complexity of contemporary news production, including periphery actors.

The goal of my analysis was to capture the important points of news production in Rwanda by casting a net broad enough to include traditional and nontraditional news producers (Anderson 2013). The starting point for this network analysis was a list of traditional news producers, but the network scraping tool captured nontraditional producers as well in the final visualization. Using a Python script, I scraped data from Twitter to construct a network composed of news outlets listed as authorized to operate in Rwanda

Table A.1 Rwanda Journalism Network Seed List

Electronic media
- Amazing Grace Radio
- BBC
- City Radio
- Contact FM
- DW
- Flash FM
- Isango Star
- Radio 10
- Radio Huguka
- Radio Isangano
- Radio Ishingiro
- Radio Izuba
- Radio Maria
- Radio Rwanda
- Radio Salus
- RC Huye
- RC Musanze
- RC Nyagatare
- RC Rubavu
- RC Rusizi
- RFI
- Rwanda Television
- Sana Radio (Restore Radio)
- Umucyo Community Radio
- Voice Of Africa
- Voice Of America
- Voice Of Hope

Print media
- Amahoro
- Amani
- Business Daily
- East African Business Week
- Gasabo
- Goboka
- Hobe
- Huguka
- Ibiyaga Bigari
- Imanzi
- Impamo
- Imvaho Nshya
- Le Reveil
- Oasis Gazette
- Rugali

Table A.1 Continued

- Rushyashya
- Rwanda Dispatch
- Rwanda News Agaency
- The New Times
- The Rwanda Focus
- Umurinzi
- Umusanzu
- Umuseke
- Umusingi
- Umwezi

Note: This network was seeded using the list of media houses (media organizations) registered with Rwanda's Media High Council as of 21 November 2016. This list includes broadcast and print media, which were the only outlets listed when I collected this information. The Media High Council has since expanded the list to include online-only outlets.

by the country's Media High Council in November 2016, mapping the official Rwandan journalism field as it appeared online in late 2016. The full seed list appears in Table A.1. I also included nodes followed by at least two of those news networks to visualize and measure the ways those news outlets were connected on Twitter. This information, shown in Figure 1.1, highlights the centrality of the *New Times* in the Rwandan journalism field. The *New Times* has the highest measure of betweenness centrality of any officially recognized news outlet in Rwanda, suggesting that this is an influential news outlet likely to serve as a role model for others in the field and best placed to relay information around the field. Figure 2.1 shows the same media map with an emphasis on eigenvector centrality rather than betweenness centrality. Eigenvector centrality is a measure of centrality that prioritizes nodes with many connections to well-connected nodes (Bonacich 2007; Borgatti 1995). This figure essentially highlights a list of the most prominent and often-consulted news subjects in Rwanda—the top five, in order, are an official Twitter handle for the Rwandan government (@RwandaGov), Rwandan president Paul Kagame (@PaulKagame), Kagame's executive office (@UrugwiroVillage), the Rwandan minister of foreign affairs (@LMushikiwabo), and the Rwanda Governance Board (@governancerw).

These two figures provided a foundation for my fieldwork and corroborate my findings. Figure 1.1 suggests that the *New Times* occupies a prominent role in the Rwandan journalism field, possibly serving as an example that other organizations in the field look to as a model of good business and news decisions. The next most prominent organizations in terms of betweenness centrality are Contact Rwanda (a radio station, @ContactRW); Umuseke (an online news outlet, @Umuseke); *Izuba Rirashe* (a print news source, @IzubaRirashe) and Rushyashya (an online-only Kinyarwanda news outlet, @rushyashya). While the *New Times* does not have the highest overall number of network connections or the most connections coming in or going out (in-degree and out-degree, respectively), it is the outlet most well placed in the network to influence others and relay information between news organizations. This made the *New Times* an ideal starting point for ethnographic study. From a practice-based perspective, the *New Times* seemed likely to influence the news practices of other organizations in the country, based on research findings that organizations on the periphery in precarious fields tend to imitate their central, successful counterparts (DiMaggio and Powell 1983). From a networking perspective, the network analysis suggested that *New Times* staff were likely to be well connected and could introduce me to other organizations for observation and interviews. In fact, the *New Times* editor, Collin Haba, was also on the board of directors of the Rwandan Association of Journalists at the time I conducted fieldwork, reinforcing the finding suggested by the network visualization. The other organizations where I spent the most time conducting observations, *KT Press* and the *East African*, are indicated with circles. *KT Press* is located on the left side of the figure and the *East African* is toward the bottom, under the *New Times*. Both are situated in strategic locations. *KT Press* is a bridge between the *New Times* and many Kinyarwanda-language outlets, including *Izuba Rirashe* and Rushyashya. The *East African* is situated among other prominent transnational organizations, including the *East African Business Week*, an outlet with many Twitter followers and a print audience in Uganda, Kenya, Rwanda, Tanzania, and Burundi.

Figure 2.1 suggests that publicly visible networks of news production in Rwanda revolve around officially established channels of information production and consumption. One could argue that this result is inevitable, given that the network started with "official" voices of news production authorized by the Rwandan Media High Council. However, the 20 or so most influential nodes ranked by eigenvector centrality are not news organizations included in the original network, so it is conceivable that they could be voices from outside the institution, or voices generating some sort of opposition. Instead, they are official government and business voices. This network configuration is not unique and perhaps not even unusual, but it does visually communicate the importance that official voices play in the public network of news production in Rwanda.

Based on these network maps along with guidance from my local research supervisor, who confirmed the importance of the *New Times* in the Rwandan news field, I began fieldwork there. From the *New Times*, I branched out to observation and interviews at other sites using a snowball sample approach, aware of how the nodes fit in the network map I had produced but flexible to include outlets not apparently prominent in that network. I conducted most of the participant observation at the *New Times* and *KT Press*, with a shorter observation period at the *East African* and tours of the *Great Lakes Voice* and a newsroom hosted by the Association of Rwandan Journalists, which is open to journalists reporting independently or working for wire services and other news outlets without offices in Kigali. *KT Press* and the *East African* are both important bridging nodes. *KT Press* is one news product from an organization that also produces news in Kinyarwanda for audiences online and via broadcast radio and television. The *East African* is, according to the network, a peripheral outlet in Rwanda but one of the only sources of news about Rwanda for rest of the East African region, making it another bridging organization. The *Great Lakes Voice* is a peripheral organization, poorly funded with a small newsroom and few staff, but is more oppositional than most Rwandan newsrooms.

The snowball sampling approach, which I chose over a random sample as the way I identified interview subjects and newsrooms to observe, allowed me to build rapport with subjects and connect with some interview subjects who would probably not have been willing to talk to a researcher who reached out via a cold call or email per a random sample. However, it also imposes limitations on my data and observations. The data I collected represents a network of journalists connected to each other who are likely to also share some similar background and experience in the field. My findings are based on the experiences, opinions, and reflections of a group of relatively elite, English-speaking journalists, most of whom work at Rwanda's elite news outlets. Most of the study participants were men, primarily because few women worked in the newsrooms I visited. While I interviewed some radio journalists, including a few who work for community radio stations, even these were elite by virtue of their English ability and their involvement with training outlets and other organizations in Kigali. The experience of the isolated local community radio station DJ or journalist who speaks only Kinyarwanda is not represented in this study. This is a loss, and future studies should explore the particular social function and role development of journalists in these more peripheral roles in diverse countries. However, by centering my interviews and observations around the power centers of Rwandan journalism, I study the values, routines, and roles important to field leaders. Thus, the findings I present are not meant to be representative of Rwandan journalism, but they are representative of the practices and thought processes guiding news production at the most politically influential and financially successful outlets. These organizations set an example for journalists throughout the country, and content they produce is also often redistributed or transmitted by smaller, local outlets.

My snowball sample began with journalists in a power center, and that shaped the sample of Rwandan journalists and media organizations I observed. The managing editor of the *New Times* is one of the most powerful journalism figures in Rwanda; he leads one of the most financially stable and well-resourced news organizations and chairs the board of the Association Rwandaise des Journalistes, which provides guidance and some protection along with best-practices recommendations for journalists throughout the country. In addition, this editor and the *New Times* more broadly have a reputation for being strongly government aligned. Because my sample started here, it took several months of fieldwork to expand my interview pool to include subjects who were outside the power center of elite, government-aligned news publications, such as community radio journalists. While a few of these journalists refused interview requests, most were happy to cooperate. However, I quickly encountered bureaucratic roadblocks when I began to include these more critical journalists in my study, and as a result I have a limited number of these interviews in my data set.

To analyze the observation and interview data, I entered it in Dedoose and coded iteratively for major themes, using an open coding process to identify and analyze my observations (Emerson et al. 2011). Some of the themes I included in my coding stood out to me as I interviewed, so when I went through data later, I looked for these things outright. Other themes only became apparent as I read through transcripts and observation later. I recorded semi-structured interviews with subjects in Rwanda, Uganda, Tanzania, and Zimbabwe. My analysis is based on verbatim quotations from these interviews as well as field notes documenting informal conversations with many of these and additional journalists whom I encountered in the course of my daily observations. The recorded interviews were transcribed; some I transcribed myself in the field, and some I sent out for transcription by confidential, professional transcription services including Rev.com and Verbal Ink. I organized the transcribed interviews and field notes through an open coding process to identify and analyze themes (Emerson et al. 2011).

While the interview protocol I used did not include any questions I considered sensitive, interviewers occasionally did share information with me that they explicitly warned would put them in danger if connected with their identities. In addition, many of the people I interviewed would be easily identifiable by looking up job titles or articles at associated publications; in the case of transnational news organizations, many wire services employ only one stringer in Kigali, so naming the wire services I included in my interviews would amount to publishing the names of certain sources. Because of this, I identify my sources with only a select amount of identifying information—the news outlet or type of news outlet (*New Times*, *KT Press*, *East African*, wire service, or radio) and the position held (reporter, photographer, or editor) To further protect my interview subjects, I do not identify interviews by date. I conducted semi-structured interviews with journalists and key observers of the news field in Rwanda and surrounding countries. Interviews ranged from 45 to 90 minutes. Most of these interviews were conducted in one-on-one, private interactions, and I recorded and took notes. I occasionally interviewed journalists in group situations, particularly when I was interacting with students who I thought would be more likely to discuss their opinions openly when they were interacting with peers. I conducted some interviews in private areas at workplaces and others at local restaurants away from workplaces. I usually suggested a location and offered to meet elsewhere at subjects' preference, to make them as comfortable as possible.

By spending my time primarily at two news outlets with shorter observation periods at the others, I sought maximum understanding of news routines while choosing a large enough sample that I could determine what news routines were shared and which might be idiosyncratic to a particular organization's practice. After I received research approval from the Rwandan Ministry of Education, I spent an average of 20 hours per week observing and interviewing journalists, primarily in Kigali, the capital of Rwanda.[1] Rwanda is a small country and most of the country's news outlets are based in the capital, making this geographic location most practical. I was based in Rwanda from January through August 2017 and conducted formal research beginning in late January. I collected data in the form of notes from participant observation and interviews; interview transcripts; WhatsApp chatroom transcripts from newsroom groups I joined, which I extracted and stored as text files; and files of news articles I edited at several outlets. In the field, I took the role of an observer and occasional volunteer, participating and observing as much as possible at the margins of the workplace (Lindlof and Taylor 2017). I attended editorial meetings regularly (these were primarily conducted in English with many side conversations in Kinyarwanda), edited news articles to provide English fluency and editorial feedback, and accompanied reporters on trips to press conferences, parliamentary hearings, and other events. I ate lunch with staff at newsroom canteens, where we typically ate some form of newsroom-subsidized local food while discussing current events and joking about reporters' personal lives. Throughout these experiences I jotted notes on paper during my observations and then spent the afternoon or evening after each field interaction transcribing and elaborating these notes. I used a general ethnographic observation guide to orient my field observations.

There are, of course, challenges with my approach, both with the method itself and with the sampling procedure. First, because social networks are not created by random sample and are intended to portray a complete network, any omission caused by missing data or an inaccurately drawn boundary alters network measurements (Kossinets 2006). Another challenge is that of ascertaining what meaning should be assigned to the observed network connections, since often the observable link only represents part of a pattern of interaction between two actors (Wasserman and Galaskiewicz 1994). For these reasons, the method can be particularly useful when paired with interviews and physical observation (Howard 2002). A second challenge of doing social network analysis lies in identifying a

---

[1] The Rwandan Ministry of Education and the University of Washington's Institutional Review Board reviewed and approved this research. It was conducted under Rwandan clearance no. MINEDUC/S&T/414/2017 and UW IRB approval no. 52693.

social network to analyze. Past network ethnographies of journalism fields have relied on software to collect links between news websites (Anderson 2013; Boyles 2016). However, the limited web presence of news outlets in Rwanda proved this network choice to be ineffective for this study's population; few Rwandan news outlets had websites in late 2016, and those that did tended not to hyperlink to other sites. Twitter networks presented a reasonable alternative to ground the social network for this study. Twitter is a commonly used social media platform whose popularity is exploding across sub-Saharan Africa, and is especially popular for its information-sharing capabilities (Hussey 2016). Journalists use the tool to share information, share breaking news, live-blog, and cultivate sources (Habel et al. 2018; Hermida 2013; Verweij and van Noort 2014). Because of this, this book builds a network ethnography from a Twitter-based social network data set.

Ethnographic research has a long tradition within journalism studies as a way to better identify and understand the process of news production (Cottle 2000). Classic newsroom ethnographic studies helped researchers better understand what news values reporters and editors rely on in deciding which stories to pursue, how editors and reporters define the value of "objectivity" and how that influences news work, and other elements of the relationships and negotiations involved in news production (Gans 1979; Tuchman 1972). Participant observation is often paired with interviews to help the researcher better understand the meaning behind observed behaviors. Using these ethnographic methods, I attempt to shed light on some underexamined newsroom realities and question some of the "orthodox ideas and heresies" of journalism (Cottle 2000, 21). This research is theoretically grounded in field theory and organizational sociology with an aim to understand journalism culture, particularly as it is shaped by technology access or lack and by the policy environment. But I also approached fieldwork with a conscious effort to remain aware of other factors at work in the field, driven by the understanding that "participant observation, perhaps more than most other methods[,] is destined to be reflexive, open to the contingencies of the field experience and therefore less than strictly linear in its execution or predictable in its findings" (Cottle 2007, 5). In unpacking the phenomenon reported here, I benefited from the strengths of ethnographic work in its ability to highlight the dynamic and embedded nature of cultural production and reveal the complex interactions of forces, constraints, and conventions that shape the news (Cottle 2007). A triangulation of research methods including observation, document analysis, and interviews shed further light on these interactions.

While my analyses draw directly from the Rwandan journalism field, this study is also informed by research interviews conducted throughout the region concurrently with the Rwandan field research. I visited Kampala, Uganda, Harare, Zimbabwe, and Zanzibar and Dar es Salaam, Tanzania, to interview journalists so that I could better understand the context for the Rwandan journalism field. These countries were selected for their variance in political environment and quality of technology infrastructure; Table A.2 outlines the variation between these fields. According to this data, Zimbabwe has a similarly restrictive policy environment but cheaper access to technology infrastructure; Tanzania has expensive technology and a more supportive policy environment; and Uganda has cheaper technology infrastructure access and a more supportive policy environment. These distinctions are not explicitly analyzed here, but they help situate the Rwandan media in geographic context. Journalists in these other countries who were familiar with Rwanda unanimously said they would prefer to be journalists in their own countries over Rwanda; one had traveled to Rwanda from Uganda to report on an environmental

Table A.2 Comparison of Journalism Fields across East Africa

Country	Tech Affordability[a]	Legal Environment[c]	Newspaper N^d	TV N^d	Radio N^d
Rwanda	3.7	23	4	1	7
Tanzania	3.7	18	11	6	9
Uganda	5.6	18	3	6	8
Zimbabwe	5.9[b]	24	8	1	7

Note: The World Economic Forum's affordability scores are calculated from data on mobile tariffs per minute, fixed broadband access per month, and a score for internet and telephone sector competition. Higher numbers are more affordable. Legal Environment scores are calculated on a 0–30 scale, with 0 being most free and 30 being most restrictive.

Source: (a) Dutta et al. (2015) (b) Gambanga (2015), WEF (2016), and Dutta et al. (2015) (c) Freedom House (2016) (d) BBC country media profiles, accessed May 2016: BBC News (2012, 2014, 2015a, 2015b).

problem recently. He had found it to be a boring and frustrating experience, spending much of his time swamped in bureaucracy waiting for permission to interview officials.

Future research can and should explore Rwanda in more comparative context, using a sample of a few nearby countries such as these to add further depth to the Rwandan case and to elaborate on factors unexplored here. A comparative study could, for instance, provide deeper insight on the roles policy and technology play in shaping journalism fields, and the ways in which their influence is incorporated by journalists.

Bibliography

Abbott, A. 2014. *The System of Professions: An Essay on the Division of Expert Labor*. University of Chicago Press.

Abuoga, J. B., and Mutere, A. 1988. *The History of the Press in Kenya*. African Council on Communication Education.

Africa Media Index. 2019, May 24. Group M Launches the Africa Media Index. https://www.groupm.com/news/groupm-launches-africa-media-index.

African Democracy Encyclopedia Project. 2013. Kenya: 2013 Presidential Election Results. Retrieved November 11 from https://www.eisa.org/wep/ken2013results.htm.

African Union. 2018, January 18. President Paul Kagame Elected as New Chairperson of the African Union for the Year 2018. https://au.int/en/pressreleases/20180128/president-paul-kagame-elected-new-chairperson-african-union-year-2018.

Agence France-Presse. 2017, August 2. Kagame Set for Sweeping Victory in Rwanda Election. http://www.theeastafrican.co.ke/news/Kagame-set-for-sweeping-victory-in-Rwanda-election/2558-4041616-cuyu86/index.html.

Aitamurto, T., and Varma, A. 2018. The Constructive Role of Journalism: Contentious Metadiscourse on Constructive Journalism and Solutions Journalism. *Journalism Practice* 12(6), 695–713.

Al-Rawi, A. K. 2013. The US Influence in Shaping Iraq's Sectarian Media. *International Communication Gazette* 75(4), 374–391.

Aldridge, M. 1998. The Tentative Hell-Raisers: Identity and Mythology in Contemporary UK Press Journalism. *Media, Culture & Society* 20(1), 109–127.

Alexis, M., and Mpambara, I. 2003. *IMS Assessment Mission: The Rwanda Media Experience from the Genocide*. International Media Support.

Allen, T., and Stremlau, N. 2005. Media Policy, Peace and State Reconstruction. Discussion Paper 8. Crisis States Discussion Papers.

Andersen, K. 2021. *Labour Market Profile Rwanda—2021/2022*. D. T. U. D. Agency.

Anderson, B. 2006. *Imagined Communities: Reflections on the Origin and Spread of Nationalism*. Versò Books.

Anderson, C. W. 2009. *Breaking Journalism Down: Work, Authority, and Networking Local News, 1997–2009*. Columbia University Press.

Anderson, C. W. 2013. *Rebuilding the News: Metropolitan Journalism in the Digital Age*. Temple University Press.

Appadurai, A. 1996. *Modernity at Large: Cultural Dimensions of Globalization*. University of Minnesota Press.

Arjomand, N. A. 2022. *Fixing Stories*. Vol. 19. Cambridge University Press.

Associated Press. 2015, December 18. Rwandan President Paul Kagame Could Rule until 2034 after Voters Lift Limits. *The Guardian*. https://www.theguardian.com/world/2015/dec/19/rwandan-president-paul-kagame-could-rule-until-2034-after-voters-lift-limits.

BIBLIOGRAPHY

AT Editor. 2017, March 28. Update: Rwanda Releases British Citizen Charged in Anti-government Crimes. *Africa Times*.

Atad, E. 2017. Global Newsworthiness and Reversed Domestication: A New Theoretical Approach in the Age of Transnational Journalism. *Journalism Practice 11*(6), 760–776.

Atanesyan, A. 2020. Media Framing on Armed Conflicts: Limits of Peace Journalism on the Nagorno-Karabakh Conflict. *Journal of Intervention and Statebuilding 14*(4), 534–550.

Baddorf, Z. 2017, August 6. Rwanda President's Lopsided Re-election Is Seen as a Sign of Oppression. *New York Times*. https://www.nytimes.com/2017/08/06/world/africa/rwanda-elections-paul-kagame.html.

Bailard, C. S. 2014. *Democracy's Double-Edged Sword: How Internet Use Changes Citizens' Views of Their Government*. Johns Hopkins University Press.

Baird, D. 2015, June 1. Rwanda Places Indefinite Ban on BBC Broadcasts over Genocide Documentary. *The Guardian*. https://www.theguardian.com/media/2015/jun/01/rwanda-places-indefinite-ban-on-bbc-broadcasts-over-genocide-documentary.

Barabási, A.-L. 2016. *Network Science*. Cambridge University Press.

Barbera, N., and Robertson, D. 2014, June 11. South Sudanese, Rwandans Share Stories of Resilience in Search of Hope. US Institute of Peace. https://www.usip.org/publications/2014/06/south-sudanese-rwandans-share-stories-resilience-search-hope.

Barker, M. J. 2008. Democracy or Polyarchy? US-Funded Media Developments in Afghanistan and Iraq Post 9/11. *Media, Culture & Society 30*(1), 109–130.

Barnett, M. 2002. *Eyewitness to a Genocide*. Cornell University Press.

Barton, G. 2001, October 4. New Beginnings in Rwanda. *Quill*. https://www.quillmag.com/2001/10/04/new-beginnings-in-rwanda/.

BBC News. 2012. Uganda Profile. Accessed May 18, 2016. http://www.bbc.com/news/world-africa-14112301.

BBC News. 2014. Zimbabwe Profile | Media. Accessed May 18, 2016. http://www.bbc.com/news/world-africa-14113511.

BBC News. 2015a. Rwanda Profile | Media. Accessed May 18, 2016. http://www.bbc.com/news/world-africa-14093244.

BBC News. 2015b. Tanzania Profile | Media. Accessed May 18, 2016. http://www.bbc.com/news/world-africa-14095831.

Bennett, W. L. 1990. Toward a Theory of Press-State Relations in the United States. *Journal of Communication 40*(2), 103–127.

Benson, R. 2013. *Shaping Immigration News*. Cambridge University Press.

Bermeo, N. 2016. On Democratic Backsliding. *Journal of Democracy 27*(1), 5–19.

Bläsi, B. 2004. Peace Journalism and the News Production Process. *Conflict & Communication 3*(1/2), 1–12.

Boje, D. M., Fedor, D. B., and Rowland, K. M. 1982. Myth Making: A Qualitative Step in OD Interventions. *Journal of Applied Behavioral Science 18*(1), 17–28.

Bonacich, P. 2007. Some Unique Properties of Eigenvector Centrality. *Social Networks 29*(4), 555–564. https://doi.org/doi:10.1016/j.socnet.2007.04.002.

Bonde, B. N., Uwimana, J.-P., Sowa, F., and O'Neil, G. 2015. The State of Media Freedom in Rwanda. *Rwanda Media Commission*. Accessed July 6, 2018. https://rsf.org/sites/default/files/6_5_2015_ib_-_final_report_on_state_of_the_media_freedom_in_rwanda_00.00.pdf.

Booth, D., and Golooba-Mutebi, F. 2012. Developmental Patrimonialism? The Case of Rwanda. *African Affairs 111*(444), 379–403.

Borgatti, S. P. 1995. Centrality and AIDS. *Connections* 18(1), 112–114.
Borgatti, S. P., Mehra, A., Brass, D. J., and Labianca, G. 2009. Network Analysis in the Social Sciences. *Science* 323(5916), 892–895. https://doi.org/10.1126/science.1165821.
Bourdieu, P. 1985. The Social Space and the Genesis of Groups. *Theory and Society* 14(6), 723–744. https://doi.org/10.2307/657373.
Bourdieu, P. 1986. The Forms of Capital. In J. Richardson, ed., *Handbook of Theory and Research for the Sociology of Education*, 241–258. Greenwood Press.
Bourdieu, P. 1991. *Language and Symbolic Power*. J. B. Thompson, ed. G. Raymond and M. Adamson, trans. Harvard University Press.
Bourdieu, P. 1999. Rethinking the State: Genesis and Structure of the Bureaucratic Field. In G. Steinmetz, ed., *State/Culture: State-Formation after the Cultural Turn*, 53–75. Cornell University Press.
Bourdieu, P., and Farage, S. 1994. Rethinking the State: Genesis and Structure of the Bureaucratic Field. *Sociological Theory* 12(1), 1–18. https://doi.org/10.2307/202032.
Bourdieu, P., and Wacquant, L. J. 1992. *An Invitation to Reflexive Sociology*. University of Chicago Press.
Bowles, M. L. 1989. Myth, Meaning and Work Organization. *Organization Studies* 10(3), 405–421.
Boyd-Barrett, O. 1980. *The International News Agencies*. Vol. 13. Constable & Robinson.
Boyles, J. L. 2016. Resiliency in Recovery: Slow Journalism as Public Accountability in Post-Katrina New Orleans. *Digital Journalism* 4(4), 478–493. https://doi.org/10.1080/21670811.2015.1104256.
Boyles, J. L. 2017. Building an Audience, Bonding a City: Digital News Production as a Field of Care. *Media, Culture & Society* 39(7), 945–959.
Bratic, V. 2008. Examining Peace-Oriented Media in Areas of Violent Conflict. *International Communication Gazette* 70(6), 487–503. https://doi.org/10.1177/1748048508096397.
Breed, W. 1955. Social Control in the Newsroom: A Functional Analysis. *Social Forces* 33(4), 326–335.
Brinkerhoff, D. W. 2005. Rebuilding Governance in Failed States and Post-conflict Societies: Core Concepts and Cross-Cutting Themes. *Public Administration and Development: The International Journal of Management Research and Practice* 25(1), 3–14.
Brown, A. D. 2006. A Narrative Approach to Collective Identities. *Journal of Management Studies* 43(4), 731–753.
Buchholz, L. 2016. What Is a Global Field? Theorizing Fields beyond the Nation-State. *Sociological Review* 64(2_suppl), 31–60. https://doi.org/10.1111/2059-7932.12001.
Bunce, M. 2010. "This Place Used to Be a White British Boys' Club": Reporting Dynamics and Cultural Clash at an International News Bureau in Nairobi. *Round Table* 99(410), 515–528.
Burrell, J. 2012. *Invisible Users: Youth in the Internet Cafés of Urban Ghana*. MIT Press.
Carlson, M. 2014. Gone, but Not Forgotten: Memories of Journalistic Deviance as Metajournalistic Discourse. *Journalism Studies* 15(1), 33–47.
Carlson, M. 2017. *Journalistic Authority: Legitimating News in the Digital Era*. Columbia University Press.
Carlson, M., and Lewis, S. C. 2015. *Boundaries of Journalism: Professionalism, Practices and Participation*. Routledge.

Carlson, M., Robinson, S., and Lewis, S. C. 2021. Digital Press Criticism: The Symbolic Dimensions of Donald Trump's Assault on US Journalists as the "Enemy of the People." *Digital Journalism* 9(6), 737–754.

Carlson, M., and Usher, N. 2016. News Startups as Agents of Innovation: For-Profit Digital News Startup Manifestos as Metajournalistic Discourse. *Digital Journalism* 4(5), 563–581.

Carter, F. 1968. The Press in Kenya. *Gazette Leiden (Netherlands) 14*(2), 85–88.

Cary, P., and D'Amour, R. 2013. US Government Funding for Media: Trends and Strategies. Report No. 19. Center for International Media Assistance. https://www.cima.ned.org/wp-content/uploads/2015/01/U.S.-Government-Funding-for-Media_Trends-and-Strategies.pdf.

Castells, M. 2009. *The Rise of the Network Society*. 2nd ed. John Wiley & Sons.

Chase-Dunn, C., Kawano, Y., and Brewer, B. D. 2000. Trade Globalization since 1795: Waves of Integration in the World-System. *American Sociological Review* 65(9), 77–95.

Chibita, M. 2010. The Evolution of Media Policy in Uganda. *African Communication Research* 3(1), 85–120.

Chibuwe, A. 2021. The Nexus of Journalism and Political Activism in Post-2000 Zimbabwe: A Field Theory Critique. *Journal of Applied Journalism & Media Studies* 10(3), 275–296.

Chopra, R. 2003. Neoliberalism as Doxa: Bourdieu's Theory of the State and the Contemporary Indian Discourse on Globalization and Liberalization. *Cultural Studies* 17(3-4), 419–444.

Chrétien, J.-P. 2006. *The Great Lakes of Africa: Two Thousand Years of History*. S. Straus, trans. Princeton University Press.

Christakis, N. A., and Fowler, J. H. 2009. *Connected: The Surprising Power of Our Social Networks and How They Shape Our Lives*. Little, Brown Spark.

CIA. 2020. *CIA World Factbook: Rwanda*. Retrieved September 1 from https://www.cia.gov/library/publications/the-world-factbook/geos/rw.html.

Clemens, E. S., and Cook, J. M. 1999. Politics and Institutionalism: Explaining Durability and Change. *Annual Review of Sociology 25*(1), 441–466.

Coddington, M. 2019. *Aggregating the News: Secondhand Knowledge and the Erosion of Journalistic Authority*. Columbia University Press.

Cohen, N., and Arieli, T. 2011. Field Research in Conflict Environments: Methodological Challenges and Snowball Sampling. *Journal of Peace Research 48*(4), 423–435. https://doi.org/10.1177/0022343311405698.

Collier, P., Hoeffler, A., and Söderbom, M. 2008. Post-conflict Risks. *Journal of Peace Research 45*(4), 461–478. https://doi.org/10.1177/0022343308091356.

Conroy-Krutz, J., and Sanny, J. A.-N. 2019. How Free Is Too Free? Across Africa, Media Freedom Is on the Defensive. Policy Paper 56. AfroBarometer. https://www.afrobarometer.org/publication/pp56-how-free-too-free-across-africa-media-freedom-defensive/.

Cook, T. E. 1998. *Governing with the News: The News Media as a Political Institution*. University of Chicago Press.

Coskuntuncel, A. 2018. Privatization of Governance, Delegated Censorship, and Hegemony in the Digital Era: The Case of Turkey. *Journalism Studies 19*(5), 690–708.

Cottle, S. 2000. New(s) Times: Towards a "Second Wave" of News Ethnography. *Communications 25*(1), 19–42. https://doi.org/10.1515/comm.2000.25.1.19.

Cottle, S. 2007. Ethnography and News Production: New(s) Developments in the Field. *Sociology Compass* 1(1), 1–16.

Cruikshank, S. A. 2017. A Developing Chasm: Oppressive Structures, Media, and Journalism in Post-genocide Rwanda. *International Communication Research Journal* 52(1), 31–56.

Dahir, A. L. 2018, May 22. Burundi Has Backed Constitutional Changes That Could See Its President Rule till 2034. *Quartz*. https://qz.com/1284514/burundi-backs-new-constitution-extending-president-term-limit/.

Davidson, R. 2013. Two Sides of the Same Coin: The Role of Boundary Work and Isomorphism in the Emergence of Financial Journalism in Israel. *Journalism Studies* 14(3), 440–455.

Davies, C. A. 2012. *Reflexive Ethnography: A Guide to Researching Selves and Others*. Routledge.

de Burgh, H. 2003. Kings without Crowns? The Re-emergence of Investigative Journalism in China. *Media, Culture & Society* 25(6), 801–820.

de Bustamante, C. G., and Relly, J. E. 2021. *Surviving Mexico: Resistance and Resilience among Journalists in the Twenty-First Century*. University of Texas Press.

de Zeeuw, J. 2015. Projects Do Not Create Institutions: The Record of Democracy Assistance in Post-Conflict Societies. In A. Croissant and J. Haynes., eds., *Twenty Years of Studying Democratization*. Vol. 1. 188–212. Routledge.

DiMaggio, P. J., and Powell, W. W. 1983. The Iron Cage Revisited: Institutional Isomorphism and Collective Rationality in Organizational Fields. *American Sociological Review* 48(2), 147–160.

Dosek, T. 2021. Snowball Sampling and Facebook: How Social Media Can Help Access Hard-to-Reach Populations. *PS: Political Science & Politics* 54(4), 651–655.

Dukalskis, A. 2021. *Making the World Safe for Dictatorship*. Oxford University Press.

Dutta, S., Geiger, T., and Lanvin, B. 2015. The Global Information Technology Report 2015: ICTs for Inclusive Growth. World Economic Forum, Geneva.

The Economist. 2019, March 30. Don't Ask, Do Tell; Ethnic Labels in Rwanda. *The Economist*. https://link.gale.com/apps/doc/A580385792/BIC?u=lln_alsu&sid=BIC&xid=5bb335e7.

The Economist. 2021. Global Democracy Has a Very Bad Year. *The Economist*, February 2. https://www.economist.com/graphic-detail/2021/02/02/global-democracy-has-a-very-bad-year.

Economist Intelligence Unit. 2020. Democracy Index 2019. A Year of Democratic Setbacks and Popular Protest. The Economist Group, London.

Eko, L. 2007. It's a Political Jungle out There: How Four African Newspaper Cartoons Dehumanized and Deterritorialized African Political Leaders in the Post–Cold War Era. *International Communication Gazette* 69(3), 219–238.

Eko, L. 2010. The Art of Criticism: How African Cartoons Discursively Constructed African Media Realities in the Post–Cold War era. *Critical African Studies* 2(4), 65–91.

Eldridge, S. A. 2014. Boundary Maintenance and Interloper Media Reaction: Differentiating between Journalism's Discursive Enforcement Processes. *Journalism Studies* 15(1), 1–16.

Ellul, J., Wilkinson, J., and Merton, R. K. 1964. *The Technological Society*. Vintage Books.

Emerson, R. M., Fretz, R. I., and Shaw, L. L. 2011. *Writing Ethnographic Fieldnotes*. 2nd ed. University of Chicago Press.

Eramian, L. 2017. Neither Obedient nor Resistant: State History as Cultural Resource in Post-genocide Rwanda. *Journal of Modern African Studies* 55(4), 623–645.

Ewick, P., and Silbey, S. S. 1995. Subversive Stories and Hegemonic Tales: Toward a Sociology of Narrative. *Law and Society Review* 29(5), 197–226.

Fenby, J. 1986. *The International News Services*. Schocken Books.

Ferguson, J. 2006. *Global Shadows: Africa in the Neoliberal World Order*. Duke University Press.

Ferris, G. R., Fedor, D. B., Chachere, J. G., and Pondy, L. R. 1989. Myths and Politics in Organizational Contexts. *Group & Organization Studies* 14(1), 83–103.

Fiedler, A., and Frère, M.-S. 2018. Press Freedom in the African Great Lakes Region: A Comparative Study of Rwanda, Burundi, and the Democratic Republic of Congo. In H. Mabweazara, ed., *Newsmaking Cultures in Africa: Normative Trends in the Dynamics of Socio-Political & Economic Struggles*, 119–143. Palgrave MacMillan.

Fiedler, C., and Mroß, K. 2017. Post-conflict Societies: Chances for Peace and Types of International Support. German Development Institute, Briefing Paper 4/2017. https://www.die-gdi.de/en/briefing-paper/article/post-conflict-societies-chances-for-peace-and-types-of-international-support/.

Fine, G. A. 1993. Ten Lies of Ethnography: Moral Dilemmas of Field Research. *Journal of Contemporary Ethnography* 22(3), 267–294.

Fligstein, N., and McAdam, D. 2012. *A Theory of Fields*. Oxford University Press.

Fourie, P. J. 2010. The Past, Present and Future of South African Journalism Research, or: In Search of a Metatheory for South African Journalism Research. *Communicatio: South African Journal for Communication Theory and Research* 36(2), 148–171.

Freedman, D. 2008. *The Politics of Media Policy*. Polity.

Freedom House. 2016. Freedom of the Press 2016 Table of Scores. Washington, DC. Accessed May 18, 2016. https://freedomhouse.org/report/freedom-press-2016/table-country-scores-fotp-2016.

Freedom House. 2017a. Freedom in the World 2017: Rwanda. Accessed June 14, 2023. https://freedomhouse.org/country/rwanda/freedom-world/2017.

Freedom House. 2017b. *Press Freedom's Dark Horizon: Freedom of the Press 2017*. Freedom House.

Frère, M.-S. 2014. Journalist in Africa: A High-Risk Profession under Threat. *Journal of African Media Studies* 6(2), 181–198.

Frère, M.-S. 2015. Francophone Africa: The Rise of "Pluralist Authoritarian" Media Systems? *African Journalism Studies* 36(1), 103–112.

Friedman, A. 2012. Kagame's Rwanda: Can an Authoritarian Development Model Be Squared with Democracy and Human Rights. *Oregon Review of International Law* 14, 253–267.

Gambanga, N. 2015. How Much to Go Online? Here Are the Prices for Zimbabwean Internet Services. Accessed May 18, 2016. http://www.techzim.co.zw/2015/04/how-much-to-go-onlinehere-are-the-prices-for-zimbabwean-internet-services/#.Vzy9mSDGkp.

Gans, H. J. 1979. Deciding What's News: Story Suitability. *Society* 16(3), 65–77.

Gans, H. J. 1999. Participant Observation in the Era of "Ethnography." *Journal of Contemporary Ethnography* 28(5), 540–548.

Gerring, J. 2004. What Is a Case Study and What Is It Good For? *American Political Science Review* 98(2), 341–354.

Gettleman, J. 2010, August 10. Rwandan Leader Heads to New Term under Shadow of Repression. *New York Times*. https://www.nytimes.com/2010/08/10/world/africa/10rwanda.html.

Gieryn, T. F. 1983. Boundary-Work and the Demarcation of Science from Non-Science: Strains and Interests in Professional Ideologies of Scientists. *American Sociological Review* 48(6), 781–795.

Giffard, C. A. 1984. Inter Press Service: News from the Third World. *Journal of Communication* 34(4), 41–59.

Glaser, B. G., and Strauss, A. L. 2017. *Discovery of Grounded Theory: Strategies for Qualitative Research*. Routledge.

Go, J. 2008. Global Fields and Imperial Forms: Field Theory and the British and American Empires. *Sociological Theory* 26(3), 201–229. https://doi.org/10.1111/j.1467-9558.2008.00326.x.

Gökgür, N. 2012. Rwanda's Ruling Party-Owned Enterprises: Do They Enhance or Impede Development? Universiteit Antwerpen, Institute of Development Policy. *IOB Discussion Papers* 2012.03. https://ideas.repec.org/p/iob/dpaper/2012003.html.

Gonza, M. 2012. *Media Sustainability Index 2012: Rwanda*. IREX.

Goodfellow, T. 2013. Planning and Development Regulation amid Rapid Urban Growth: Explaining Divergent Trajectories in Africa. *Geoforum*, 48, 83–93.

Goodfellow, T., and Smith, A. 2013. From Urban Catastrophe to "Model" City? Politics, Security and Development in Post-conflict Kigali. *Urban Studies* 50(15), 3185–3202.

Granovetter, M. S. 1973. The Strength of Weak Ties. *American Journal of Sociology* 78(6), 1360–1380. https://www.jstor.org/stable/2776392.

Gros, J.-G. 1996. Towards a Taxonomy of Failed States in the New World Order: Decaying Somalia, Liberia, Rwanda and Haiti. *Third World Quarterly* 17(3), 455–472.

Guariso, A., Ingelaere, B., and Verpoorten, M. 2017. *Female Political Representation in the Aftermath of Ethnic Violence: A Comparative Analysis of Burundi and Rwanda*. Working Paper 74/2017. United Nations University World Institute for Development Economics Research. https://doi.org/10.35188/UNU-WIDER/2017/298-4.

Guliyev, F. 2009. End of Term Limits. http://hir.harvard.edu/article/?a=1823.

Habel, P., Moon, R., and Fang, A. 2018. News and Information Leadership in the Digital Age. *Information, Communication & Society* 21(11), 1604–1619.

Hallin, D. C. 2009. Not the End of Journalism History. *Journalism* 10(3), 332–334.

Hallin, D. C., and Mancini, P. 2004. *Comparing Media Systems: Three Models of Media and Politics*. Cambridge University Press.

Hallin, D. C., and Mancini, P., eds. 2012. *Comparing Media Systems beyond the Western World*. Cambridge University Press.

Hamilton, J. M., and Jenner, E. 2004. Redefining Foreign Correspondence. *Journalism* 5(3), 301–321.

Hamilton, J. T. 2010. The (Many) Markets for International News: How News from Abroad Sells at Home. *Journalism Studies* 11(5), 650–666.

Hanitzsch, T. 2004. Journalists as Peacekeeping Force? Peace Journalism and Mass Communication Theory. *Journalism Studies* 5(4), 483–495.

Hanitzsch, T. 2019. Journalism Studies Still Needs to Fix Western Bias. *Journalism* 20(1), 214–217.

Hanitzsch, T., and Mellado, C. 2011. What Shapes the News around the World? How Journalists in Eighteen Countries Perceive Influences on Their Work. *International Journal of Press/Politics* 16(3), 404–426.

Hanitzsch, T., and Vos, T. P. 2017. Journalistic Roles and the Struggle over Institutional Identity: The Discursive Constitution of Journalism. *Communication Theory* 27(2), 115–135.

Hanitzsch, T., and Vos, T. P. 2018. Journalism beyond democracy: A New Look into Journalistic Roles in Political and Everyday Life. *Journalism* 19(2), 146–164.

Hanna, S. F. 2005. Hamlet Lives Happily Ever After in Arabic: The Genesis of the Field of Drama Translation in Egypt. *The Translator* 11(2), 167–192. https://doi.org/10.1080/13556509.2005.10799197.

Hannan, M. T., and Freeman, J. 1984. Structural Inertia and Organizational Change. *American Sociological Review* 49(2), 149–164. https://doi.org/10.2307/2095567.

Hanusch, F., and Uppal, C. 2015. Combining Detached Watchdog Journalism with Development Ideals: An Exploration of Fijian Journalism Culture. *International Communication Gazette* 77(6), 557–576. https://doi.org/10.1177/1748048515597873.

Harber, A. 2014. *Legacy of Rwanda Genocide Includes Media Restrictions, Self-Censorship*. Special report. Committee to Protect Journalists. https://cpj.org/reports/2014/12/legacy-of-rwanda-genocide-includes-media-restricti/.

Hasty, J. 2005. *The Press and Political Culture in Ghana*. Indiana University Press.

Hellmueller, L. 2017. Gatekeeping beyond Geographical Borders: Developing an Analytical Model of Transnational Journalism Cultures. *International Communication Gazette* 79(1), 3–25.

Herbst, J. 2014. *States and Power in Africa: Comparative Lessons in Authority and Control*. Princeton University Press.

Heritage Foundation. 2021. *2021 Index of Economic Freedom: Rwanda*. The Heritage Foundation. Retrieved January 14 from https://www.heritage.org/index/country/rwanda.

Hermida, A. 2013. #Journalism: Reconfiguring Journalism Research about Twitter, One Tweet at a Time. *Digital Journalism* 1(3), 295–313.

Herod, A. 1999. Reflections on Interviewing Foreign Elites: Praxis, Positionality, Validity, and the Cult of the Insider. *Geoforum* 30(4), 313–327.

Hess, K. 2013. Tertius Tactics: "Mediated Social Capital" as a Resource of Power for Traditional Commercial News Media. *Communication Theory* 23(2), 112–130. https://doi.org/10.1111/comt.12005.

Hess, K. 2015. Making Connections: "Mediated" Social Capital and the Small-Town Press. *Journalism Studies* 16(4), 482–496.

Higiro, J.-M. V. 2007. Rwandan Private Print Media on the Eve of the Genocide. In A. Thompson, ed., *the Media and the Rwandan Genocide*, 73–89. Pluto Press.

Hintjens, H. M. 1999. Explaining the 1994 Genocide in Rwanda. *Journal of Modern African Studies* 37(2), 241–286.

Höhne, M. V. 2008. Newspapers in Hargeysa: Freedom of Speech in Post-conflict Somaliland. *Africa Spectrum* 43(1), 91–113.

Howard, P. N. 2002. Network Ethnography and the Hypermedia Organization: New Media, New Organizations, New Methods. *New Media & Society* 4(4), 550–574.

Howard, R. 2003. *International Media Assistance: A Review of Donor Activities and Lessons Learned*. Working Paper 19. Netherlands Institute of International Relations "Clingendael" Conflict Research Unit.

Hughes, S. 2003. From the Inside Out: How Institutional Entrepreneurs Transformed Mexican Journalism. *Harvard International Journal of Press/Politics* 8(3), 87–117.

Hughes, S. 2006. *Newsrooms in Conflict: Journalism and the Democratization of Mexico.* University of Pittsburgh Press.

Hughes, S., Garcés, M., Márquez-Ramírez, M., and Arroyave, J. 2017. Rethinking Professional Autonomy: Autonomy to Develop and to Publish News in Mexico and Colombia. *Journalism* 18(8), 956–976. https://doi.org/10.1177/1464884916659409.

Human Rights Watch. 2010, August 2. Rwanda: Silencing Dissent Ahead of Elections. https://www.hrw.org/news/2010/08/02/rwanda-silencing-dissent-ahead-elections.

Human Rights Watch. 2017, August 18. Rwanda: Politically Closed Elections—a Chronology of Violations. https://www.hrw.org/news/2017/08/18/rwanda-politically-closed-elections.

Hussey, M. 2016. Why Twitter Should Pay More Attention to Africa. *Next Web*, April 6. https://thenextweb.com/africa/2016/04/06/twitter-finds-political-side-africa/.

Ingelaere, B. 2010. Do We Understand Life after Genocide? Center and Periphery in the Construction of Knowledge in Postgenocide Rwanda. *African Studies Review* 53(1), 41–59.

International Development Association. 2009, August 1. Rwanda: From Post-Conflict Reconstruction to Development. Brief No. 51957. The World Bank. http://documents1.worldbank.org/curated/en/954801468108536137/pdf/519570BRI0ida1148B01PUBLIC11PUBLIC1.pdf.

International Trade Union Confederation. 2019. List of Affiliated Organizations. International Trade Union. Accessed June 14, 2023. https://www.ituc-csi.org/list-of-ituc-affiliates.

Ireri, J. K. 2015. *Constructing a Portrait of Kenyan Journalists in the 21st Century: Demographics, Job Satisfaction, Influences on News Values and Autonomy, and Standards of Journalism Training.* Indiana University.

Ireri, J. K. 2016. High Job Satisfaction Despite Low Income: A National Study of Kenyan Journalists. *Journalism & Mass Communication Quarterly* 93(1), 164–186.

Ireri, J. K. 2017. A National Survey on the Professional Role Conceptions of Journalists in Kenya. *Journalism Practice* 11(8), 1042–1061.

Jessee, E. 2011. The Limits of Oral History: Ethics and Methodology amid Highly Politicized Research Settings. *Oral History Review* 38(2), 287–307.

Jordaan, M. 2020. An Open Mind, Not an Empty Head: Towards Perpetual Waves of Newswork Ethnography. *African Journalism Studies* 41(4), 51–67.

Jose, A. B. 1975. Press Freedom in Africa. *African Affairs* 74(296), 255–262.

Jukes, S., Charles, M., and Fowler-Watt, K. 2021. Rethinking Journalism Practice through Innovative Approaches to Post Conflict Reporting. *Journalism Practice* 15(6), 767–784.

Kagire, E. 2010, July 30. Media High Council to Crack Down on Unregistered Media Houses. *New Times*. http://www.newtimes.co.rw/section/read/22455/.

Kagire, L. 2021, May 4. What to Consider When Choosing a Career in Journalism. *New Times*. https://www.newtimes.co.rw/lifestyle/what-consider-when-choosing-career-journalism.

Karlowicz, I. 2003. The Difficult Birth of the Fourth Estate: Media Development and Democracy Assistance in the Post-conflict Balkans. Policy Analysis. Central European University Center for Policy Studies. 115–135. http://pdc.ceu.hu/archive/00002252/01/media_5_karlowicz.pdf.

Karlsson, M., and Clerwall, C. 2019. Cornerstones in Journalism: According to Citizens. *Journalism Studies* 20(8), 1184–1199.

Kasoma, T. 2009. Development Reporting as a Crumbling Tower? Impact of Brown Envelope Journalism on Journalistic Practice in Zambia and Ghana. *Global Media Journal-African Edition* 3(1), 18–32.

Kelley, T. 2017. Maintaining Power by Manipulating Memory in Rwanda. *Fordham International Law Journal* 41, 79–134.

Kellow, C. L., and Steeves, H. L. 1998. The Role of Radio in the Rwandan Genocide. *Journal of Communication* 48(3), 107–128.

Kielbowicz, R. B. 1983. The Press, Post Office, and Flow of News in the Early Republic. *Journal of the Early Republic* 3(3), 255–280.

King, E. 2010. Memory Controversies in Post-genocide Rwanda: Implications for Peacebuilding. *Genocide Studies and Prevention* 5(3), 293–309.

King, G., Pan, J., and Roberts, M. E. 2013. How Censorship in China Allows Government Criticism but Silences Collective Expression. *American Political Science Review* 107(2), 326–343.

Kluttz, D., and Fligstein, N. 2016. Varieties of Sociological Field Theory. In S. Abrutyn, ed., *Handbook of Contemporary Sociological Theory*, 185–204. Springer International Publishing.

Konieczna, M. 2018. *Journalism without Profit: Making News When the Market Fails.* Oxford University Press.

Kossinets, G. 2006. Effects of Missing Data in Social Networks. *Social Networks* 28(3), 247–268.

Kotisova, J., and Císařová, L. W. 2023. "I Know Which Devil I Write For": Two Types of Autonomy among Czech Journalists Remaining in and Leaving the Prime Minister's Newspapers. *International Journal of Press/Politics* 28(1), 238–256. https://doi.org/10.1177/19401612211045229.

Krabill, R. 2010. *Starring Mandela and Cosby: Media and the End(s) of Apartheid.* University of Chicago Press.

Krause, M. 2017. The Patterns in between: "Field" as a Conceptual Variable. In C. E. Benzecry, M. Krause, and I. A. Reed, eds., *Social Theory Now*, 226–250. University of Chicago Press.

Kumar, K. 2006. International Assistance to Promote Independent Media in Transition and Post-conflict Societies. *Democratization* 13(4), 652–667.

Lacey, M. 2003, August 26. Rwandan President Declares Election Victory. *New York Times.* https://www.nytimes.com/2003/08/26/world/rwandan-president-declares-election-victory.html.

Lacey, M. 2004, April 9. A Decade after Massacres, Rwanda Outlaws Ethnicity. *New York Times.* https://www.nytimes.com/2004/04/09/world/a-decade-after-massacres-rwanda-outlaws-ethnicity.html.

Laplante, L. J., and Phenicie, K. 2009. Mediating Post-conflict Dialogue: The Media's Role in Transitional Justice Processes. *Marquette Law Review* 93, 251–283.

Lareau, A., and Lamont, M. 1988. Cultural Capital: Allusions, Gaps and Glissandos in Recent Theoretical Developments. *Sociological Theory* 6(2), 153–168.

Leeds, T. 2022. The Journalistic Field in the Platform Economy: The *New York Times* and the Inverted Pyramid. *Social Problems* 00, 1–20. https://doi.org/10.1093/socpro/spac045.

Levitsky, S., and Way, L. A. 2002. Elections without Democracy: The Rise of Competitive Authoritarianism. *Journal of Democracy* 13(2), 51–65.

Lewis, S. 2010. Journalism Innovation and the Ethic of Participation: A Case Study of the Knight Foundation and Its News Challenge. PhD diss., University of Texas at Austin.

Li, S.-C. S., and Lee, C.-Y. 2010. Market Uncertainty and Mimetic Isomorphism in the Newspaper Industry: A Study of Taiwan's Mainstream Newspapers from 1992 to 2003. *Asian Journal of Communication 20*(3), 367–384.

Lim, J. 2012. The Mythological Status of the Immediacy of the Most Important Online News: An Analysis of Top News Flows in Diverse Online Media. *Journalism Studies 13*(1), 71–89.

Lindlof, T. R., and Taylor, B. C. 2017. *Qualitative Communication Research Methods*. Sage Publications.

Lowrey, W. 2005. Commitment to Newspaper-TV Partnering: A Test of the Impact of Institutional Isomorphism. *Journalism & Mass Communication Quarterly 82*(3), 495–515.

Loyle, C. E. 2018. Transitional Justice and Political Order in Rwanda. *Ethnic and Racial Studies 41*(4), 663–680.

Lundy, P., and Mcgovern, M. 2001. The Politics of Memory in Post-conflict Northern Ireland. *Peace Review 13*(1), 27–33.

Maares, P., and Hanusch, F. 2022. Interpretations of the Journalistic Field: A Systematic Analysis of How Journalism Scholarship Appropriates Bourdieusian Thought. *Journalism 23*(4), 736–754.

Mabweazara, H. M. 2010. Researching the Use of New Technologies (ICTS) in Zimbabwean Newsrooms: An Ethnographic Approach. *Qualitative Research 10*(6), 659–677.

Mabweazara, H. M. 2011. Between the Newsroom and the Pub: The Mobile Phone in the Dynamics of Everyday Mainstream Journalism Practice in Zimbabwe. *Journalism 12*(6), 692–707.

Mabweazara, H. M. 2013. Normative Dilemmas and Issues for Zimbabwean Print Journalism in the "Information Society" Era. *Digital Journalism 1*(1), 135–151.

Mabweazara, H. M. 2018. *Newsmaking Cultures in Africa*. Springer.

Mabweazara, H. M., and Mare, A. 2017. Researching the Fluid and Multisited Appropriations of Digital Technologies in African Newsrooms. In J. Tong and S.-H. Lo, eds., *Digital Technology and Journalism*, 317–345. Palgrave MacMillan.

Mahoney, J., and Thelen, K. 2009. *Explaining Institutional Change: Ambiguity, Agency, and Power*. Cambridge University Press.

Mamdani, M. 2001. *When Victims Become Killers: Colonialism, Nativism, and the Genocide in Rwanda*. Princeton University Press.

Mann, L., and Berry, M. 2016. Understanding the Political Motivations That Shape Rwanda's Emergent Developmental State. *New Political Economy 21*(1), 119–144.

Mano, W. 2015. *Racism, Ethnicity and the Media in Africa: Mediating Conflict in the Twenty-First Century*. Bloomsbury Publishing.

Mano, W. 2017. Press Freedom, Professionalism and Proprietorship: Behind the Zimbabwean Media Divide. *Westminster Papers in Communication and Culture 2*, 56–70.

Mari, W. 2021. *The American Newsroom: A History, 1920–1960*. University of Missouri Press.

Matfess, H. 2015. Rwanda and Ethiopia: Developmental Authoritarianism and the New Politics of African Strong Men. *African Studies Review 58*(2), 181–204.

Mattes, R., and Bratton, M. 2007. Learning about Democracy in Africa: Awareness, Performance, and Experience. *American Journal of Political Science* 51(1), 192–217.

McIntyre, K., and Skjerdal, T. 2022. *Investigating the Gap between Journalists' Role Conceptions and Role Performance in Rwanda and Ethiopia*. Paper presented at Association for Education in Journalism and Mass Communication conference, Detroit, MI.

McIntyre, K., and Sobel, M. (2018). Reconstructing Rwanda: How Rwandan Reporters Use Constructive Journalism to Promote Peace. *Journalism Studies* 19(14), 2126–2147.

McIntyre, K., and Sobel, M. 2019. How Rwandan Journalists Use Whatsapp to Advance Their Profession and Collaborate for the Good of Their Country. *Digital Journalism* 7(6), 705–724.

McIntyre, K., and Sobel Cohen, M. 2021. Public Trust in State-Run News Media in Rwanda. *Journalism & Mass Communication Quarterly* 98(3), 808–827. https://doi.org/10.1177/1077699021998647.

Means, G. P. 1996. Soft Authoritarianism in Malaysia and Singapore. *Journal of Democracy* 7(4), 103–117.

Mechkova, V., Lührmann, A., and Lindberg, S. I. 2017. How Much Democratic Backsliding? *Journal of Democracy* 28(4), 162–169.

Media Council of Kenya. 2021. Journalist Accreditation List. Retrieved December 15 from https://accreditation.mediacouncil.or.ke:882/active-journalists?page=1.

Mellado, C. 2015. Professional Roles in News Content: Six Dimensions of Journalistic Role Performance. *Journalism Studies* 16(4), 596–614.

Mellado, C., and Humanes, M. L. 2012. Modeling Perceived Professional Autonomy in Chilean Journalism. *Journalism* 13(8), 985–1003.

Merton, R. K. 1995. The Thomas Theorem and the Matthews Effect. *Social Forces* 74, 375–424.

Meyer, J. W., and Rowan, B. 1977. Institutionalized Organizations: Formal Structure as Myth and Ceremony. *American Journal of Sociology* 83(2), 340–363.

Michener, G. 2011. FOI Laws around the World. *Journal of Democracy* 22(2), 145–159.

Migdal, J. S. 1988. *Strong Societies and Weak States: State-Society Relations and State Capabilities in the Third World*. Princeton University Press.

Mills, J. 2020. Toward a Theory of Myth. *Journal for the Theory of Social Behaviour* 50(4), 410–424. https://doi.org/10.1111/jtsb.12249.

Mitra, S., and Paterson, C. 2019. Reporting Global While Being Local: Local Sources of News for Distant Audiences. *Journalism Studies* 20(12), 1671–1678.

Mitra, S., Witherspoon, B. L., and Creta, S. 2022. Invisible in This Visual World? Work and Working Conditions of Female Photographers in the Global South. *Journalism Studies* 23(2), 149–166.

Molt, P. 2017, October 18. Rwanda as a Model. International Report No. 3 for Konrad-Adenauer-Stiftung. http://www.kas.de/wf/en/33.50364/.

Moon, R. 2019. Beyond Puppet Journalism: The Bridging Work of Transnational Journalists in a Local Field. *Journalism Studies* 20(12), 1714–1731. https://doi.org/10.1080/1461670x.2019.1638293.

Moon, R. 2022. Moto-Taxis, Drivers, Weather, and WhatsApp: Contextualizing New Technology in Rwandan Newsrooms. *Digital Journalism* 10(9), 1569–1590.

Moon, R. 2023. Preparing to Publish: How Journalists Negotiate Content Restrictions in Semi-Authoritarian States. *International Communication Gazette* 85(2), 120–140. https://doi.org/10.1177/17480485221118501.

Munoriyarwa, A., and Chiumbu, S. H. 2019. Big Brother Is Watching: Surveillance Regulation and Its Effects on Journalistic Practices in Zimbabwe. *African Journalism Studies* 40(3), 26–41.

Murphy, S. M., and Scotton, J. F. 1987. Dependency and Journalism Education in Africa: Are There Alternative Models? *African Media Review* 1(3), 11–35.

Musandu, P. 2018. *Pressing Interests: The Agenda and Influence of a Colonial East African Newspaper Sector.* McGill-Queen's University Press.

Mutsvairo, B., Borges-Rey, E., Bebawi, S., Márquez-Ramírez, M., Mellado, C., Mabweazara, H. M., Demeter, M., Głowacki, M., Badr, H., and Thussu, D. 2021. Ontologies of Journalism in the Global South. *Journalism and Mass Communication Quarterly* 98(4), 996–1016.

Muvunyi, S. 2017, August 8. Rwanda: Presidential Elections Were Free, Fair and Transparent—Governance Board. *New Times.* http://www.newtimes.co.rw/section/read/217555.

Mwambari, D. 2017. Women-Led Non-governmental Organizations and Peacebuilding in Rwanda. *African Conflict and Peacebuilding Review* 7(1), 66–79.

Mwizerwa, J., Robb, W., Namukwaya, C., Namuguzi, M., and Brownie, S. 2017. Improving Response Rates to an Alumni Survey in East Africa. *Advances in Social Sciences Research Journal* 4(20), 120–127.

Ndlela, N. 2009. African Media Research in the Era of Globalization. *Journal of African Media Studies* 1(1), 55–68.

Nduhura, D., and Prieler, M. 2017. Citizen Journalism and Democratisation of Mainstream Media in Rwanda. *African Journalism Studies* 38(2), 178–197.

Newbury, C. 1995. Background to Genocide: Rwanda. *African Issues* 23(2), 12–17.

Ngok, M. 2007. State-Press Relationship in Post-1997 Hong Kong: Constant Negotiation amidst Self-Restraint. *China Quarterly* 192, 949–970. https://doi.org/10.1017/s0305741007002111.

Nielsen, R. K. 2014. "Frozen" Media Subsidies during a Time of Media Change: A Comparative Analysis of Media Policy Drift in Six Western Democracies. *Global Media and Communication* 10(2), 121–138.

Nkie Mongo, C. 2021. The Practice of Envelope Journalism in the Republic of the Congo. *Newspaper Research Journal* 42(1), 111–126.

Nkurunziza, J. D. 2008. Civil War and Post-conflict Reconstruction in Africa. United Nations Conference on Trade and Development. Geneva, Switzerland.

Nyamnjoh, F. B. 2005. *Africa's Media: Democracy and the Politics of Belonging.* Zed Books.

Nyamnjoh, F. B. 2015. Journalism in Africa: Modernity, Africanity. *African Journalism Studies* 36(1), 37–43.

Oberschall, A. 2000. The Manipulation of Ethnicity: From Ethnic Cooperation to Violence and War in Yugoslavia. *Ethnic and Racial Studies* 23(6), 982–1001.

Ofori-Parku, S. S., and Botwe, K. 2020. "This Is (Not) Journalism": Corruption, Subterfuge, and Metajournalistic Discourses on Undercover Journalism in Ghana. *Journalism Studies* 21(3), 388–405.

Oliver, C. 1991. Strategic Responses to Institutional Processes. *Academy of Management Review* 16(1), 145–179. https://doi.org/10.5465/amr.1991.4279002.

Oluoch, F. 2017. August 19. Tyranny of Numbers in Kenya Parliament Agenda. http://www.theeastafrican.co.ke/news/tyranny-of-numbers-in-kenya-parliament-agenda-/2558-4063752-4cp2nxz/index.html.

Overholser, G., and Jamieson, K. H. 2005. *The Press.* Vol. 2. Oxford University Press.

Owen, W. M. 1986. *Autopsy of a Merger.* WM Owen.

Palmer, L. 2019. *The Fixers: Local News Workers and the Underground Labor of International Reporting.* Oxford University Press.

Paluck, E. L., and Green, D. P. 2009. Deference, Dissent, and Dispute Resolution: An Experimental Intervention Using Mass Media to Change Norms and Behavior in Rwanda. *American Political Science Review 103*(4), 622–644.

Paterson, B. L. 1994. A Framework to Identify Reactivity in Qualitative Research. *Western Journal of Nursing Research 16*(3), 301–316.

Pax Press. 2017. *Media and Policy Making in Rwanda: Findings from a Survey.* Research report. Kigali, Rwanda.

Pejic, N. 1996. Media's Responsibility for the War in Former Yugoslavia. Zentrum für Europastudien.

Pepinsky, T. B. 2009. *Economic Crises and the Breakdown of Authoritarian Regimes: Indonesia and Malaysia in Comparative Perspective.* Cambridge University Press.

Pepinsky, T. B. 2017, January 9. Life in Authoritarian States Is Mostly Boring and Tolerable. https://www.vox.com/the-big-idea/2017/1/9/14207302/authoritarian-states-boring-tolerable-fascism-trump.

Pezalla, A. E., Pettigrew, J., and Miller-Day, M. 2012. Researching the Researcher-as-Instrument: An Exercise in Interviewer Self-Reflexivity. *Qualitative Research 12*(2), 165–185.

Picard, R. G. 1998. Measuring and Interpreting Productivity of Journalists. *Newspaper Research Journal 19*(4), 71–84.

Prunier, G. 1997. *The Rwanda Crisis: History of a Genocide.* Columbia University Press.

Puddington, A. 2017. *Breaking Down Democracy: Goals, Strategies, and Methods of Modern Authoritarians.* Freedom House.

Purdeková, A. 2015. *Making Ubumwe: Power, State and Camps in Rwanda's Unity-Building Project.* Berghahn Books.

Purdeková, A. 2016. "Mundane Sights" of Power: The History of Social Monitoring and Its Subversion in Rwanda. *African Studies Review 59*(2), 59–86.

Putnis, P. 2004. Reuters in Australia: The Supply and Exchange of News, 1859–1877. *Media History 10*(2), 67–88.

Reese, S. D. 2016. The New Geography of Journalism Research: Levels and Spaces. *Digital Journalism 4*(7), 816–826.

Reich, Z. 2013. The Impact of Technology on News Reporting: A Longitudinal Perspective. *Journalism & Mass Communication Quarterly 90*(3), 417–434.

Reich, Z., and Hanitzsch, T. 2013. Determinants of Journalists' Professional Autonomy: Individual and National Level Factors Matter More Than Organizational Ones. *Mass Communication and Society 16*(1), 133–156.

Repnikova, M. 2017. *Media Politics in China: Improvising Power under Authoritarianism.* Cambridge University Press.

Reyntjens, F. 2011. Constructing the Truth, Dealing with Dissent, Domesticating the World: Governance in Post-genocide Rwanda. *African Affairs 110*(438), 1–34.

Reyntjens, F. 2013. *Political Governance in Post-Genocide Rwanda.* Cambridge University Press.

Rønning, H., and Kupe, T. 2000. The Dual Legacy of Democracy and Authoritarianism: The Media and the State in Zimbabwe. In J. Curran and M.-J. Park, eds., *De-Westernizing Media Studies,* 157–177. Routledge.

Roudakova, N. 2017. *Losing Pravda: Ethics and the Press in Post-Truth Russia*. Cambridge University Press.

Rwanda Governance Board. 2021. *Rwanda Media Barometer 2021: The State of Media Development in Rwanda*. Kigali, Rwanda.

Rwanda Media High Council. 2014. *Media Business Growth with Capacity Needs Assessment*. Kigali, Rwanda.

Rwandan Media Fraternity. 2011. *Code of Ethics Governing Journalists, Other Media Professionals, and the Media in Rwanda*. Rwandan Media Fraternity: Kigali, Rwanda.

Rwandan Parliament. 2009. Law number 22/2009 of 12/08/2009 on media. Retrieved June 14, 2023 from https://aceproject.org/ero-en/regions/africa/RW/rwanda-law-nb022-2009-of-12-08-2009-regulating-the.

Rwandan Parliament. 2013. Official Gazette nº 10 of 11 March 2013. Retrieved June 14, 2023 from https://rura.rw/fileadmin/Documents/ICT/Laws/Media_Law_Official_Gazette_no_10_of_11_03_2013.pdf.

Ryfe, D. M. 2006. Guest Editor's Introduction: New Institutionalism and the News. *Political Communication* 23(2), 135–144.

Ryfe, D. M. 2018. A Practice Approach to the Study of News Production. *Journalism* 19(2), 217–233.

Samset, I. 2011. Building a Repressive Peace: The Case of Post-Genocide Rwanda. *Journal of Intervention and Statebuilding* 5(3), 265–283.

Sassen, S. 2007. *A Sociology of Globalization*. Norton.

Schoon, A., Mabweazara, H. M., Bosch, T., and Dugmore, H. 2020. Decolonising Digital Media Research Methods: Positioning African Digital Experiences as Epistemic Sites of Knowledge Production. *African Journalism Studies* 41(4): 1–15.

Schudson, M. 1978. *Discovering the News*. Basic Books.

Schudson, M. 1994. Question Authority: A History of the News Interview in American Journalism, 1860s–1930s. *Media, Culture & Society* 16(4), 565–587.

Schudson, M. 2005. Autonomy from What? in R. Benson and E. Neveu, eds., *Bourdieu and the Journalistic Field*, 214–223. Polity Press.

Schudson, M. 2011. *The Sociology of News*. Norton.

Schultz, I. 2007. The Journalistic Gut Feeling: Journalistic Doxa, News Habitus and Orthodox News Values. *Journalism Practice* 1(2), 190–207.

Scott, J., and Carrington, P. J. 2011. *The Sage Handbook of Social Network Analysis*. Sage Publications.

Scott, M., Bunce, M., and Wright, K. 2017. Donor Power and the News: The Influence of Foundation Funding on International Public Service Journalism. *International Journal of Press/Politics* 22(2), 163–184.

Scotton, J. F. 1973. The First African Press in East Africa: Protest and Nationalism in Uganda in the 1920s. *International Journal of African Historical Studies* 6(2), 211–228.

Semujju, B. 2014. Participatory Media for a Non-Participating Community: Western Media for Southern Communities. *International Communication Gazette* 76(2), 197–208. https://doi.org/10.1177/1748048513504166.

Serwornoo, M. Y. W. 2021. The Coverage of Africa in Ghanaian Newspapers: The Dominant Western Voice in the Continent's Coverage. *Journalism* 22(12), 3013–3030.

Shamlal, P. 2014, April 8. For Rwanda's Media, the State Plays a Dominant Role. International Press Institute. https://ipi.media/for-rwandas-media-the-state-plays-a-dominant-role/.

Shapiro, A. 2017, August 3. Decline in Democracy Spreads across the Globe as Authoritarian Leaders Rise. *NPR All Things Considered*. https://www.npr.org/2017/08/03/541432445/decline-in-democracy-spreads-across-the-globe-as-authoritarian-leaders-rise.

Shaw, I. S., Lynch, J., and Hackett, R. A. 2011. *Expanding Peace Journalism: Comparative and Critical Approaches*. Sydney University Press.

Shoemaker, P. J., and Cohen, A. A. 2006. *News around the World: Content, Practitioners, and the Public*. Routledge.

Shoemaker, P. J., and Reese, S. D. 2013. *Mediating the Message in the 21st Century: A Media Sociology Perspective*. Routledge.

Silberstein-Loeb, J. 2014. *The International Distribution of News: The Associated Press, Press Association, and Reuters, 1848–1947*. Cambridge University Press.

Singer, J. B. 2003. Who Are These Guys? The Online Challenge to the Notion of Journalistic Professionalism. *Journalism* 4(2), 139–163.

Singer, J. B. 2007. Contested Autonomy: Professional and Popular Claims on Journalistic Norms. *Journalism Studies* 8(1), 79–95.

Sjøvaag, H. 2013. Journalistic Autonomy. *Nordicom Review* 34(S1), 155–166.

Skjerdal, T. S. 2010. Research on Brown Envelope Journalism in the African Media. *African Communication Research* 3(3), 367–406.

Skjerdal, T. S., and Ngugi, C. M. 2007. Institutional and Governmental Challenges for Journalism Education in East Africa. Ecquid Novi: African Journalism Studies 28(1–2), 176–190. https://doi.org/10.1080/02560054.2007.9653365.

Smith, A.-M. 1997. *A Forced Agreement: Press Acquiescence to Censorship in Brazil*. University of Pittsburgh Press.

Sobel, M., and McIntyre, K. 2019. The State of Journalism and Press Freedom in Postgenocide Rwanda. *Journalism & Mass Communication Quarterly* 96(2), 558–578.

Srivastava, M., and Wilson, T. 2019. Inside the WhatsApp Hack: How an Israeli Technology Was Used to Spy. *Financial Times* October 30. https://infoweb.newsbank.com/apps/news/document-view?p=awnb&docref=news/176e70b5b3cc9ec0.

Ssentanda, M., and Nakayiza, J. 2015, November 4. English Rules in Uganda, but Local Languages Should Not Be Side-Lined. *The Conversation*. https://theconversation.com/english-rules-in-uganda-but-local-languages-shouldnt-be-sidelined-49381.

Stapleton, S. 2014, May 26. Journalists' Pay and Conditions in Rwanda. http://democracyinafrica.org/making-press-count-pay/.

Starr, P. 2004. *The Creation of the Media: Political Origins of Modern Communications*. Basic Books.

Steinmetz, G. 2008. The Colonial State as a Social Field: Ethnographic Capital and Native Policy in the German Overseas Empire before 1914. *American Sociological Review* 73(4), 589–612.

Stockmann, D., and Gallagher, M. E. 2011. Remote Control: How the Media Sustain Authoritarian Rule in China. *Comparative Political Studies* 44(4), 436–467.

EFA Global Monitoring Report Team. 2011. *Education for All Global Monitoring Report: The Hidden Crisis: Armed Conflict and Education*. UNESCO, Paris, France.

Straus, S. 2007. What Is the Relationship between Hate Radio and Violence? Rethinking Rwanda's "Radio Machete." *Politics & Society* 35(4), 609–637.

Straus, S. 2013. *The Order of Genocide: Race, Power, and War in Rwanda*. Cornell University Press.

Straus, S. 2015. *Making and Unmaking Nations: War, Leadership, and Genocide in Modern Africa*. Cornell University Press.

Stroh, A. 2010. Electoral Rules of the Authoritarian Game: Undemocratic Effects of Proportional Representation in Rwanda. *Journal of Eastern African Studies* 4(1), 1-19.

Strömbäck, J., and Dimitrova, D. V. 2006. Political and Media Systems Matter: A Comparison of Election News Coverage in Sweden and the United States. *Harvard International Journal of Press/Politics* 11(4), 131-147. https://doi.org/10.1177/1081180x06293549.

Sturmer, M. 1998. *The Media History of Tanzania*. Ndanda Mission Press.

Suchman, M. C. 1995. Managing Legitimacy: Strategic and Institutional Approaches. *Academy of Management Review* 20(3), 571-610.

Sundaram, A. 2016. *Bad News: Last Journalists in a Dictatorship*. Bloomsbury Publishing.

Takševa, T. 2018. Building a Culture of Peace and Collective Memory in Post-conflict Bosnia and Herzegovina: Sarajevo's Museum of War Childhood. *Studies in Ethnicity and Nationalism* 18(1), 3-18.

Tapsell, R. 2012. Old Tricks in a New Era: Self-Censorship in Indonesian Journalism. *Asian Studies Review* 36(2), 227-245.

Thompson, A. 2007. *Media and the Rwanda Genocide*. Pluto Press.

Thomson, S. 2010. Getting Close to Rwandans since the Genocide: Studying Everyday Life in Highly Politicized Research Settings. *African Studies Review* 53(3), 19-34.

Thomson, S. 2017, May 2. How Rwanda Beats the United States and France in Gender Equality. *World Economic Forum*. https://www.weforum.org/agenda/2017/05/how-rwanda-beats-almost-every-other-country-in-gender-equality/.

Tong, J. 2018. Journalistic Legitimacy Revisited: Collapse or Revival in the Digital Age? *Digital Journalism* 6(2), 256-273.

Tong, J., and Sparks, C. 2009. Investigative Journalism in China Today. *Journalism Studies* 10(3), 337-352.

Tripp, A. M. 2004. The Changing Face of Authoritarianism in Africa: The Case of Uganda. *Africa Today* 50(3), 3-26.

Tuchman, G. 1972. Objectivity as Strategic Ritual: An Examination of Newsmen's Notions of Objectivity. *American Journal of Sociology* 77(4), 660-679.

US Bureau of Labor Statistics. 2021. *News Analysts, Reporters, and Journalists*. September 9, 2021. Retrieved December 15 from https://www.bls.gov/ooh/media-and-communication/mobile/reporters-correspondents- and-broadcast-news-analysts.htm.

US Department of State. 2019. *Rwanda 2019 Human Rights Report*. Country Reports on Human Rights Practices for 2019. U.S. Department of State Bureau of Democracy, Human Rights, and Labor. Washington, DC.

Usher, N. 2014. *Making News at the New York Times*. University of Michigan Press.

Uwiringiyimana, C. 2018, September 5. Two Opposition Lawmakers Elected in Rwanda for the First Time *Reuters*. https://www.reuters.com/article/us-rwanda-politics/two-opposition-lawmakers-elected-in-rwanda-for-the-first-time-iduskcn1ll2hi.

Vachudova, A. M. 2020. Ethnopopulism and Democratic Backsliding in Central Europe. *East European Politics* 36(3), 318-340.

Vandevoordt, R. 2017. Why Journalists Covered Syria the Way They Did: On the Role of Economic, Social and Cultural Capital. *Journalism* 18(5), 609-625.

Vauchez, A. 2008. The Force of a Weak Field: Law and Lawyers in the Government of the European Union for a Renewed Research Agenda. *International Political Sociology* 2(2), 128-144.

Vauchez, A. 2011. Interstitial Power in Fields of Limited Statehood: Introducing a "Weak Field" Approach to the Study of Transnational Settings. *International Political Sociology* 5(3), 340–345.

Verweij, P., and Van Noort, E. 2014. Journalists' Twitter Networks, Public Debates and Relationships in South Africa. *Digital Journalism* 2(1), 98–114. https://doi.org/10.1080/21670811.2013.850573.

Vision Group. n.d. Share Holders. Retrieved June 18, 2023 from https://www.visiongroup.co.ug/shareholder-faqs/

Vos, T. P., and Singer, J. B. 2016. Media Discourse about Entrepreneurial Journalism: Implications for Journalistic Capital. *Journalism Practice* 10(2), 143–159.

Wahutu, J. S. 2017. "In the Case of Africa in General, There Is a Tendency to Exaggerate": Representing Mass Atrocity in Africa. *Media, Culture & Society* 39(6), 919–929.

Wahutu, J. S. 2018a. The Politics of Representation: Wire Agencies and Local News Organizations in the Coverage of Darfur. *Sociological Forum* 33, 465–481.

Wahutu, J. S. 2018b. Representations of Africa in African Media: The Case of the Darfur Violence. *African Affairs* 117(466), 44–61.

Wahutu, J. S. 2018c. What African Media? Rethinking Research on Africa's Press. *Global Media and Communication* 14(1), 31–45.

Wahutu, J. S. 2019. Fake News and Journalistic "Rules of the Game." *African Journalism Studies* 40(4), 13–26.

Wahutu, J. S. In press. *In the Shadow of the Global North: Journalism in Postcolonial Africa.* Cambridge University Press.

Waisbord, S. 2000. *Watchdog Journalism in South America: News, Accountability, and Democracy.* Columbia University Press.

Waisbord, S. 2013. *Reinventing Professionalism: Journalism and News in Global Perspective.* John Wiley & Sons.

Waldner, D., and Lust, E. 2018. Unwelcome Change: Coming to Terms with Democratic Backsliding. *Annual Review of Political Science* 21(1), 93–113.

Waldorf, L. 2009. Revisiting Hotel Rwanda: Genocide Ideology, Reconciliation, and Rescuers. *Journal of Genocide Research* 11(1), 101–125. https://doi.org/10.1080/14623520802703673.

Wasserman, S., and Galaskiewicz, J. 1994. *Advances in Social Network Analysis: Research in the Social and Behavioral Sciences.* Sage.

Waters, S. 2018. The Effects of Mass Surveillance on Journalists' Relations with Confidential Sources: A Constant Comparative Study. *Digital Journalism* 6(10), 1294–1313.

WEF. 2016. World Economic Forum on Africa. Retrieved from https://www.weforum.org/events/world-economic-forum-on-africa-2016/.

Winsbury, R. 2013. The Print Journalist, UK and Africa. In H. Tumber, ed., *Media Power, Professionals and Policies*, 247–258. Routledge.

Wolf, T. P. 2013. International Justice vs Public Opinion? The ICC and Ethnic Polarisation in the 2013 Kenyan Election. *Journal of African Elections* 12(1), 143–177.

Workneh, T. W. 2020. Journalistic Autonomy in Voice of America's Amharic Service: Actors, Deterrents, and Safeguards. *Journalism Studies* 21(2), 217–235. https://doi.org/10.1080/1461670x.2019.1634484.

World Bank. 2021. GDP Per Capita (Current US$)—Rwanda. Retrieved December 17 from https://data.worldbank.org/indicator/ny.gdp.pcap.cd?locations=rw.

Yale University. n.d. Genocide Studies Program: Rwanda Project. Yale University. Retrieved June 18, 2023 from https://gsp.yale.edu/case-studies/rwanda-project.

Yeo, T. E. D. 2016. Communicating Legitimacy: How Journalists Negotiate the Emergence of User-Generated Content in Hong Kong. *Journalism & Mass Communication Quarterly 93*(3), 609–626.

Yesil, B. 2014. Press Censorship in Turkey: Networks of State Power, Commercial Pressures, and Self-Censorship. *Communication, Culture & Critique 7*(2), 154–173.

Yuezhi, Z. 2000. Watchdogs on Party Leashes? Contexts and Implications of Investigative Journalism in Post-Deng China. *Journalism Studies 1*(4), 577–597.

Zelizer, B. 1993. Journalists as Interpretive Communities. *Critical Studies in Media Communication 10*(3), 219–237.

Zirugo, D. 2021a. Audiences as Agents of Collective Memory—Implications for Press Criticism and Journalism Boundaries. *Journal of Broadcasting & Electronic Media 65*(2), 270–288. https://doi.org/10.1080/08838151.2021.1933984.

Zirugo, D. 2021b. Journalism Hybridization in Postcolonial Societies: Paradigm Adaptation Tensions in Post-apartheid South Africa. *Journalism Studies 22*(7), 860–877.

Index

For the benefit of digital users, indexed terms that span two pages (e.g., 52–53) may, on occasion, appear on only one of those pages.

advertising, 115–17, 140–41
Afghanistan
   media assistance programs in, 167–68
   moderate authoritarianism in, 165–66
   post-conflict journalism in, 166–67
African Union, 166
Agence France-Presse, 12–13, 136–37, 144, 151, 153–54, 156
Airtel, 115–16
Aldridge, M., 17
Algeria
   extension of presidential term in, 165–66
   moderate authoritarianism in, 165–66
Al Jazeera, 136–37
Associated Press, 12–13, 14, 136–37, 144, 151, 153–54
Association-Rwandaise des Journalistes (Rwandan Journalists' Association)
   generally, 92, 171
   business pressure and, 115, 119
   code of ethics, 87–88, 104–5
   investigative journalism and, 131
   representation of journalists' rights by, 141
authoritarianism
   collectivity and, 36–37
   complexity of media under, 169–70
   conformity, pressure for, 38–39
   consensus-based decision-making and, 28–29, 158–59, 170
   elections, uncontested nature of, 2, 36–37
   globalization of journalism field and, 13–14
   impact on journalism, 2–3, 160–61
   investigative journalism and, 163
   Kenya compared, 2
   obedience to central authority and, 36–37
   one-party rule in Rwanda, 83–84, 94–95
   semiauthoritarian state, Rwanda as, 164–67
   surveillance and, 37–38
   symbolic democracy and, 8–9, 11–12, 35
   Western influence as exacerbating, 27
   worldwide prevalence of, 8–9, 165–66
autonomy of media
   assumptions regarding, 4–5, 10
   complexity of, 52–54
   defined, 53
   lack of, 69, 162
   limited autonomy (*see* limited autonomy of media)
   professionalism, relation to, 84–85
Azerbaijan, extension of presidential term in, 165–66

BBC, 29–31, 38–39, 100, 136–37
BBC Rwanda, 142
Belarus, extension of presidential term in, 165–66
Bloomberg, 153–54
Bolivia, extension of presidential term in, 165–66
Booth, D., 117
Bosnia–Herzegovina, post-conflict journalism in, 8, 166–67
Bourdieu, Pierre, 13, 44–45, 62, 161
bribery, 40–41
Burundi, extension of presidential term in, 165–66

business pressure on media
  generally, 26–27, 111, 158–59
  advertising and, 115–17, 140–41
  compensation of journalists,
    inadequacy of, 112–13, 114
  contradictory communications,
    110, 121–24
  corporations, avoidance of criticism
    of, 118
  deadlines, 111, 126–29
  decline in critical news stories
    and, 92–93
  East African and, 120–21
  "financial logic," 110, 112–13, 114, 116,
    124, 128–29, 131–32
  financial stability, incentive of, 113–17
  government, avoidance of criticism
    of, 118–19
  government control over media,
    relation to, 112–13
  investigative journalism,
    discouragement of, 125–26
  isomorphism, 114, 131
  KT Press and, 120–21
  limited autonomy and, 163–64
  mid-level management, avoidance of
    criticism of, 119–20
  mimetic isomorphism, 114, 115
  "no-go" areas, 117–18
  normative isomorphism, 114
  organizational routines, 131–32
  orthodoxy, as solidifying, 129–31
  quotas, 124–26
  self-censorship and, 112–13, 121–24, 164–65
  standardization of news, 129–31
  transnational news organizations
    insulated from, 145
byline recognition, social capital and, 48

Cambodia, moderate authoritarianism
  in, 165–66
Cameroon
  extension of presidential term
    in, 165–66
  globalization and journalism in, 14–15
  moderate authoritarianism in, 165–66
  political cartoons in, 93–94

Canada
  development journalism paradigm, lack
    of, 98–99
  media assistance programs, 27
  watchdog role of media in, 100–1
Carlson, Matt, 171
censorship, 112
challenges facing journalists, 156–57
China
  censorship in, 112
  investigative journalism in, 163
  state and media in, 15–16
The Chronicles
  critical analysis by, 92, 170–71
  limitations of, 92
CNN, 70, 100, 136–37
code of ethics, 87–88, 104–5
collusion between media and
  government, 3
Colombia, post-conflict journalism in, 8
compensation of journalists, inadequacy
  of, 40–41, 113
Congo, Democratic Republic of, Twa
  advocacy groups in, 67–68
Congo, Republic of
  bribery in, 40–41
  moderate authoritarianism in, 165–66
Congrès du Travail et de la Fraternité
  au Rwanda (Labor and Worker's
  Brotherhood Congress)
  (COTRAF), 43
counternarratives, 141, 171
credibility. *See* vocational legitimacy
Croatia, post-conflict journalism in, 166–67
Cuba, moderate authoritarianism
  in, 165–66
cultural capital, 50–52, 104, 154

data collection, 19–21
deadlines, 111, 126–29
democratic backsliding, 8–9
Democratic Green Party, 2
Deutsche Welle, 13–14, 153–54
development journalism
  generally, 108
  development-centered social
    role based on perceived lack of
    professionalism, 93–95

INDEX 203

KT Press, at, 95, 97–98, 102
New Times, at, 95, 97, 98, 100, 101–2
1994 genocide, impact of, 95, 96–97, 101–2
partnering with government and, 99–100
personal motivations for, 100–1
prioritization of development based on perceived lack of professionalism, 95–100
unity as motivation for, 100–2, 159–60
watchdog role of media contrasted, 100–1
Western influence, effect of, 94–95
digital media, 34
divisionism, 35
doxa, 17, 18, 57, 61–63, 68–69

East African
advertising and, 140–41
business pressure on, 120–21
criticism of government in, 89–90, 91–92
data collection and, 19–20
deadlines at, 126
elections, coverage of, 133–35, 156
globalization of journalism field and, 152
journalistic independence at, 45, 46–47
journalistic practice at, 133–35
newsroom, 133
organizational identity and, 45
watchdog role of, 145–46, 147, 153–54
East Timor, post-conflict journalism in, 166–67
economic capital, 154
Economist Intelligence Unit, 165–66
Ecuador, moderate authoritarianism in, 165–66
Egypt, moderate authoritarianism in, 165–66
elections
conduct of, 165
East African, coverage in, 133–35, 156
fraud in, 36–37
KT Press, coverage in, 134–35
New Times, coverage in, 134–35, 156
uncontested nature of, 2, 36–37

empirical analysis, 5–6
employment contracts for journalists, lack of, 41–43
ethics
code of ethics, 87–88, 104–5
unethical behavior by journalists in attempt to counteract public mistrust arising from myths, 75–76
Ethiopia
compensation of journalists, inadequacy of, 112–13
moderate authoritarianism in, 165–66
ethnography, 18–19
existing theories of journalism practice, inadequacy of, 6–7

Facebook, 142
field theory
generally, 5–6, 13
application to Rwandan media, 161
changing fields, 162–64
communities in journalism field, 19–20, 20f
comparison of journalism fields across East Africa, 180t
cultural capital, 50–52, 104, 154
globalization and, 12–15 (see also globalization of journalism field)
horizontal capital, 43
relationship of actors in, 13
setting field boundaries, 15–17 (see also setting field boundaries)
social capital (see social capital)
vertical capital, 43–44, 139
"financial logic," 112–13
Fligstein, N., 163
forces shaping Rwandan journalism
generally, 25
bribery, 40–41
compensation, inadequacy of, 40–41, 113, 114
cultural capital, 50–52
employment contracts, lack of, 41–43
graphic representation, 39f
health insurance, lack of, 42–43
horizontal capital, 43
networks, 44–45
organizational identity, 45–47

forces shaping Rwandan journalism (*cont.*)
    personal brand, 47–50
    social capital (*see* social capital)
    state, 34–40 (*see also* state and media)
    trade unions, 43
    vertical capital, 43–44
    vocational legitimacy, 50–52
France, transnational news organizations and, 151
Freedom House, 52, 165–66
freedom-of-information laws, 16–17, 35–36
freedom of press, 35–36, 83–84

gacaca (transitional justice program), 38–39
game approach. *See* field theory
genocide in Rwanda. *See* 1994 genocide
Genocide Memorial, 58–59
Ghana
    bribery in, 40–41
    development journalism in, 94
    historical background of media in, 83–84
globalization of journalism field, 12–15
    authoritarian context and, 13–15
    East African and, 152
    integration of democratic values and, 14–15
    local news organizations and, 136–39
    overlapping fields, 14
    setting field boundaries and, 16–17
    transnational news organizations and, 152 (*see also* transnational news organizations)
    Western influence, 12–13
global outlook
    investigative journalism, effect on, 160
    utilitarian approach of journalists with, 159–60
Golooba-Mutebi, F., 117
Great Lakes Voice
    critical analysis by, 92, 170–71
    limitations of, 92, 151
    mission of, 102

Habineza, Frank, 36–37, 134
Habyarimana, Juvénal, 58, 83–84

health insurance for journalists, lack of, 42–43
Hess, Kristy, 44–45
Hong Kong, state and media in, 165
horizontal capital, 43
human rights, media coverage of, 148–49
Human Rights Watch, 148–49, 165
Hungary, moderate authoritarianism in, 165–66
Hutus
    development journalism and, 97–98
    1994 genocide and, 57–60
    restrictions on use of ethnic labels, 35
hybrid governance, 8–9

independence. *See* journalistic independence
Indonesia, state and media in, 165
international correspondents, 137–38
Inter Press Service, 12–13, 136–37
interviews, 22*t*, 24, 163
investigative journalism
    authoritarianism and, 163
    discouragement of, 125–26
    global outlook, effect of, 160
    journalistic independence and, 85
    KT Press, at, 81
    New Times, at, 81
    perceived lack of professionalism, effect of, 85–93
    transnational news organizations, in, 144, 159–60
Iraq
    media assistance programs in, 167–68
    post-conflict journalism in, 166–67
Ireland, post-conflict journalism in, 8
IRIN, 136
isomorphism, 114, 131

journalism network seed list, 174*t*
journalistic credibility. *See* vocational legitimacy
journalistic independence
    East African, at, 45, 46–47
    investigative journalism and, 85
    New Times, at, 45
    transnational news organizations, of, 141, 144

Kagame, Paul
  African Union, as president of, 166
  extension of presidential term and, 165
  media coverage of, 130, 134–35, 139–40
  1994 genocide and, 38–39
  reelection of, 2, 36–37, 156, 157
  treatment of media, 23–24
Kangura, 59
Kasoma, T., 40–41
Kazakhstan, extension of presidential term in, 165–66
Kellow, C. L., 59
Kenya
  advertising funds from, 140–41
  compensation of journalists, inadequacy of, 112–13
  development journalism in, 94, 108
  Jubilee Party, 2
  Media Council of Kenya, 31–32
  number of journalists in, 31–32
  Orange Democratic Party, 2
  post-conflict journalism in, 5–6
  Rwanda contrasted, 2
  transitional democracy in, 2
  transnational news organizations and, 136–37
  watchdog role of media in, 100–1
Kigali Today
  pro-government stance of, 49–50
  self-censorship at, 121
Kosovo, post-conflict journalism in, 166–67
KT Press
  business pressure on, 120–21
  data collection and, 19–20
  deadlines at, 111, 126, 127
  development journalism at, 95, 97–98, 102
  economic capital and, 154
  editorial control over journalists at, 109–11
  elections, coverage of, 134–35
  investigative journalism at, 81
  journalistic practice at, 109–11
  lack of training at, 107–8
  Ministry of Health story, 118–19
  mission of, 102

  New Times compared, 111
  organizational identity and, 45–46
  pro-government stance of, 49–50, 111
  Rwandan Stock Exchange story, 118, 119
  self-censorship at, 121
  unethical behavior in attempt to counteract public mistrust arising from myths, 75
Kwibuka (genocide memorial week), 109

legitimacy. *See* vocational legitimacy
Le Messager (Cameroon), 93–94
limited autonomy of media
  business pressure and, 163–64
  myths, arising from, 70–71
  post-conflict journalism and, 10
  state and media and, 163–64
local news organizations. *See also specific outlet*
  critical analysis by, 171
  future research, 154–55
  globalization of journalism field and, 136–39
  protection of journalists by, lack of, 143–45
  transnational news organizations contrasted, 135, 170
  vocational legitimacy and, 139–40
  watchdog role, lack of, 147–49, 151
local practices and context
  effect of neglecting on studies of journalism, 10
  importance of, 7
  myths and, 27

Mabweazara, H. M., 40–41
Macedonia, post-conflict journalism in, 166–67
Malaysia, state and media in, 112–13
mapping Rwandan media
  digital media, 34
  journalists, 31–32, 32t
  media outlets, 29–31, 30t
  print media, 32–33
  radio, 33–34
  television, 33–34
McAdam, D., 163

media assistance policy
  generally, 167–68
  business practices, consideration of, 169
  diversity of journalist motivations, consideration of, 168–69
  economic reality, consideration of, 169
Media Barometer, 29–32, 33–34
Media High Council (MHC), 29–34, 35–36
methodology of study, 173–80
Mexico, changes in media in, 163
Michener, Greg, 16–17
Millennium Challenge Corporation, 167–68
mimetic isomorphism, 114, 115
"mindset" issue, 76
Ministry of Health, 118–19
Montenegro, post-conflict journalism in, 166–67
MTN, 115–16, 118
Myanmar, moderate authoritarianism in, 165–66
myths
  generally, 17–18, 25–26, 158–59
  avoidance of conflict by media arising from, 71
  collective memory and, 61
  defined, 18, 60–61
  doxa and, 17, 18, 57, 61–63, 68–69
  impact on journalism, 69–70, 77–78, 79–80
  limited autonomy arising from, 70–71
  local practices and context and, 27
  "mindset" issue, 76
  1994 genocide, arising from, 25–26, 63–64, 166–67
  organizational culture, impact on, 79, 80–81
  power of regarding journalism, 171–72
  pressure on media arising from, 158–59
  public trust in media, impact on, 72–75
  responsibility of media arising from 1994 genocide, 63–64, 66–68, 69, 78–79, 80
  role of media in 1994 genocide, 3–4, 57–60, 63–66, 69, 72–74, 76, 78–79
  setting field boundaries through, 17–18, 60–63
  sources, impact on trust in media by, 72–74, 76–77
  unethical behavior by journalists in attempt to counteract public mistrust arising from, 75–76
  watchdog role of media, reluctance to assume arising from, 71–72
  weakness of journalism field, impact on, 69–77
mzungu (white foreigner), 23

networks, social capital and, 44–45
New Times
  generally, 12–13
  advertising at, 116
  audience of, 33
  compensation of journalists at, 40
  data collection and, 19–20
  deadlines at, 126–28
  development journalism at, 95, 97, 98, 100, 101–2
  economic capital and, 154
  editorial control over journalists at, 86, 91–92
  elections, coverage of, 134–35, 156
  employment contracts for journalists at, 42
  investigative journalism at, 81
  journalistic independence at, 45
  journalistic practice at, 82–83
  KT Press compared, 111
  lack of training at, 107–8
  newsroom, 82–83
  organizational identity and, 45
  pro-government stance of, 49–50
  quotas at, 125–26
  role of media and, 70
  self-censorship at, 121, 123
New Vision (Uganda), 15–16
New York Times, 156
1994 genocide
  avoidance of discussion of, 35, 67–68
  development journalism, impact on, 95, 96–97, 101–2
  discouragement of discussion of, 38–39
  Genocide Memorial, 58–59
  impact on journalism, 8, 35–36, 83–84

myths arising from, 25–26, 63–64, 166–67
origins of, 58
pre-1994 genocide journalists, effect of lack of, 106
responsibility of media arising from, myth of, 63–64, 66–68, 69, 78–79, 80
role of media, myth of, 3–4, 57–60, 63–66, 69, 72–74, 76, 78–79
tensions regarding portrayal of, 57–60
visual reminders of, 55–57, 56f
Nkie Mongo, C., 40–41
"no-go" areas, 117–18
normative isomorphism, 114
Ntawukuriyayo, Jean Damascene, 2

organizational culture, impact of myths on, 79
organizational identity, social capital and, 45–47
organizational routines, 131–32

parachute journalists, 137–38
Pax Press, 41, 165
Pepinsky, Thomas, 164–65
personal brand, social capital and, 47–50
political cartoons, 93–94
political role of media, 157–58
post-conflict journalism
  generally, 7–12, 166–67
  international intervention to support, 10–11
  limited autonomy and, 10
  strong states, in, 5–6
print media
  generally, 32–33
  historical background in East Africa, 83–84
  1994 genocide, myth of role of media in, 65–66
professionalism in media
  generally, 11, 26, 108, 158–59
  autonomy, relation to, 84–85
  code of ethics, 84–85, 104–5
  criticism of government and, 87–88, 89–90
  decline in critical news stories, 91–93

development-centered social role based on perceived lack of, 93–95
development journalism and (see development journalism)
hierarchy-based consensus based on perceived lack of, 83, 85–93
investigative journalism, effect of perceived lack of professionalism on, 85–93
lack of training, effect of, 86–87, 88–89, 104, 105–8
perceived lack of, 83
pre-1994 genocide journalists, effect of lack of, 106, 107
prioritization of development based on perceived lack of, 95–100
self-censorship and, 93
vocational legitimacy, relation to, 103–8
watchdog role of media, relation to, 87–88, 89, 90–92, 103
"puppet journalism," 154–55

quotas, 124–26

radio
  generally, 33–34
  1994 genocide, myth of role of media in, 65–66
Radio-Télévision Libre des Milles Collines (RTLM), 59
Rapid City Journal (US), 23–24
reactivity, 24
registration of media
  journalists, 31–32, 32t
  media outlets, 29–31, 30t
  requirement, 35–36
Reuters, 12–14, 136–38, 144, 151, 153–54
Russia
  extension of presidential term in, 165–66
  moderate authoritarianism in, 165–66
  state and media in, 15–16, 163
Rwandan Election Commission (REC), 134
Rwandan Governance Board (RGB), 29–33, 34
Rwandan Media Commission, 1

Rwandan Patriotic Front (RPF)
  business holdings of, 117
  elections, in, 2
  power of, 36
  rise of, 58
Rwandan Stock Exchange, 118, 119
Rwigara, Diane, 134

Schudson, Michael, 131
self-censorship
  business pressure and, 112–13, 121–24, 164–65
  Kigali Today, at, 121
  KT Press, at, 121
  New Times, at, 121, 123
  reasons for, 93
semiauthoritarian state, Rwanda as, 164–67
Serbia, post-conflict journalism in, 166–67
setting field boundaries, 15–17
  economic systems, by, 15–16
  freedom-of-information laws and, 16–17
  globalization and, 16–17
  governments, by, 15
  myths, through, 17–18, 60–63
  stories, through, 17–18
Singapore, state and media in, 112–13
Slovenia, post-conflict journalism in, 166–67
social capital
  generally, 161
  byline recognition and, 48
  networks and, 44–45
  organizational identity and, 45–47
  personal brand and, 47–50
  social media and, 48
  sources and, 47–48
  transnational news organizations and, 146–51
  watchdog role of media and, 150–51
social media, social capital and, 48
social role of media, 157–58
sources
  myths, impact on trust in media, 72–74, 76–77
  social capital and, 47–48
  transnational news organizations and, 144

South Africa
  development journalism in, 94
  social and political role of media in, 157–58
Stapleton, Sally, 40–41
state and media, 34–40. *See also* authoritarianism
  business pressure, relation to government control over media, 112–13
  censorship, 112
  collectivity and, 36–37
  conformity, pressure for, 38–39
  consensus-based decision-making and, 28–29, 158–59, 170
  divisionism, 35
  freedom of press, 35–36, 83–84
  harassment of journalists, 105–6, 107–8
  historical background, 83–84
  laws regarding media, 35–36
  limited autonomy and, 163–64
  methods of state control over media, 8–9
  1994 genocide, impact on journalism, 8, 35–36
  obedience to central authority and, 36–37
  surveillance of media, 37–38
Steeves, H. L., 59
stories
  myths (*see* myths)
  power of, 17
  setting field boundaries through, 17–18
study of Rwandan journalism, 18–25
  comparison of journalism fields across East Africa, 180*t*
  data collection, 19–21
  ethnography, 18–19, 21–22
  grounded theory analytical framework, 19
  interviews, 22*t*, 24
  journalism network seed list, 174*t*
  language, difficulties involving, 23
  methodology, 173–80
  outsider status, difficulties involving, 23
  reactivity, accounting for, 24
  shared identity and, 23–24
surveillance, 37–38

Taarifa
  limitations of, 151
  mission of, 102
  MTN story, 118
Tanzania
  advertising funds from, 140–41
  bribery in, 40–41
  compensation of journalists, inadequacy of, 112–13
  data collection in, 19–20
television, 33–34
trade unions, 43
transnational news organizations. *See also specific outlet*
  generally, 158–59
  business pressure, insulation from, 145
  counternarratives and, 141
  criticism of government by, 139–41
  employment advantages, 152–53
  future research, 154–55
  globalization of journalism field and, 152
  insulation of journalists from criticism, 143–44
  international correspondents, 137–38
  investigative journalism in, 144, 159–60
  journalistic independence of, 141, 144
  local journalists working in, 136–39
  local news organizations contrasted, 135, 170
  parachute journalists, 137–38
  policy, influence on, 149
  protection of journalists by, 142–43, 144–45
  relative power of, 140–41, 145
  social capital and, 146–51
  sources and, 144
  stability of, 142
  vertical capital and, 139
  vocational legitimacy and, 139–46
  watchdog role of, 146–51
  Western audience of, 136–37
  Western origins of, 151
Trump, Donald, 7–8, 23–24, 70
Turkey
  moderate authoritarianism in, 165–66
  state and media in, 15–16, 112–13, 165
Tutsis
  development journalism and, 97–98
  1994 genocide and, 38–39, 57–60
  restrictions on use of ethnic labels, 35
Twas, 58, 67–68
Twitter, 142

Ubuntu, 6
Uganda
  advertising funds from, 140–41
  data collection in, 19–20
  experienced journalists in, 107
  extension of presidential term in, 165–66
  historical background of media in, 83–84, 94–95
  language in, 37
  public trust in media in, 74
  state and media in, 15–16, 38–39, 52
  Twa advocacy groups in, 67–68
Ukraine, moderate authoritarianism in, 165–66
umudugudus (community organizations), 38–39
umuganda (community work groups), 37–38
underdevelopment, 11, 158–59
United Kingdom, transnational news organizations and, 136–37, 151
United Nations
  freedom-of-information laws and, 16–17
  Human Development Index, 166
United States
  aid to Rwanda, 9
  Bureau of Labor Statistics, 31–32
  development journalism paradigm, lack of, 99
  McCarthyism, 17
  media assistance programs, 27, 167–68
  myths in, 171–72
  number of journalists in, 31–32
  political intrigue, media coverage of, 158–59
  profit motive in media in, 15, 131
  stories in, 17
  transnational news organizations and, 136–37, 151
USAID, 167–68
watchdog role of media in, 100–1
Watergate scandal, 17

University of Rwanda, 19–20
Uzbekistan, extension of presidential term in, 165–66

Venezuela
  extension of presidential term in, 165–66
  moderate authoritarianism in, 165–66
vertical capital, 43–44, 139
violence, power of media to influence, 3–4
Virginian-Pilot (US), 23–24
vocational legitimacy
  cultural capital, as, 104
  impact on Rwandan journalism, 50–52
  local news organizations and, 139–40
  professionalism, relation to, 103–8
  transnational news organizations and, 139–46
  watchdog role of media and, 153–54
Voice of America, 38–39, 153–54

Wahutu, James, 6
watchdog role of media
  generally, 6–7
  development-centered social role contrasted, 93–95
  development journalism contrasted, 100–1
  East African, 145–46, 147, 153–54
  financial independence and, 153–54
  local news organizations, lack in, 147–49, 151
  myths, reluctance to assume arising from, 71–72
  patriotism, false dichotomy with, 146–47, 150, 153–54
  policy, influence on, 149
  professionalism, relation to, 87–88, 89, 90–92, 103
  social capital and, 150–51
  social pressure regarding, 149–50
  transnational news organizations, 146–51
  vocational legitimacy and, 153–54
WhatsApp, 37–38, 111
wire services. *See* transnational news organizations
World Bank, 16–17

Xinhua, 12–14

Yugoslavia
  media assistance programs in, 167–68
  post-conflict journalism in, 166–67

Zambia, bribery in, 40–41
Zimbabwe
  bribery in, 40–41
  data collection in, 19–20
  experienced journalists in, 107
  freedom-of-information law in, 16–17
  state and media in, 53